# Landscape with Machines

# Landscape with Machines

## The First Part of his Autobiography

## L.T.C. ROLT

ALAN SUTTON PUBLISHING LTD

First published in the United Kingdom in 1971

First published in this edition in 1984
Alan Sutton Publishing Limited
Phoenix Mill · Far Thrupp · Stroud · Gloucestershire

First published in this edition in the United States of America in 1994
Alan Sutton Publishing Inc.
83 Washington Street · Dover · NH 03820

Reprinted 1986, 1994, 1995

British Library Cataloguing-in-Publication Data

Rolt, L.T.C.
        Landscape with machines.
        1. Rolt, L.T.C. 2. Engineers—England—Biography
        I. Title
        620'.0092'4  TJ140.R55

        ISBN 0-86299-140-4

Library of Congress Cataloging in Publication Data applied for

*Cover picture: detail from a painting by Felix Kelly*

Typesetting and origination by
Alan Sutton Publishing Limited.
Printed in Great Britain by
WBC, Bridgend, Mid Glam.

# Contents

## Part I

## Part II

## Part III

# List of Illustrations

## Acknowledgements

Thanks are due to the following for granting reproduction permission: the Montagu Motor Museum for No. 24 which is from the W.J. Brunell Collection; John Snell for No. 26; James Brymer for No. 31. Mrs Barbara Curwen very kindly supplied Nos. 19 and 20 from the Willans family album. The other illustrations are from the author's collection.

# Foreword

This Autobiography is intended to reflect the two sides of my own nature and the varied interests that have stemmed from them. They have often been at war with each other and have seldom achieved more than an uneasy truce. For this reason I have never found myself a particularly easy person to live with; I ask myself too many awkward questions.

That small minority who care for such things have for years been fighting to save something of the beauties of England and the English Tradition from the barbarity and philistinism of science and technology. Whose side am I on? There has never been any doubt in my mind, but I fear that, in this conflict which reflects the conflict within myself, I must seem to both sides an equivocal figure like that egregious vicar of Bray.

The battle is the more tragic because the gulf of non-understanding between the two sides seems to be so unbridgeable. For this reason, this book may fall with a dull thud in the no-man's-land between the two opposing forces. I wonder ruefully whether it should not be printed in two colours or two contrasting type faces, thus enabling each side to skip the part that they prefer to ignore. But that would be to admit defeat in a desperate situation. For where there is no mutual understanding there can be no hope of remedy.

L. T. C. R.

Of dying man
His living mind
By writing deeds
His children find.

*Inscription over a cottage doorway
at Welcombe, North Devon*

# Part I

# Chapter 1

# Poverty, Powder and Gold

No one with any sense of place could fail to be aware that Chester is a Roman city. To stand on the red rampart of its walls and look south-westward over the great defensive loop of the Dee towards the blue mountains of Wales on the far horizon is to comprehend the reason for the city's foundation as a legionary fortress. Chester, like its counterpart Caerleon-upon-Usk at the opposite end of the Welsh Border, was a stronghold of Imperial Rome, designed to impose the Pax Romana on the turbulent mountain country of the Celt. It was in this ancient city that I was born and it was on the Welsh March between Chester and Caerleon that the most impressionable years of my childhood were spent.

My birthplace, and my home for the first four years of my life, was a house in Eaton Road in what was then the respectable outer suburban fringe of the city, poised between extremes of wealth and poverty. Eaton Road follows part of the line of a Roman highway. Heading due south, this passes through the village of Eccleston and by Eaton Hall, then the seat of the Duke of Westminster, a vast, pretentious Victorian pile by Alfred Waterhouse whose demolition even the most enthusiastic devotee of nineteenth-century architecture could scarcely lament. Northwards, the road went through the parish of Handbridge, falling steeply towards the old sandstone bridge over the Dee, and thence entered the city by the south gate. On the right of the road as it stooped towards the bridge there was then a malodorous huddle of slum property which I suspect had once housed a colony of Dee fisherfolk but had since become notorious for its squalor. The crumbling brick cottages, leaning crazily against one another as though for mutual support, appeared in imminent danger of plunging down the steep slope towards the river in a torrent of rotten brick and shattered slates.

When pushing me in my pram towards the city, my nurse

always hurried past this squalid rookery with averted eyes, clinging to the opposite side of the road. Sometimes, if the odour of poverty was particularly strong, she would spit upon the pavement and enjoin me urgently to do likewise. 'Spit! Spit!', she would hiss at me. I realise now that this strange ritual was a survival of those pre-Pasteur Victorian days when the frightful epidemics of cholera and typhus were attributed to what was politely called 'the miasma'. Spitting was not a superstitious warding off of the evil eye, but a practical precaution to prevent one swallowing the supposedly deadly stench. Another precaution of my nurse's which I remember was the spreading of sheets of newspaper on the seats of railway carriages before one sat down.

On one occasion when we were scuttling past Handbridge, I recall seeing two middle-aged women fighting viciously on the pavement opposite before an audience of rough looking men who lounged in cottage doorways, jeering and egging them on. Their work-worn, dirty hands were hooked like a hawk's talons as they clawed at each other's eyes or tore at the ragged curtains of greying hair that hung loose over their faces. Not surprisingly, this scene of primitive violence was indelibly imprinted on my infant mind.

Other random recollections emerge from the dark glass of these earliest years. One is of a journey by motorcycle combination with my father and mother—quite a venturesome one it must have been in those days—to take luncheon with my great-uncles and aunt, brothers and sister to my paternal grandmother 'Grannie Garnett'. Four bachelor brothers, they lived together in a great square house of blackened stone known as Wyreside Hall in the Lancashire Pennines above Garstang with their spinster sister 'Aunt Louis' to preside over the household. One of them was a director of the London and North Western Railway and wore his director's gold pass on his watch chain. And a most potent talisman it was, for at his bidding even the lordliest West Coast Scotch express would stop at the little wayside station of Bay Horse to pick him up. But their lives at Wyreside seem to have been mainly devoted to shooting on the moors and fishing the waters of the Wyre.

Of that awesome family luncheon party I remember only one thing: the footmen who waited at table. With their powdered wigs, velvet breeches, white stockings and buckled shoes, they were far more attractive to my childish eye than my great-uncles and aunt of whom I have not the slightest recollection. I discovered much later, however, that they formed my only tenuous family link with engineering history, for their father, Henry Garnett, had been the financial partner of the celebrated James Nasmyth, inventor of the steam hammer, in his famous engineering business at the Bridgewater Foundry, Patricroft. Nasmyth referred to him as: 'my excellent friend Henry Garnett, Esq., of Wyre Side, near Lancaster. He had been my sleeping partner or "Co." for nearly twenty years, and the most perfect harmony always existed between us.'[1] It was in memory of this happy association that one of my great-uncles was christened Frank Nasmyth.

But I think my earliest recollection of all was of the silver half-sovereign case that my father habitually wore on one end of his watch chain. He would draw it from his waistcoat pocket, press the catch which released the spring lid, and hold it out for my investigation. As my questing forefinger slid out one of the little golden coins, another would move up to replace it, impelled by the action of the spring beneath. It seemed to me a magic box, ever brim-full with an inexhaustible fount of gold.

These three recollections, of ragged women fighting in the street, of powdered footmen and gold coins, preserved by chance from these my earliest years in the rag-bag of the mind, seem now to be strangely apposite, typifying for me the world into which I was born in February 1910, a world destined so soon to vanish utterly away. That a social conscience was already astir was something I only learned later from the history books. From those about me I accepted such evidences of the extremes of wealth and poverty as something inevitable like sunlight or storm. They were part of the unalterable common lot of man; the outward manifestations of innate inequality.

Of the grown-ups among whom I moved, I saw and remember little of my mother's family. They were not very thick upon the ground anyway. For my maternal grandmother was an orphan who had married at an early age an obscure elderly gentleman named Clarke of Cogshall Hall near Comberbatch where my mother Jemima and her only sister, my aunt Augusta, were born in quick succession. After achieving this remarkable feat— he was over seventy years of age at the time—Mr Clarke understandably passed away. This frustrated the optimistic hopes of my grandmother's guardian who, it is said, had made the match in the expectation that she would provide an heir for

[1] James Nasmyth, *Autobiography*, pp. 371-2 f.

Cogshall. Long before I was born, my grandmother had taken as her second husband a dubious clergyman of good family named Timperley, of Hintlesham in Norfolk. He had objected strenuously but unavailingly to my father's marriage to his step-daughter, the reason being, as my father subsequently discovered, that the reverend gentleman had been cheerfully making away with the handsome dowry left to my mother by the munificent Mr Clarke.

Not surprisingly, therefore, with the exception of my aunt Augusta, my mother's family did not figure largely in my life. With the Rolts, however, it was quite otherwise for there was a positive legion of Rolt uncles and aunts. The two favourite pastimes of my grandfather, Thomas Francis Rolt, who died nine years before I was born, appear to have been hunting and procreation. He and his elder brother Henry, always known in my family as 'Uncle Hen.', were the only sons of Sir John Rolt, a mysteriously elusive Anglo-Irish figure of whom I gave some account in an earlier book.[1] My grandfather moved from house to house about the English Shires, sampling the pleasures of different hunting countries, accompanied by a string of hunters, a lengthening string of children and his long-suffering wife. Apparently, his brother, who was in holy orders, frequently upbraided him for what he considered the wanton extravagance of this way of life. He pointed out that his private means, supplemented only by the half-pay he received from his regiment (the Coldstream Guards), was not adequate to support both his horses and his family. Though this was patently true, it had no moderating influence whatsoever upon my grandfather. Judging from the indifferent education that my father received and his very meagre patrimony, the horses consumed the lion's share of the family fortunes.

It seems my grandfather had a particular fondness for the Heythrop country, for no less than six of his family of twelve, including my father, were born at Stow-on-the-Wold, between the years 1865 and 1874, in a house that stands back from the central square and is now a hotel. An earlier sojourn in Worcestershire proved far less successful, for the house the Rolts took in the village of Cropthorne was so heavily haunted that they were compelled to leave after only one child had been born there. Almost every night the family was awakened by the sound of heavy footfalls tramping up the stairs and through the cor-

---

[1] *Green and Silver*, 1949, p. 23.

ridors. This recurrent perambulation invariably ended with two resounding thumps from the attic, suggesting that the visitor had violently flung off a pair of heavy boots. My grandfather, who was no coward, lay in wait for the visitor, armed to the teeth, but although the footsteps passed him by, nothing could be seen. An untitled water-coloured drawing in one of my grandfather's numerous sketch books purports to show this haunted house, but I have not succeeded in identifying it on the ground. No doubt it was pulled down.

At a time when the more avant-garde were already using cameras, my grandfather preferred his pencil and water-colours. The many sketch books of his now in my possession are the equivalent of the family photograph album and contain portraits, hunting scenes and landscapes. The latter predominate to show that he travelled widely in Europe, Algeria and Morocco. One of these water-colour sketches appeals to me particularly. It was made early in his married life when he was living at Tor Grove, Plymouth, and it shows Brunel's great bridge over the Tamar under construction.

If the Edwardian world into which I was born appears as remote and fantastic as some half-remembered dream, the Rolt uncles and aunts with which my grandfather so liberally endowed me seem in recollection to belong to an extinct species. Their like does not exist today, certainly not in my experience. Perhaps this is just as well. An old nobleman once remarked to me sadly in 1947 that 'Today I am a hawk pursued by sparrows' and I fear that those Rolts would have found the modern world equally hostile—and not without justice. For some inexplicable reason, no blue-blooded aristocrats could have been more intensely proud of their ancestry and this gave them a sublime self-assurance which today would be regarded as intolerable. Each was enviably certain of the rightness of his own views on any subject, but as these opinions were seldom shared by brothers or sisters, when two or more Rolts were gathered together, loud voiced and animated arguments invariably developed. Such disputes were conducted in a strange dialect (gairl for girl, larndry for laundry, etc.) which had little in common with the so-called upper class accent of today and seems to have died out with their generation. Whereas my aunts all possessed unusually deep voices, curiously enough, those of my uncles were light and high-pitched. This trait was particularly marked in my uncle Wilfred who spoke in a high falsetto and was nicknamed 'Squeaker' in consequence. With his extremely long and narrow face, I always looked upon Wilfred as a kind of caricature of a Rolt uncle in whom all the family characteristics were exaggerated. In old age he became so absent-minded that he frequently forgot where he had parked his car and used to invoke the aid of the police to help him to find it.

Serene self-confidence allied to the conviction that they knew best not infrequently involved my uncles and aunts in incidents which, even at that time, caused some consternation. Of these one example will suffice. On an occasion when my aunt Dorothy, a keen animal lover, was travelling by rail, her train drew up at a large station where she espied an unfortunate nanny goat, with a label round its neck, tethered to an awning column. Observing that this goat was in obvious discomfort, its udder swollen with milk which was dripping from its teats, she let down her compartment window with a bang and, leaning out, called in a loud clear voice which drew many passengers to the train windows: 'Porter! Can't you see that that goat needs milking? Attend to it at once!' Seeing that the porter only gazed at her in mute bewilderment, she threw open the carriage door, strode across the platform, hitched up her long skirts and, squatting down upon her haunches, proceeded to milk the goat, oblivious alike to her wondering audience and to the discomfiture of the guard, who stood by, fiddling nervously with his whistle, while little rivulets of milk flowed down the platform. Not until my aunt's errand of mercy was completed and she had regained her compartment could the train proceed on its way.

The surprising thing is that such imperious behaviour was not the product of great wealth. Thanks to my grandfather's profligacy, his children were left as poor as church mice. At the same time he took no steps to ensure that they could earn their livings in any gainful occupation. They were brought up to be ladies and gentlemen but were denied the means to be independent. That they were thus so severely handicapped can only have been due to that absurd Victorian snobbery that to be 'in trade' was unworthy of a gentleman. This attitude was wholly illogical since it would be difficult to find a Victorian gentleman without a tradesman or a business tycoon somewhere in his family tree. This was certainly true of the Rolts. Their ancestor Sir Thomas Rolt (d. 1722) of Sacomb Park, High Sheriff of Hertfordshire and 'President of India', whose portrait, wearing an extraordinary eastern costume, was painted by Reynolds, was certainly a successful, and probably unscrupulous, tycoon. But subsequent Rolt generations seem to have done little more than erode the fortune he amassed. As a start, they lost a packet when the South Sea Bubble burst.

Thus, although I liked and admired my Rolt uncles, I can now see that, lacking both money and training, they all led fairly unsatisfactory and frustrating lives. It is true that my uncle Vivian became quite a successful artist in water-colour and a member of the so-called 'Sussex School', a county in which he eventually settled; also that my uncle Harry, in the face of strong family disapproval, became an actor, appearing on the London stage under the name of Henry Bayntun though not with any conspicuous success. Uncle Harry's curious ability to consume the smoke of an entire cigarette and later to exhale it slowly through his ears was a source of considerable wonderment to me. He liked to perform the second part of this trick in the non-smoking compartments of trains to the consternation of his fellow passengers.

It was apparently in order for a gentleman to stoop to trade provided he was safely out of sight abroad, for both my uncles Neville and Wilfred became tea planters in Ceylon. But my favourite uncle Algernon was probably the most successful in the worldly sense. Somehow, I know not how, he obtained the job of tutor to the heir of the Maharajah of Cooch Behar, schooling him to the manners of an English gentleman. A strikingly handsome man, my uncle must have been well paid by the maharajah for he subsequently retired to London where he led a life of slightly raffish bachelordom as a man-about-town. I remember as a boy being taken by him on a visit to his first cousin Bernard Rolt who was a bird of somewhat similar feather and a close and devoted friend of Dame Nellie Melba. He is said to have been the only man who could cope with her tantrums with complete equanimity. In 1929 Bernard published a single novel, *Kings Bardon*, which I suspect, like many first novels, was partly autobiographical.

As for my father, Lionel, he went foot-loose about the world, gaining much varied experience but little profit. After working on an Australian cattle ranch and an indigo plantation in India, his last exploit was to set out on the famous 'Trail of '98' to the Yukon Territory. I have a faded photograph of him beside the shore of Great Slave Lake looking like a character in an early Western film, heavily bearded, guns in holsters at hip. I have two of those revolvers still, a ·38 Colt automatic and non-automatic Smith and Wesson of the same calibre. The ensuing sad story is related in the pages of his faded journal. Finding no gold and betrayed by his companions, he was left practically penniless in that bitter country but managed to make his way to Herschel Island. Here he was able to pick up a whaler on which he worked his passage back to civilisation and so home to his widowed mother who was by then living at Holly Bank, Christleton, near Chester. Five years later he married at the age of 39 and after another five years, in February 1910, I, his only child, was born.

Meanwhile my uncle Harry had left the stage and bought himself a house near Hay, Welsh Hay, or Hay-on-Wye as it is now called. Here he devoted the remainder of his life to the growing of roses, a hobby of which he was passionately fond. He sent us such glowing accounts of that country and of the fishing on the Wye that my father asked him to look for a suitable house in the district for us. Such a house was eventually found and, on the eve of the outbreak of war in August 1914, when I was four years old, we moved from Chester to the southern marches of Wales.

# Chapter 2

# Kilvert's Country

An important literary event occurred in July 1938 when the *Diary* of Francis Kilvert was published. As most people now know, from 1865 to 1872 Kilvert was curate at Clyro, a Radnorshire village just across the Wye from Hay. As a result of the acclaim with which this *Diary* was rightly received, Kilvert has become a minor literary celebrity and there is even a Kilvert Society whose members make an annual pilgrimage to what is now often referred to as Kilvert's Country. Naturally, when we moved into the Hay district in the fateful summer of 1914 this was all in the future and, so far as I know, we never even heard the name of Kilvert mentioned. Although this simple, kindly man was evidently beloved in his parish, his short life would have ended in oblivion had he not shyly recorded, with no thought of publication, his great love for the people and the landscape of this part of the Welsh Border.

Kilvert was neither the first nor the last man to be influenced by the powerful magic of this mountain country. I know that in my early boyhood its beauty and wildness was capable of inducing in me a strange feeling of intense exaltation that was part awed reverence and part terror. It could make my spine tingle and the hair on my head stand up. It was from such experiences and not from the teachings of any organised religion that there has stemmed my conviction that there is a God beyond human conceptions of good and evil. The reverse of this medal is that I believe these same experiences to be the source of my lifelong interest in supernatural evil. When, much later in life, I discovered the great mystical writings of the Silurist Henry Vaughan and his contemporary Thomas Traherne, I realised with shock of wonderment that they had been similarly influenced by the same landscape. And when, at about the same time, I read those short stories of Arthur Machen, *The Novel of the Black Seal*,

*11*

*The Great God Pan, The Shining Pyramid* and *The White People*, I knew that he, born at Caerleon, had experienced its darker side. Yet Machen also has expressed his belief 'that man is made a mystery for mysteries and visions, for the realisation in his consciousness of ineffable bliss, for a great joy that transmutes the whole world, for a joy that surpasses all joys and overcomes all sorrows'.

Although there are several references to Wordsworth in his *Diary*, Kilvert never mentions Henry Vaughan, while Machen was still unborn. As for Traherne, the seventeenth-century incumbent of the nearby parish of Credenhill, he, like Kilvert himself, enjoys a posthumous fame, for his greatest work, *The Centuries of Meditations*, was only discovered by chance in 1895, sixteen years after Kilvert's untimely death at Bredwardine. Yet a single terse and otherwise inexplicable sentence: 'An angel satyr walks these hills', which suddenly appears in his *Diary* between mundane trivialities under the date 20 June 1871 reveals that Kilvert, too, was of this company. But whereas the ordinary mortal cannot exist for very long on the mystical plane that Vaughan and Traherne inhabit, the great merit of Kilvert's *Diary* is that it is a faithful reflection of life itself in its rapid shifts from pathos to bathos, from the sublime to the ridiculous and from prose of visionary quality to homespun detail or country gossip. It is for this reason and also because no other book has the power to evoke such vivid memories of my childhood that his *Diary* has become one of my favourite bedside books.

In 1914, so little had changed in the district during the forty-four years that had passed since Kilvert wrote, that his world became my world, and by this I mean not only the landscape but the way of life of the folk who peopled it. The men and women I remember, riding their sure-footed ponies down from their lonely mountain farms to crowd the little streets of Hay on market days, were still such people as Kilvert knew and described so affectionately. Many of the local landowners and middle-class families bore the same names as they did in his day, and in summer they still joined forces in communal walks and pinics such as he describes. I took part in many of these neighbourly excursions. Even today, the district has changed less than anywhere else I know outside western Ireland.

Kilvert's *Diary* has its darker side. Reading it, one cannot but be aware that the writer was always acutely conscious of life's transience. It could scarcely have been otherwise when it fell to the lot of that sentimental and susceptible curate to read the burial service over many of those rosy country girls about whose charms he waxed so eloquent. Like so many early faded flowers, he would watch them sicken and die. Tuberculosis was then the arch enemy of youth and in 1914 the disease was still rife in the district, particularly in the mountain farms. Tombstones in the local churchyards reveal that the people either succumbed to this scourge before they were thirty or they lived to a ripe old age.

Kilvert's characteristic Victorian reticence and inhibition, not to say prurience, on the subject of sex was offset by a realistic attitude towards death which we now find morbid. We do so because our way of thinking on these subjects has turned topsy-turvy since Kilvert's day. Obsessively frank about sexual matters, we are extremely reticent about death as though trying to pretend it does not exist. This is misguided. So far from being morbid, a constant awareness that 'all flesh is grass' makes us appreciate the beauty of the world and the potential riches of life the more keenly. Kilvert's *Diary* is a proof of this. His love of natural beauty and his zest for the small, homely pleasures of life would not shine so brightly from his pages were it not for an awareness of life's brevity which he makes his readers share.

I learnt to appreciate this myself during my years at Hay, for I was then a sickly small boy who occasioned his parents considerable anxiety. I suffered from recurrent bouts of bronchitis which confined me to bed with a 'low fever' for weeks on end each winter. It was feared I had fallen a victim to the prevalent disease and there was dark whispered talk about a suspected 'patch' on my lungs. But my blood seemed to respond like sap to the lengthening days. Spring spelled convalescence and summer full health. Consequently I savoured these far off spring and summer days so intensely that memories of them now seem ineffably sweet.

I should like to be able to say that my home during these years was some romantic old house in the mountains, but the truth is far more prosaic. The architecture of every small town along the Welsh Marches reveals the fact that there was a sudden increase in their moneyed population in late Victorian or early Edwardian times bringing a brief period of prosperity. The more wealthy of these immigrants emparked land and built themselves considerable mansions, but the majority were content with neat detached villas surrounded by large gardens. This influx was reflected in the towns by the building of new shops, hotels and public buildings: market halls, town halls and clock towers. By contrast with the bleak and characterless cubes of today, many of these buildings have now acquired a certain period charm, but in 1914 we regarded them as hideously over ornate. No book that I have read about the Welsh Border even mentions this social phenomenon. I suspect the reason for it was that the belated coming of railways to the Marches made such small towns suddenly accessible. At a time when it was becoming more difficult and more expensive to lead the life of a country gentleman, railways opened up a new territory where property was cheap, where there was no shortage of domestic servants and where good fishing and rough shooting could be had for the asking. These were certainly the considerations that drew, first my uncle Harry and then my father to Hay.

In the scattered parish of Cusop, lying a little to the south of Hay, a small housing estate had been built at the turn of the century which was known locally as 'the Forty Acres'. The houses, which an agent would describe as 'desirable detached residences standing in own grounds' were served by a rectangle of narrow road that enclosed a single green field. This central field has since been built upon and there are other examples of what the planners call 'judicious infilling', but in 1914 there were, at most, a dozen houses and my father acquired one of the more retired of these. It was called 'Radnor View'. Instead of facing the central field as most of the others did, it stood apart at the furthest corner of the estate at the end of a short drive fringed by pine trees that have long since been cut down. These trees became so many eyries for me, the ladder-like set of their branches a positive invitation to climb them. My knees would be sticky and scented by the clear resinous gum their trunks exuded and as I lay in bed I could hear their branches, heavy-laden with dark pine needles, soughing on windy nights with a sound like the sea. In winter those branches would bow to the ground beneath their burden of snow.

These trees made a somewhat gloomy approach to what was a not unattractive house. From the end of the drive one could see its front porch of green-painted wood framed in an arc of dark trees. But the house was set at such an angle to the drive that its plain sash windows looked out across a tennis lawn and over the little town in the valley below to the gentle slope of Radnor, a mosaic of fields and copses that rose behind the village of Clyro beyond the Wye. Unlike the 'Sea Views' of so many coastal resorts, at least the house was honestly named. Beyond the house, the drive led to a small coach-house and stable with a hayloft above which fronted a paddock intended to furnish the necessary winter fuel supply for the horse transport. This stable was a singularly ugly building of cream-painted corrugated iron with green doors and windows. But at a time when the motor-car was beginning to oust the horse-drawn carriage for private transport, it must have been one of the latest buildings of its kind. In our time the only appropriate occupant of the stable was Meg, a diminutive Shetland pony which my parents bought for me in a misguided moment. She proved to be a vicious little brute with the habits of biting her rider in the leg, or crushing his foot against any convenient wall or tree. This effectually put me off riding for good and all. I have ever since preferred wheels to hooves.

My father, who at one time had been a keen amateur racing cyclist, greatly favoured two wheels (or at the most three) to four and throughout the war years the coach-house at Radnor View housed the two motorcycles he had brought with him from Chester: a 2¾ h.p. solo A.J.S. for personal transport, and a huge unwieldy Williamson combination for family use. This last was a somewhat rare breed. It was powered by a flat twin water-cooled Douglas engine and had radiators mounted beside the front forks as on a Scott. In my recollection it was not particularly reliable and as a family we never motored very far afield. I cannot think what had prompted my father to buy it, as he was a devotee of A.J.S. motorcycles, maintaining that they were the finest machines in the world.

The house had a red-tiled roof and walls of rough-dressed local old red sandstone with brick quoins. At the front, these walls were practically invisible under a dense tangle of white flowering clematis and ivy. If one looks at old photograph albums it is surprising how many houses were densely clothed in creepers at this time. It cannot have been good for the masonry, making it impossible to see when it needed repointing, while many unwelcome insect visitors found their way in through the windows. These included earwigs of which I had a positive horror, having been told by nurse that they were liable to crawl into my ears and drive me mad.

As one entered the front door, my mother's drawing-room lay to the right while on the left was my father's smoking-room. This had a high fender topped by a padded leather seat surrounding the fireplace. On walls and shelves were numerous memorials of his roving life: an Australian boomerang and nulla-nulla of aborigine origin and a long stock-whip to remind him of his days 'down under'; a silver trophy won when playing polo

*15*

for the Behar Light Horse in India; a length of whalebone, and the broken head of a harpoon recalling his empty-handed return from the Yukon expedition; a pelican's head mounted on a wooden shield from heaven knows where. A mahogany glass-fronted gun case housed his revolvers (one fitted with a long saloon barrel), a ·22 Winchester repeating rifle and a magnificent pair of shot guns—16-bore Holland and Holland Royals. My father was a deadly shot who spurned a 12-bore as though it had been a blunderbuss. Shooting with the smaller 16s he could hold his own with any man. Much later, after my father's death, I became a sufficiently good shot myself to be able to appreciate the superb quality and balance of these guns, but since I could not use them in the manner my father had, I regretfully decided to sell them at a time when I was particularly hard-up. I should have got a great deal more for them had they been 12-bores.

Sometimes, to entertain his small son and to prove to himself that he still had the knack, my father would take his stock-whip down from its hook and out on to the tennis lawn. There, while I watched him goggle-eyed from a safe distance, he would whirl the long whip faster and faster about his head until it made a loud whistling noise. Then, with a quick flick of the wrist, the spinning circle would suddenly become a straight line and the lash would crack with a noise like a gun shot.

At the back of the house facing south were the dining-room, the kitchen and the servants' quarters where dwelt a housemaid and my beloved Welsh nurse, Mary Gwynne. The dining-room had a pair of French windows opening on to a small lawn, sunny and sheltered, where we frequently sat out in basket chairs in summer. A grass path flanked by herbaceous borders led away from this lawn and from it one could look across green fields to the foothills of the Black Mountains: wooded Mouse Castle to the left, Cusop Hill, with a solitary white cottage halfway down its steep slope, directly opposite and, away to the right beyond the deep cleft of Cusop Dingle, the hill oddly named the Haynault which had a curious crest of outcropping rocks. Of these three hills, only the first was a true outlier; the other two were merely the steep faces of a high, wide moorland which we called the plateau, a great windy, unenclosed and curlew-haunted sheepwalk of close, springy turf and bracken which served as a plinth for those two northern gables of the Black Mountain ridges, Pen y Beacon (or Hay Bluff) and Rhiw Wen.

Although the Black Mountains are in reality of no great height, nowhere substantially exceeding 2,000 ft, they appear to be far higher and wilder. There are two reasons for this. First, their most prominent escarpments face north and east and are therefore nearly always in shadow. Hence they appear to loom over the rich red fields, the pastures and orchards of Herefordshire as darkly menacing as a thunder cloud. Secondly, they have a perfection of outline and symmetry that is incomparably grand. So majestic are the curves by which their projecting bluffs stoop towards the plain below that one is reminded of a succession of great waves, petrified upon the instant of breaking.

Seen from beyond the Wye, from Clyro or from the Radnor Hills beyond, these mountains with their outer rampart of foothills compose what I always consider to be one of the finest landscapes in all Britain. It was a scene that continually drew Kilvert's eye while he was at Clyro. He gives one particularly fine description of a stormy late afternoon in March 1870 when, as he watched, the clouds that had veiled the mountains from sight all day suddenly lifted and dissolved to reveal the whole range glistening with snow in the light of a setting sun. 'One's first involuntary thought in the presence of these magnificent sights,' he wrote, 'is to lift up the heart to God and humbly thank Him for having made the earth so beautiful . . . I could have cried with the excitement of the overwhelming spectacle . . . it seemed to me as if one might never see such a sight again.'

From our much closer vantage at Cusop we were denied such splendours. With the exception of one portion of the high shoulder of Pen y Beacon which appeared in the cleft of Cusop Dingle, the mountains lay hidden behind their foothills. But at least it was that much easier to explore their high solitudes and somehow I was always conscious of their presence.

Gradually, I came to know this country intimately. My first walks were necessarily confined to the more immediate neighbourhood, but as I slowly gained stature and strength I was able to range further afield. From what my father subsequently told me, my birth had been a traumatic experience for my mother. Consequently, it was some time after I was born before she could be persuaded even to look at me. In the meantime, I would have died but for my father's affection and the care of my nurses. Hence it was upon the latter, and in particular my Welsh nurse, Mary Gwynne, that my affections were at first centred. It was she who accompanied me on my first walks at Cusop. Initially these were part walk, part pram ride and they almost invariably took us along the narrow road that closely followed the Dulas Brook up Cusop Dingle. Perhaps I should explain

*17*

that 'dingle' means a deep and narrow valley, the equivalent of
the Welsh 'cwm'. Like other local terms such as 'glat', meaning
a stile or any other form of climbable gap in a hedge, 'dingle'
became a part of my growing vocabulary. No matter how many
times I went that way, I never grew tired of Cusop Dingle,
for the flowers in the cottage gardens beside the road and the
changing foliage of the many and varied trees that overhung the
brook ensured that on no two occasions did it look the same. But
above all I loved the Dulas Brook. It fell down its narrow valley
in a succession of small waterfalls, shadowed pools and boulder-
strewn stickles. It was spanned by many narrow wooden foot-
bridges by which the people from the cottages and farms on
the opposite bank gained access to the road. I loved to stand on
these bridges, gazing down into dark pools, flecked with moving
patterns of gold by the sunlight that filtered through the hazels
overhead, looking for trout. I would spot them sinuously
breasting the clear water with the lazy motion of trailing water
weeds, swayed by the current. There were birds, too, to look
for; wagtails and white-throated dippers bobbing on the boulders
in mid-stream, shy ring-ouzels, and occasionally the azure flash
of a kingfisher flying fast and low over the water.

At such times the brook seemed half asleep, its voice sunk to
a murmur as soothing as the hum of bees. But after a heavy
storm on the mountains where it had its source the Dulas
would become suddenly and violently awake and this I found
terribly exciting. A great torrent of tawny water would come
rushing down, filling the whole valley with its thunder. Tree
branches were varnished by the spray that rose from the larger
falls like drifting steam and, on the surface of the pools, gobbets
of foam spun giddily in the eddies. When such sudden spates
subsided as quickly as they had come there were always changes
to look for; here a tree had been undermined and had fallen
across the stream, there a miniature landslide of red earth had
altered the shape of a familiar pool.

When I was recovering from my recurrent bouts of bronchitis
in the spring, Mary used to push me up the Dingle in an old Bath
chair which I steered by the long handle that controlled the
single pivoting front wheel. On such occasions I would persuade
Mary to let me coast down on the return journey. Good-
naturedly, though somewhat rashly, she would consent to this
practice, allowing me to disappear rapidly out of her sight.
Although the gradient was nowhere steep, it was almost continuous, the road rough and the elderly vehicle quite unsuited

to such speeds, having a high centre of gravity and no form of brake. Why it did not overturn I do not know, but, as there was no risk of meeting wheeled traffic, I was able to pick the best line through the corners. When I had eventually rolled to rest I would wait for the faithful Mary to appear, somewhat flushed and breathless, brushing her brown hair out of her eyes.

That the Dingle road was rough is not strictly a true statement. One stretch of about 150 yards on the lower and more frequented portion had been given a tarred surface by the wealthy owners of a neighbouring house, partly to silence the iron-tyred wheels of passing carts and partly to prevent white road dust from blowing over their garden. It was then the only road of its kind for many miles around and although it was apt to become disconcertingly soft and sticky in hot weather, I used to regard with wonderment its smooth and dustless surface.

Later, when my mother realised that I was approaching the age of rationality and was fully in control of my bodily functions, she began to take the place of Mary as my companion on these walks. Sometimes my father would accompany us, but usually he was too preoccupied in shooting or fishing. In this way we established a normal relationship and she began to usurp my father's place in my affections. In retrospect, this seems a little unfair, but it was simply a reversal of the normal shift in the proportion of affection a boy feels for his parents as he grows up.

These walks with my mother took us further and further afield; to the tree-crowned mound and vallum of Mouse Castle, to the top of Cusop Hill and finally to 'the plateau' and the Black Mountains beyond. In order to reach the latter we had to walk up Cusop Dingle to the point where the metalled road ended, turn right-handed, cross the Dulas by a footbridge, and then climb steeply by a rough track, now a completely overgrown watercourse, to a farm called New Forest. It was by this farm that we gained a track that led up to the high plateau past the little lonely shepherd's holding that we knew as Cock-a-Lofty.[1] Although it entailed a considerable climb, it cannot have been much more than three miles from our house to the plateau and we often went up in late summer to pick whinberries or the rarer cranberries. But the occasion I remember most vividly must have been in early spring. All was fresh green below, but when we had climbed to Cock-a-Lofty it was to be rewarded with a sight such as had ravished Kilvert so many years before. For

---

[1] Many of these local names are corruptions of Welsh words.

under a sky of cloudless blue all the wide plateau and the slopes beyond were white with new-fallen snow and lay glittering in the sunshine, the folds on the flanks of the mountains shadowed to an unbelievable shade of deepest blue. I remember sliding over the black surface of a small, frozen tarn.

The track that we struck at New Forest Farm on these occasions led down to Hay in one direction and in the other it climbed ever higher up the side of Pen y Beacon until it finally curved out of sight between the two peaks to cross the high saddle between them by the Gospel Pass. This is known in Welsh as Bwlch yr Efengel, the Pass of the Evangelists, because, it is said, the Apostles Peter and Paul once crossed it on their mission to bring the gospel of Christ to the Silures. The summit of this pass was too far for my small legs and I used often to wonder what undiscovered country lay beyond those gables of the mountains until, on one memorable summer's day, I saw it for the first time.

My mother's mother, 'Grannie Timperley', was staying with us and, as a special treat, my father had hired an open two-horse wagonette to take us over the pass. A large wicker picnic hamper was stowed on board and we all set off on a perfect morning in June. When we reached the plateau, the clink of hooves and the grinding of the steel-shod wheels fell silent on the smooth close-bitten turf of the track so that one could hear the creaking of the harness as the two horses toiled steadily upward along the flank of Pen y Beacon. As we climbed ever higher, a breath-taking view unfolded over the valley of the middle Wye to Radnor Forest and the mountains of Wales beyond. But when we eventually turned left-handed and passed quickly through the narrow defile of the Gospel Pass, we turned our backs upon this familiar country and I found myself translated into a landscape much smaller in scale but in my eyes far more fascinating because it appeared so lonely, so secret and so strange. This was my first glimpse of the Vale of Ewyas, that deep and rich valley that the Black Mountains harbour in their heart. The child is always captivated by the miniature, and, after the broad prospect, suddenly to come upon this small and exquisite landscape that the mountains guarded so jealously was an experience I never forgot.

The head of the valley into which we had come was wild and treeless, its steep slopes furrowed by a fan of converging streams, but I could see below the first small green fields with a glimpse of distant trees beyond and as we slowly descended towards the valley floor we soon left the open mountain for a narrow high-banked lane where arching hazels made a tunnel of green shade. And so we came to the lost hamlet of Capel-y-ffyn with its tiny church and Baptist chapel. Here we turned aside to visit the Monastery, scene of that ill-starred attempt by Joseph Leycester Lyne, self-styled 'Father Ignatius', to found a community of Anglican Benedictine monks. Though tenantless, the Monastery buildings still appeared externally to be in good order, for Father Ignatius had died only some ten years before. The high roof of the choir—the only portion of the great church he planned that was actually built—still looked sound and secure, though eventually its vaulting would fall, covering the tomb of Ignatius, who lies buried beneath the central aisle, under tons of masonry. Beside this church, we saw the monastery bell, 'Big Bernard', still hanging within its wooden framework; how it was ever got up the narrow valley road is still a mystery to me. We saw, too, the white marble statue of Our Lady standing incongruous and ghostly in the corner of a field below the Monastery, marking the spot where she is alleged to have appeared to the brothers. This happening is commonly attributed to wishful thinking. Maybe so, but I will only say that if ever it is vouchsafed to man to see visions, then it would be in such a place as this valley whose very air seemed to a child to be numinous and charged with magic. That one of the remote mountain holdings nearby is called the Vision Farm is nothing to do with nineteenth-century mysticism but recalls some far older tradition.

I thought the Monastery, on the dark side of the valley and surrounded by gloomy pines, a sad, depressing place and was glad when we were rumbling on our way again along the narrow winding lane down the valley. The sun shone down out of a clear sky; there were wild strawberries and foxgloves growing in the hedge banks and through gateways in the hazels there were occasional glimpses of meadows carpeted with wild flowers; the creamy froth of meadowsweet; the purple spires of orchis. The further we went, the stronger sounded the voice of the stream below the lane, the taller and richer grew the trees until at length we turned aside and came to our destination—the ruined Priory of Llanthony, or 'The Abbey' as it is called in the valley. Here the picnic basket was unpacked and we lunched on the green turf beside the columns of the ruined nave.

No building in Britain has so majestical a setting as Llanthony. The valley hereabouts is at its widest and most luxuriant. Like some gigantic outflung lion's paw, the high, bracken-furred

wall of Hatterall Hill encloses its richness in a majestic protective arc terminating in a steep fall. Its slopes were thickly sewn
with sheep and in that breathless summer stillness the sound of
their distant bleating mingled with the singing of birds in the
valley below. Everything seemed to conspire to charm my five
senses. Nor was this first childish impression in any way
delusive. For since this first ever-memorable visit I have returned to the Vale of Ewyas countless times at all stages of my
life and have seen it in every kind of weather and seasonal
mood. Yet its beauty has never failed to equal my expectation;
in fact and in recollection it was to prove an unfailing source of
spiritual solace to me from that day to this.

It was after this first visit to Llanthony that I began to take
part in those communal, Kilvert-like walks and picnic parties to
which I have already referred. Among those who joined us on
these outings were our neighbours, Major Herbert Armstrong
and his wife, who lived in a large and ugly house of yellow brick
called Mayfield on the road down to Hay. He was a solicitor
though he usually wore his uniform and had what was called a
'military bearing'. He had singularly piercing blue eyes and
used to read the lessons in Cusop church. I stood rather in awe
of him. Little did we realise then that in the dapper Major we
were harbouring a dangerous viper with poisoned fangs in our
peaceful country nest. But of this, more later.

A much more likeable companion on these picnics was Thomas
Southwick, a retired inspector of schools, a mild, scholarly and
kindly man with a grey beard and pince-nez. My father took to
him although the two men were quite dissimilar in character. He
used to stroll down the road on summer evenings for a quiet
game of bowls with my father on our tennis lawn. I used to
listen to the click of the woods and the soothing murmur of male
voices as I lay in bed. Thomas Southwick became my tutor and
each morning I trotted up the road through the Forty Acres to
take my lessons in his study. He was an inspired teacher who
taught me more than I ever learned subsequently at school.

I remember sitting at my mid-morning lesson in Mr
Southwick's study when the steam hooter at the sawmills near
Hay Station suddenly and unexpectedly blared. Why was it
sounding so loud and so long at such a time? Thomas Southwick
leaned back in his chair and sighed: 'Well, it's over at last,' he
said. The date was 11th November 1918 and the Armistice had
just been declared.

Later, when I came to realise fully the terrible carnage and

agony of the Great War and that these years had been a time of
the breaking of nations, it used to make me feel guilty to think
how little the even tenor of our lives had been affected by it. I
remember only my father, who was too old to serve, shaking his
head over the headlines in the newspaper and the dark green
blinds which we put up as a precaution against air raids, although
no Zeppelin ever came within a hundred miles of Hay. Thanks
to my father's proficiency with rod and gun, plus the produce of
a large vegetable garden, we hardly felt the effects of food
rationing. Our larder was always kept well supplied with fish
and game in season. I recall sitting on the bank of the Wye and
watching my father, within two hours, take three salmon, none
of them under 15 lb, from the Wyecliff pool just above Hay.
But, although he was an expert salmon fisherman, he much preferred trout fishing as calling for the greater skill and when my
uncle Neville came to stay they would go off on trout fishing
expeditions, fishing the Kentchurch Court water on the Monnow
or, latterly, the Usk at Brecon. It was a disappointment to my
father that I never took up fishing; I think I reacted against his
total commitment to the sport.

Although there were—and still are—grouse on the Black
Mountains, the population was never very great and as the
'Twelfth' came round my father's 'Royals' would be carefully
dismantled and packed in their fitted travelling case ready for his
annual pilgrimage to Scotland. There he would join a wealthy
shooting friend named Holmes who each year rented Methven
Castle in Perthshire. Highly coloured postcards of purple moors
briefly reporting the 'bag' would arrive together with several
brace of grouse to festoon our larder. Lack of refrigeration never
worried my father who liked his game high. He used to maintain that grouse should hang until maggots appeared on the
flags below. At other seasons my father found plenty of rough
shooting locally. In Norfolk jacket, breeches, puttees and
shooting boots, with a capacious shooting bag on his back and a
cartridge belt round his waist, he would set off for a day's
shooting, gun under arm and cocker spaniel trotting at heel.
His cockers 'Don' and 'Flora' successively inhabited a kennel
behind the stable and were not permitted to cross the threshold
of the house. He never returned from these expeditions without
at least a brace of pheasants or partridges, depending on the
season.

We salted down farm butter in a great earthenware crock and
my father bought two small piglets to fatten for the table. This,

his only venture in livestock keeping, was only partially successful. For one of the pigs somehow contrived to fall into our
compost pit where it proceeded to gorge itself on decaying
lawn mowings until it practically burst and the local vet had to
be called to put it out of its misery. Such misfortunes my father
would dismiss with a sigh and a shrug as an example of what he
termed the 'Rolt luck'. In fact this luck, or rather ill-luck, was
really due to the fact that the Rolt ability to excel in any form of
field sport was matched by an almost total incapacity to deal
efficiently with anything which had to do with the practical business of living.

The seasons also brought the fruits of the field: wild strawberries in profusion on the high hedge banks at midsummer;
mushrooms in quantity from the old pastures; whinberries from
the mountains and, of course, blackberries. Gathering hazel-nuts
was a favourite pastime of mine on autumn walks in the deep
lanes. When I brought the nuts home I used to pack them into
tins and then bury them in the earth of the garden, like a squir-
rel, digging them up at Christmas. I used to think they tasted
better that way.

From the boundary hedge of our small paddock, one looked
across a couple of meadows to a farm beneath the slopes of
Mouse Castle. This farm, which I used to call 'Lididiway' (it
was really Lidiart-y-Wain), was unusually large for this district of small farms. It was of very ancient origin. There were
traces of a moat and ranges of barns, bartons and stables all of
local old red sandstone with walls of massive thickness. Local
people used to say that they had originally been built to keep
out the wolves. Whether this was true or no, it was like a
farm in a story book, a mixed farm of the traditional kind with
arable fields under oats, wheat and roots and with green pastures
heavily stocked with red Hereford bullocks, milking cows and,
of course, the ubiquitous sheep. At the farm there were pigs in
the styes and a great stable full of horses, for everything was
done by horse-power. Ducks and geese swam in the large pond
which was part of the old moat, while the farmyard was full of
scratching chickens, turkeys strutting among them with an air
of affronted dignity.

I became friendly with the son of this farmer (I cannot now
recall his name), a boy of about my own age, and used often to
slip away across the fields to join him. Wet or fine, that farm
with its great barns was a wonderful place for boys. On one
occasion we succeeded in mounting and riding a couple of rams.

I returned home reeking with the smell of their oily fleeces to the consternation of my mother and Mary. In the cart shed was every kind of horse-drawn vehicle from light gigs and traps to great four-wheeled Herefordshire harvest wagons whose massive wheels were not tyred but shod with a double row of iron strakes. There was also a type of two-wheeled harvest cart which we called a gambo.[1]

We used to help at haysel and harvest, pitching until the load grew too high for our small arms, or setting the corn sheaves in stook. And we loved to ride back to the farm, sprawled on top of the loaded wains, their loads brushing the hazels as they lumbered down the narrow lanes. I remember—it must have been at the height of the U-boat blockade in 1917, I think—that I first saw a Fordson tractor at plough on this farm. I little thought then that this was the thin end of a very large wedge that would drive the horse from the farm altogether within my lifetime, leaving gaily painted wagons and harness bright with polished ornament to rot and to tarnish.

Apart from my friend the farmer's boy, I knew few local children for I was, and still am, an unsociable animal and I always disliked children's parties. Occasions of this sort were reserved for Christmas when we invariably went to Chester to stay with my aunt Augusta and her doctor husband. Our neighbours may have thought me a lonely child, but solitary would have been a better word for I was never consciously lonely. Nor do I recall reading much as lonely children are apt to do. For although Thomas Southwick had given me an excellent grounding in the first two of the three Rs, I never felt the need to escape into imaginary worlds conjured up by other minds. Of my first four years in Chester I retained only a few shadowy memories like a random collection of faded snapshots. It was this little world of the Welsh Border that I discovered for myself and made peculiarly my own. When, years later, I first read that famous meditation of Thomas Traherne which begins: 'The corn was orient and immortal wheat, which never should be reaped, nor was ever sown', I knew it to be a superbly articu-

---

[1] The true gambo, however, originated in Radnorshire where it was designed for use in steeply sloping fields. This Radnorshire gambo was part cart part sledge with a pair of massive fore-wheels and a pair of large bosses behind to act as runners. It would be drawn uphill on its wheels and come down on its runners with the wheels locked.

late expression of all that I had felt as a child. It is said that the child is father to the man; certainly this 'first Light which shined in my infancy' affected me profoundly for the rest of my life. It was something which I learned to set my course by.

But I could not live in paradise forever, or, as my nurse would say tritely when I was reluctant to come to bed on a summer evening: 'All good things have got to come to an end, Master Tom.' I had to go to school; I had to learn, as Traherne puts it, 'the dirty devices of this world'.

# Chapter 3

# Holidays and Schooldays

If I saw any cars in the Hay neighbourhood during the First World War I do not remember them. There must have been a few, though doubtless their use was severely restricted by the petrol shortage. It was an entirely horse-drawn world that I recall; indeed most of the minor roads in the district were too rough and too steep for the cars of those days. In most country districts, the local doctor was usually the first to adopt the motor-car for obvious reasons, but our doctor, Tom Hinks, habitually rode on his rounds wearing a hacking jacket, cord breeches and leggings of polished leather. On the rare occasions when we went away as a family we hired an ancient four-wheeled 'growler' from Hay to convey us to the station, luggage piled upon its roof and straw on the floor.

We had no gas or electric light. Our cook/housemaid tended a voracious coal range and lighting was by wick paraffin lamps with bead-fringed shades of pleated silk. There were no telephones in Cusop and I doubt if there were any in Hay either, certainly I never saw one. Sometimes on clear nights the sky over the mountains would glow a faint but angry red. I was told that this was the reflection of the iron furnaces of industrial South Wales, Ebbw Vale, or Dowlais, but this information held no meaning for me. For there was no industry in Hay apart from the steam sawmills and the local railway was the only evidence that an Industrial Revolution had ever come about.

With my unprofessional and non-technical family background, brought up as I was in such a completely rural environment, it has always been a wonder to me that I should have begun so soon to take a keen interest in all things mechanical. I wanted to become an engineer, mysteriously acquiring this sense of vocation in that pre-industrial world whose natural beauty, simplicity and order influenced me so deeply. That by making this inexplicable choice I was sowing the seeds of future inner conflict I then had no inkling.

I think it must have been *Katie* that first seduced me into the world of machines. Built in 1890 and long since scrapped, *Katie* was a tiny four-wheeled steam locomotive which worked over the three miles of fifteen-inch gauge line that had been laid out and equipped by Sir Percival Heywood for the Duke of West-minster. It linked Eaton Hall with exchange sidings at Balderton station on the Great Western Shrewsbury–Chester line. I cannot remember exactly when it was, perhaps it was on a visit to Eaton Park with my nurse before we moved from Chester, but the first sight of this diminutive engine puffing energetically along between the trees of the park was enough. I became a railway enthusiast from that moment.

Hay station was not a very rewarding place for a railway-minded small boy, for no great expresses thundered through it. Like the small town it served, its atmosphere of somnolent calm was but rarely disturbed. Trains were few, and for most of the day there was no louder sound to be heard than the cool voice of the Wye flowing over rock-shelving rapids just behind the up platform. The station was served by two single track branches, the Hereford, Hay and Brecon line of the Midland Railway and the Great Western's Golden Valley branch from Pontrilas. Both were relics of wildly optimistic territorial ambitions that had remained completely unfulfilled. The Hereford, Hay and Brecon had originally been a creation of that inveterate Welsh railway promoter and contractor Thomas Savin of Oswestry, whose policy it was to promote and to build railways in the expectation that one or other of the great companies would subsequently acquire them. In this case the line had been amalgamated with the Midland in the teeth of the bitterest opposition from the Great Western. By the exercise of running powers, the Midland Company had rosy visions of its acquisition forming part of a new through route between its own system and the industrial riches of South Wales. But the dream of train loads of Northamp-tonshire iron ore rumbling through Hay en route for Ebbw Vale was never realised and the line had remained a remote and isolated backwater of the Midland system. When I knew it the train service—and indeed the trains themselves—can have changed very little since Kilvert's day. He was, as his diary reveals, a frequent passenger, often using the railway for sur-prisingly short journeys such as that between Hay and Whitney-on-Wye, the next station up the line. One would think it might have been quicker to walk. Little 0-4-4 passenger tank engines drew trains that, even by the standards of 1916, were archaic. There were a few clerestory-roofed, gas-lit six-wheeled coaches, but these were exceptional; usually the trains were made up of four-wheelers with pot lamps in their elliptical roofs. There was no steam heating. Footwarmers covered in brilliantly hideous scarlet and green carpeting were slid into the compartments on winter mornings.

Although the first sod of the Golden Valley Railway was cut with no little pomp and ceremony at Peterchurch in 1876, three years before Kilvert's death at Bredwardine, it was not completed until thirteen years later after a protracted struggle to overcome difficulties that were financial rather than physical, for it was not a difficult line to build. A prospectus announcing an issue of debentures in 1888 was accompanied by a map which was a masterpiece of mendacious cartography. It showed the nineteen miles of this remote rural railway between Pontrilas and Hay (together with a projected extension down the Monnow valley to Monmouth which was never built) as a vital link in a new direct through route between Bristol and Liverpool. What the map did not reveal was that this 'direct' route was not only longer than those already existing but that it consisted almost entirely of heavily graded and sharply curved single line along the Welsh Border and that in order to make such a journey a through train would have to make more than one reversal.

The line was eventually opened from Pontrilas to Hay in 1889 and struggled along in the face of mounting financial difficulties until 1898 when it closed down only to be rescued and re-opened in 1901 by the Great Western Railway Company to which it was sold for a fraction of its cost. Despite such distinguished ownership, however, the Golden Valley remained the most bucolic and dilatory of rural branch lines. To a small boy it formed an unflattering first introduction to a great railway company which was later to win my devoted allegiance. Trains on the Midland line might be archaic but at least they kept reasonable time whereas on the Golden Valley time seemed to be of no account at all. Although an intermediate passing loop had originally been provided at the half-way station at Dorstone, it was never used as such, traffic being conducted on the 'one engine only in steam' principle. This single locomotive used to work three mixed trains of passengers and goods daily in each direction. These performed desultory shunting operations at intermediate stations, dropping empties and picking up truckloads of cattle or timber. The conveyance of passengers was of secondary importance. I remember one frustrating occasion when my mother and I went to Hay station intending to take the afternoon train to Pontrilas. As we stood on the platform we could see our train, the little green tank engine with the single coach attached, performing seemingly interminable shunting operations in Hay goods yard, its every movement punctuated by a prolonged pause. At each sign of animation our hopes rose; now, surely, the train was coming to pick us up. But alas, although we waited until long after departure time, it never did so until, much to my disappointment, we were compelled to abandon our proposed excursion.

Although they had been comparatively lately built, no doubt the coming of these railways was something of a nine days' wonder, for in such remote country there must have been many who had never seen a railway train before. Yet by the time I knew them, these byways of the steel rail with their leisurely train services, their sleepy stations bright with flowers and staffed by stolid slow-moving countrymen, had become an accepted part of the country scene. They taught me nothing of that distant Industrial Revolution which had brought them to birth. To me, as I lay in bed of an evening, the distant cry of a Midland whistle as the last train from Hereford ran up the Wye valley seemed as natural a sound as the hoot of an owl from the fir trees outside my window. It was on our occasional visits to Chester that I formed my first clear impressions of that larger world of which our local railways were the only evidence.

Each year we went to Chester to spend Christmas with my mother's only sister, her doctor husband and their two young daughters. I cannot recall the precise date when this custom began, and as it continued for some years, recurring visits cannot now be separated in memory but have left a composite impression. My uncle, Dr George Taylor, lived in a large, rambling house called Grey Friars. It was very old, but had been rebuilt and encased in brickwork in Georgian times. For an impressionable small boy there could have been few more romantic houses, and certainly no more romantic city, in which to spend Christmas. After the simplicities of Hay, the brightly lit shop fronts in the old streets and rows seemed so many glittering Aladdin's caves filled with rich treasure.

One grocer's shop especially fascinated me. This was in an ancient building and its counters, laden at Christmas time with glittering crystallised fruits, candied peel and other magical wares, occupied the length of a long, narrow, stone-vaulted crypt-like hall below street level. A complex system of miniature aerial railways connected each counter to the cashier's office right at the back of the shop. If change was required, the shop assistant would place your money in a round wooden canister, screw it on to the two-wheeled traveller that ran on the wire, and pull the handle of the cord that sent it whizzing away down the length of the shop. In due course it would come singing back along the wire with the change, reaching its terminus with a satisfying *clunk*. I was fascinated by this device and could have played with it for hours. Sometimes a kindly assistant would allow me to be held up so that I might pull the cord.

But one recollection stands out in memory above all. It is of walking back to Grey Friars through the snow after a Christmas Eve carol service at the cathedral. Our way took us down Watergate Street. This was a narrow cobbled road flanked by even narrower pavements and shadowed by the over-sailing timbered gables of the houses. Because both street and pavements were thickly carpeted by new-fallen snow, we climbed the stone steps to the shelter of the row. Unlike the more frequented rows with their gay shop fronts, Watergate Row was a dim, mysterious place after dark, lit only by infrequent flickering gas lamps. It was inhabited—as it doubtless had been since the Middle Ages—by small craftsmen, coopers, tinsmiths and the like. The windows of their workshops were shuttered now, though some showed chinks of light and there were sounds of unknown activity within. Occasionally the mouth of a narrow alley, dark as midnight and leading who knows where, opened up between them. Perhaps it was the tunes of the already familiar carols which I had just heard sung in the candle-lit choir of the cathedral, the anticipations of Christmas and the contrasting whiteness of the snow outside that combined to induce a receptive mood in which my recollection of this dim tunnel of Watergate Row was registered and stored away in some most profound level of conscious memory. I could not have said why this was so. For a child's apprehensions spring from some mysterious source—racial memory perhaps—which becomes harder to tap as the years pass. The adult must needs rationalise and formulate what the child grasped intuitively. Attempting to formulate at this distance of time I would say that what I perceived then was an embodiment of the continuing life of an ancient city, labyrinthine, dark, mysterious yet not sinister but

intensely human. I think I was born just in time, for which of
our modern cities, I wonder, could make such an impression
upon a child?

My recollections of Grey Friars House are a random mixture
of ancient and modern. There was electric light, dim carbon
filament bulbs glowing redly in the long corridors. They were
operated by switches with covers of fluted brass. There was that
magical instrument the telephone, hidden away in a little forbidden room, the size of a downstairs lavatory, next door to my
uncle's consulting room. The inside of the bowl of the w.c. was
decorated in blue willow pattern and discreetly concealed
beneath the lid of a built-in chest of polished mahogany. A
second smaller lid opened to disclose a pull-up flushing handle.
The bath, with its big brass taps, was of enormous proportions
and similarly encased in mahogany, like an outsized coffin. Its
interior felt somewhat rough to the bare behind. It occupied one
end of a large, cold and otherwise empty room with a polished
wooden floor. This seemed to me an ideal place in which to
discharge a small cannon which I had rashly been given as a
Christmas present. Having stuffed the barrel to the mouth with
black powder, it went off with a tremendously satisfying report,
filling the room with smoke. Unfortunately, though successful,
this experiment spread instant alarm and despondency through
the entire household; they became convinced that the antiquated
heating system had exploded and I fell into dire disgrace.

Grey Friars was a large warren of a house with the traditional baize doors on both floors which sealed off the servants'
quarters and back stairs. Every room, even the bathroom,
seemed to have two doors and this feature, combined with
mysterious corridors and many dark corners, made an ideal
setting for hide-and-seek and other Christmas games. The house
was held on good authority to be haunted by an apparition in a
habit (presumably a Grey Friar) which frequented the back
stairs. On the occasion of one Christmas visit when foundations
for two new buttresses, one on either side of the front door, were
being dug, a number of human bones were unearthed. Some
held that this betokened the Friary graveyard, others an old
plague pit.[1] My two young cousins and I made off with a skull

[1] Chester suffered a terrible visitation of the plague in the
seventeenth century. 'God's Providence House' in Watergate
Street was so named because it is said to have been the only
house to escape.

and placed it at the head of the back stairs, arguing with childish logic that the ghost would be sure to come and claim it. We took special precautions to ensure that the slightest movement of the skull could be detected and were keenly disappointed next morning to find that, apart from disconcerting the female domestic staff, the result of our ghost-baiting experiment had been completely negative.

The house stood on the western walls of the city. The big bay window of the long first floor drawing-room and the smaller barred window of the children's nursery looked out over the walls on to the Roodee, a great level expanse of green on which agricultural shows and the annual Chester Cup race meeting were held. This was bounded on the south-west by the river Dee and on the north-west by the railway which crossed the Roodee on a long viaduct of squat brick arches terminating in a steel girder bridge over the river. Although distant, I could hear from the nursery the hollow booming sound that the trains made as they passed from the viaduct on to the bridge. Here there was plenty of traffic for me to watch, for the bridge carried four tracks, two of them the Great Western Shrewsbury–Chester line over which I travelled on my visits to Chester from Hay, and the other two the London and North Western main line to Holyhead. The two diverged at Saltney Junction, just out of sight beyond the bridge. I would watch the trains through binoculars from the nursery window, the gleaming black locomotives of the North Western contrasting with the more familiar green ones of the Great Western. Sometimes I would see strange coaches with salmon pink upper panels. These, I learned, were London and South Western stock, working over Great Western metals on through trains between Chester and the South Coast. Hankering for a closer look, my favourite walk was across the Roodee to the footway beside the railway bridge. On the further side of the river, this footway ascended to the road bridge above by a flight of wooden steps which provided an ideal vantage point. Later, as I grew more independent, I used frequently to take a tram to Chester General station and haunt its platforms by the hour. It was here, armed with a new No. 2 Brownie box camera, that I took my first successful photograph —of a shining North Western 'Precursor' standing in a bay platform at the head of a train for Manchester.

For Chester Northgate station I had little time, I chiefly remember it for the remarkable notice over the gentlemen's lavatory which read:

CHESHIRE LINES.
NOTICE.
These closets are intended for the convenience of passengers only, workmen, cabmen, fishporters and idlers are not permitted to use them.                    BY ORDER.

But I thought the Cheshire Lines trains poor things compared with the great expresses whose arrival and departure at the General Station I watched with awed admiration. Best of all were the Euston–Holyhead expresses of the North Western which were usually double-headed, a 'Precedent' piloting a 'GeorgeV' or a 'Precursor'. I found their arrival more thrilling than their departure. As the two locomotives came drifting into the great station with steam shut off and their long train snaking behind them, their coupling rods rang with a continuous reverberation, like a tintinnabulation of tenor bells, that re-echoed from the station roof. I can hear this sound still and it will forever be associated in my mind with the locomotives of the London and North Western Railway. In fact, it may have been a symptom of technical imperfection but to a small boy it was a brave and thrilling sound; the proud voice of power, proclaiming sonorously: 'I have travelled fast and far; make way, here I come!'

After the railway, my second greatest enjoyment on these visits to Chester was to be allowed to accompany my uncle on his professional rounds. They were the first journeys by car that I can recall. My uncle owned two Daimlers. One was a mud-coloured open two-seater with what seemed to me brass head-lamps of enormous size flanking its brass finned radiator. This car, which was of pre-war origin, he drove himself. For his rounds he used a 20 h.p. six-cylinder Daimler of later date. An enclosed drive landaulette in battleship grey with black head and nickel-plated radiator and lamps, it was always driven by his faithful chauffeur Ellis who lived in a cottage over the garage in a nearby mews where my uncle kept his cars. On these expeditions I sat in front on the black leather seat beside Ellis while behind the glass division my uncle reclined in solitary state amid Bedford cord and polished wood panelling. With his keen dark eyes and hawk-like nose, my uncle George would have looked perfect in the part of Sherlock Holmes. He always wore high, white stand-up collars that came close up under his chin and jaw and looked to me extremely uncomfortable. This somewhat

formidable appearance was misleading for he was the mildest
and kindest of men. This made him a very good doctor for, in
a G.P., personality and humanity matter more than medicine.
He was a capable but extremely cautious driver. Even on the
uncluttered roads of those days he would never exceed 30 m.p.h.
and would slow down and sound his bulb horn at even the most
minor side turning. His chauffeur Ellis was, needless to say, a
very proficient driver who found his master's excessive caution
somewhat irksome. Sometimes if the round had been long and
had taken us far afield, Ellis would obviously be anxious to get
home for, no matter how late his return, his first act was always
to leather down the car ready for the morning. With a sly
sidelong glance at me he would let the car very gradually gather
speed above the permitted limit of 30 m.p.h. But although my
uncle was unable to see the speedometer from where he was
sitting, this ruse was never successful. Sooner rather than later,
he would lean forward and tap peremptorily on the glass division with his stethoscope whereupon Ellis, with a sigh of resignation, would return to the regulation speed.

On these trips with my uncle I became familiar with the
countryside around Chester, but although this was far less built-
up than it is today it never appealed to me. Whether it was due
to the influence that the Black Mountains had upon me during
the impressionable years of my childhood or to some deeper,
primitive instinct I do not know, but I have never felt happy or
at home in flat country. I must have hills or mountains about me.
Some people have the same sense of mysterious affinity for the
sea which maybe springs from a similarly ancient source, but
though I can appreciate the beauties of the sea, I am aware that
this is a conscious, aesthetic appreciation very different from that
strange exaltation that I can only call a sudden awareness of the
numinous, of the recognition of some profound reality behind
appearances, that certain mountain country is capable of awaken-
ing within me. Even on these comparatively brief visits to
Chester, enjoyable though they were and rich with fresh and
exciting experiences, I used to miss my mountains and suffer
occasional twinges of home-sickness. But whenever the weather
was clear the far peak of Moel Fammau, sometimes blue, sometimes white with snow, became visible to the south-west from
the window of the nursery. I found the sight of it reassuring.
The mountains, after all, were not far away. It would remind
me that the ancient reason for the city's existence was to keep
the mountain people in check; its walls still watched Wales and

I would imagine myself some hawk-eyed Roman legionary, pacing the parapet below the window.

Chester's link with Wales was emphasised in my mind by the fact that my uncle owned a country house there to which his family would annually migrate for long periods during the summer months accompanied by their numerous animals, dogs and cats, goats and donkeys. My aunt's excessive fondness for animals was shared by her younger daughter, Rosalind, but by no one else. Like the goats, the domestic dogs and cats smelled abominably. They were grossly overfed, they moulted all over the chairs and carpets and were never house-trained so that one was always made unpleasantly aware of their existence. My aunt's misplaced affection would never permit them to be 'put down' so that they seemed to me to be in a perpetual state of advanced decrepitude that was at once painful and obscene. My father used to regard these wretched creatures with ill-concealed disfavour, muttering that the only proper place for a dog was in a kennel, but my uncle George bore his burden with saint-like resignation. It must have been a considerable expense to transport this seedy menagerie annually to Wales, but he paid up gladly as it ensured him at least a few weeks' peace from pets. For he would remain in solitary state at Grey Friars looking after his practice and make only brief visits to see his family, driving himself in the two-seater Daimler. On one occasion my aunt had the happy notion of transporting her goats to Wales in the back of the big Daimler, but this proved too much for the patience of the faithful chauffeur Ellis who threatened to give notice if the car upon which he lavished so much loving care was ever again used as a cattle truck.

When my uncle George finally retired to a small manor house in Hertfordshire, he found himself accompanied by a strange and gruesome assortment of live and dead stock. The former included two donkeys, bought for my cousins when they were small girls but now so senile that they could scarcely walk. A series of soap boxes filled with ashes contained the remains of pets that had passed on. The annual summer pilgrimage to Wales still continued. A motor horse box was hired to convey thither the two superannuated donkeys. My uncle and aunt followed by car accompanied by the latest pet dog. They habitually broke their journey at Bridgnorth, and as dogs were not permitted in the hotel where my uncle slept, my aunt remained all night in the car.

The house in Wales was called Plas-y-Garth. It could be described as a large *cottage ornée* of white-painted woodwork and walls of pink-washed pebbledash and it stood high on the steep south-facing slope of the Ceiriog valley in Denbighshire overlooking the slate roofs of the village of Glynceiriog. It was approached from this village by a lane which was then far too rough, narrow and steep to be passable by any car, a fact which considerably magnified the difficulties of the Taylor family's annual migration. In front of the house a high retaining wall of unbonded slate had been built in order to form a broad level terrace. In my recollection, this was the most pleasant and memorable feature of Plas-y-Garth. It included a deep embrasure built as though for a cannon and large enough to admit a table and garden seat, in which one could have al fresco meals while enjoying magnificent views, eastwards down the valley towards Chirk, westwards through the narrower defile that led to Llanarmon. The front door of Plas-y-Garth opened on to this terrace, but the hill slope was so steep that the back door was on the first floor and gave on to a lane, terraced along the hillside. Whoever had built the house had omitted to include any plumbing or the essential mod. cons. that go with it. This deficiency had been partially overcome at some later date by means of a structure of quite extraordinary eccentricity and ugliness. This consisted of a bathroom perched on wooden stilts on the opposite side of the back lane, the whole crazy edifice being clad in sheets of corrugated iron. This remarkable bathroom was reached from the top floor of the house by a kind of covered bridge of sighs of similar construction spanning the lane. I cannot recall that I ever took a bath at Plas-y-Garth. This is scarcely surprising for naturally each winter the plumbing was put out of action by frost and even in summer the most furious stoking would only produce tepid water from so remote a bath tap. If the bath was unusable, the w.c. was non-existent. Instead, a reeking earth privy, known to the family as the Fairy Glen, lurked in the midst of a dense laurel shrubbery at the eastern end of the terrace. It was cleared so infrequently and stank so dreadfully that a stay at Plas-y-Garth usually left me acutely constipated.

On my occasional visits to this house, the greatest source of attraction for me was undoubtedly the narrow-gauge Glyn Valley Tramway which linked Glynceiriog with the Great Western station at Chirk. As our train from Hereford drew in to Chirk station, I would look out eagerly for the rake of box-like four-wheeled coaches, a long tail of empty granite or slate wagons coupled in the rear, and the little tramway-type locomotive, *Sir Theodore*, *Dennis* or *Glyn*, at its head, standing at the parallel platform waiting to take us up the valley. Some of the coaches were open above the waistline and others closed, both with two compartments and the latter sharing a single pot lamp in the roof. Soon we would set off, swaying and rattling down a steep gradient through thick woods to the floor of the valley at Pontfaen where the line crossed the road which it then accompanied all the way to Glynceiriog.

On the hillside above the village was the Wynne Slate Quarry which was connected to the railway by a rope-worked incline. From the foot of this, loaded slate trains in charge of brakesmen were worked by gravity over a short mineral spur that crossed the village street on its way to join the main line. The Wynne Quarry was of the underground type and the manager, Mr Roper, once allowed us to visit it. This was a great thrill. Crouched in empty slate wagons hauled by a tiny, cabless steam locomotive, we travelled through what seemed to be miles of dark and mysterious underground caverns. However, the most important traffic on the Glyn Valley Tramway was not slate but granite road stone from the Hendre Quarry, situated two miles above Glynceiriog in the direction of Llanarmon. Passenger trains terminated at Glynceiriog, so the line beyond was a mineral extension only. It did not follow the road but was a reserved track and thus, to my eyes, a true railway. From the station platform it could be seen curving enticingly away out of sight up the narrow valley.

On my last visit to Plas-y-Garth from Gloucestershire in 1922 I had an experience even more exciting than the underground journey through the slate quarries. By dint of hanging around looking wistfully expectant while a driver topped up his tank at the station water column preparatory to taking a train of empties up to Hendre, I achieved my first ride on a locomotive footplate. With a jerk of his head and a terse 'Come on up then', the overalled king of the footplate condescended to let me share his throne. I was speechless with gratitude and wonderment. The locomotive was not one of the original tram engines but a later acquisition, one of the five hundred 4-6-0 side tank engines built by the Baldwin Locomotive Company of Philadelphia for service on the Western Front. After the war she had been bought by the G.V.T. and after re-gauging and other modifications, went into service in 1921. Unlike the older engines she was not given a name but was simply referred to in the valley as 'the Baldwin'. My chief impressions were of great heat, tremendous mechanical commotion (she had very small driving wheels) and of a ride so rough that it seemed incredible that we managed to stay on the rails. Later, I learned that these engines were notoriously rough riders. The load which we brought back from the Hendre Quarry that day represented only a minute fraction of the many thousands of tons of roadstone that were carried over the railway during its lifetime. In this fashion the G.V.T. literally paved the way for its own death. It was finally closed down in 1935 and today its surviving traces are so slender that only the initiated would guess that there had ever been a railway up the Ceiriog Valley.

Just after the war, my father skidded and crashed when returning home from Hereford on his A.J.S. Although he was unhurt apart from a few bruises, he evidently decided that the time had come to take to four wheels and the two motorcycles were sold. There could not have been a worse time to buy a car. Prices were inflated and manufacturers had long waiting lists. My father fancied a Calthorpe but because he could obtain no promise of early delivery, he finally bought the only new car that was then readily available, an Overland 'four', a black four-seater tourer which was Willys Overland's reply to the ubiquitous Model T Ford that it in many ways resembled. Though reasonably reliable, it was a very dreary car even by the standards of 1920, so as it cost my father nearly £500 by the time he had bought the various essential 'extras' like the headlamps and the horn, it was not a good buy. However, it did make us more mobile and I remember going off in the Overland for a summer holiday at St David's in Pembrokeshire. Although that part of Pembrokeshire is relatively flat, its narrow roads had numerous steep little pitches on them and I recall seeing the English light cars of the period failing on these hills and being compelled to tackle them in reverse. At least our Overland would go up anything in bottom gear, albeit slowly. It is the only time I can remember feeling snobbish about that car.

That holiday in Pembrokeshire was a bright spot in what was for me the blackest of black years. For, having reached the age of ten, my parents decided it was time I went to school and at the end of May 1920 I was sent to the Junior School of Cheltenham College as a boarder for the summer term. I think Cheltenham was chosen for its family associations, for although my father had not been there, a number of his brothers were old Cheltonians, and my uncle Vivian's son John was already in the senior school. I suppose that Cheltenham Junior School was no worse than other preparatory schools of the period and probably a great deal better than some, but to me, who had never been away from home by myself before, that first term was a traumatic experience. The school was an ugly barrack of red brick with the school playing field on one side and on the other a bleak expanse of asphalt surrounded by a high brick wall like some prison yard. Except on Sundays when we attended the College chapel in the morning and went for a walk in charge of a master in the afternoon, we were never allowed out, so that playing field and yard were the limits of our world. To one side of the playing field there was a small ornamental lake with an island linked by an ornamental bridge to a circumferential path. Even this was out of bounds. Occasionally some venturesome boy would be 'dared' by his fellows to run round this lake and over the bridge, but the strictest watch was maintained at all times and he was usually caught and beaten by the headmaster.

Most of the boys slept in two large dormitories divided into individual cubicles by partitions of varnished pitch-pine, their tops bristling with nails to discourage climbers. Bare, unpolished board floors could send long splinters into unwary feet. The narrow window of my cubicle in the upper dormitory overlooked the school yard and from its high vantage I could see over its wall into the garden of a large private house in the Grecian style which has since become part of the college. There was a wide expanse of smooth green lawn shaded by a great cedar tree and on hot summer evenings when I was unable to sleep I would see a small group of fortunate strangers reclining in basket chairs under the cedar. The sight reminded me of my father and my old tutor playing bowls on the tennis lawn at home, part of another world that now seemed infinitely far away. No banished Adam recalling lost Eden could have felt more desolate.

From late-coming and uneasy sleep I was awakened to face another day's purgatory by the school porter, Nash, a lugubrious and taciturn individual with a black walrus moustache who clumped along the corridor between the cubicles in his heavy boots clanging a large hand-bell. The first ritual of the day was a wash in cold water poured from a ewer into a tin washbasin. In my case this was usually perfunctory, consisting of creating enough lather to cloud the water suitably. This was particularly the case in winter when I often had to break the ice in my ewer, for the dormitories, though insufferably hot in summer, became bitterly cold in winter. Hot baths were taken only once a week by rota, but even this rare luxury was marred by another horrible ritual designed to ensure that every boy's bowels were kept open. With great jugs of senna tea, the matron and assistant matron stood guard before the upper and lower dormitories and each boy, as he returned from the bath, was given an enamelled tin mug filled with the disgusting stuff. The ruse for evading this was always to approach the hazard in couples. Then, while one boy engaged the matron's attention, either by a beguiling display of false charm or by detailing dire imaginary symptoms ('I think I've got spots on my chest, Matron') the other would covertly pour the contents of his mug into his sponge. With expertise and a sufficiently large sponge, most of the senna tea could be absorbed in this way, the sponge being subsequently wrung out of one's cubicle window.

What astonished me was the fact that most of the boys appeared to be quite resigned to such a way of life, while some seemed to find it positively enjoyable. To me, school was a prison which excluded me from all the wonder, beauty and excitement of the world outside its walls and when I contemplated the long vista of school terms lying ahead of me I despaired; it was as though I had been sentenced to penal servitude for life. It seemed incredible that my elders and betters, the masters, could have created such a barbarous little world and should appear to be so satisfied with it. It seemed to have been planned on the assumption that small boys were so many beasts who, if every waking minute of work or play were not ordered, dragooned and disciplined, would run riot and commit fearful crimes. I did not realise that the majority of my masters took school life for granted because they had known no other. They seemed to have none of that mature and kindly wisdom that had made my old tutor such a good teacher and consequently I learned nothing from them, or if I did I speedily forgot it.

Even if school life had been more civilised I believe it would still have been anathema to me. For I was a solitary boy who hated any form of hearty, communal life. Days so organised that I was never allowed a moment to myself were an endless torment. The only time I was alone was in my cubicle at night. There I would lie, open-eyed in the darkness, thinking by the hour of my lost freedom, of Cusop Dingle, of the Black Mountains and Llanthony. For most people home-sickness is merely a figure of speech, but for me that first term it became a physical illness. Utterly miserable, I pined so intensely that I became feverish and had to be moved into the sick bay. Since I revealed no obvious physical symptoms, the school doctor could not understand what was wrong with me and but for the evidence of his thermometer I should doubtless have been accused of malingering. But because I muttered repeatedly 'Take me away . . . take me *away*' the school authorities eventually gave me up as a bad job and wrote to my parents. They came to fetch me home early in July and I thus got an extra-long summer holiday. By the end of it I was not only in perfect health but had grown another skin which made it possible for me, if not to look forward to the coming term, at least to contemplate the prospect with stoical resignation.

# Chapter 4

# Gloucestershire

It must have been towards the end of my summer holidays in 1920 that 'The Misfortune' occurred and it was a little ironical that my favourite uncle Algy should have been the agent of it. Urbane and charming as ever, he came down from London bearing bad tidings. I overheard raised Rolt voices arguing at length in my father's smoking room and later noticed that my mother had been in tears. I subsequently learned that, on my uncle's advice, my father had invested a sizeable slice of his meagre capital in a company which had just failed. My mother was extremely angry with both of them, perhaps unjustifiably; angry with my father for allowing himself to be led astray and with my uncle for leading him. My father was more resigned, attributing the loss to the inscrutable workings of fate; the 'Rolt luck' had struck again.

The drastic economies that became necessary as a result of this misfortune led to a number of changes, the most important of which was the decision to sell the house at Cusop and move to some smaller house, nearer to civilisation in England, which could be run without staff. My parents determined to look for such a house in the vicinity of Cheltenham, not because they intended to economise to the extent of making me a day boy, but because they had taken a fancy to the town and to the Cotswold country around it.

After a protracted search, they finally settled upon a house in the tiny hamlet of Stanley Pontlarge on the lower slopes of the north Cotswold scarp, eight miles from Cheltenham and three from Winchcombe. Known as 'the Cottage', in fact it consisted of two roomy attached cottages of Cotswold stone which had been converted into one house immediately after the war to the order of an elderly maiden lady who had not lived long to enjoy it. The two cottages were of widely different dates, the one being late eighteenth century and the other of great antiquity— fourteenth century if not earlier. My mother purchased this house, which included a large garden and an orchard, paying for it out of her dowry, or rather as much of it as had remained to her following the depredations of her step-father. Although comparatively near Cheltenham, the house stood in what was then deep country, reached by narrow, dusty, single-track white roads between high hedgerows. Apparently other members of my family thought my parents mad to bury themselves in such a remote place and considered that they had paid far too high a price for the property.

Our house at Cusop was sold to a young solicitor named Martin, who had recently put up his plate in Hay and who promptly changed its name from 'Radnor View' to 'Bredon'. Meanwhile our neighbour Mrs Armstrong at 'Mayfield' had become so seriously ill that she had to be removed to a nursing home in Gloucester. Almost the last social engagement that my mother fulfilled before we left the district was to attend a tea-party at Mayfield given by Mrs Armstrong to celebrate her remarkably rapid recovery and return. The congratulations of the local ladies on this occasion proved sadly premature, however, for their hostess shortly afterwards suffered a sudden relapse and died in a matter of days. The full significance of these events, however, was not revealed until later.

We moved to Gloucestershire in the spring of 1921. Although I soon learned to appreciate this country, particularly its incomparable stone buildings, it remained always very much a second love. It was the Welsh Border that had my heart. Even the spacious stone-walled uplands of Cotswold seemed tame to me when I compared them with the wildness and grandeur of the Black Mountains. From our new house a rough trackway led to the top of Stanley Mount, a promontory of the Cotswold edge. On clear evenings from his high vantage point I could see the Black Mountains on the skyline to the west, a high wall looming dark as a damson against the sunset over the nearer folds of the foothills. At least they were not so very far away. There were also other consolations. The ancient stone house fired my imagination in a way that the Edwardian villa we had left could never do. I used to speculate about the many forgotten generations who must have been born, lived and died in the house: what clothes they had worn, what they cooked and ate and how they spent their working lives. The more I learned of English history the more incredible did it seem that, since the Middle Ages, my new home had survived such an immensity of change practically unaltered. On what strange, wild landscape had its windows first looked? They may not even have been glazed then, for some of their stone sills still bore the squared mortice holes for the uprights of their original iron grilles. It gave me a strange sense of satisfaction to follow with my fingers the chamfer of an oak beam or the concave curve of a stone mullion and to think of the men who had fashioned them with adze and chisel at least five centuries ago.

Looking back, I believe that this house, in a different but related way, influenced me as profoundly as the landscape of the Welsh Border had earlier done. That country had revealed to me the heart-stopping beauty and permanence of the natural world. Now, the old house not only quickened my appreciation of craftsmanship, but taught me how man can make a positive and enduring contribution to the beauty of this world. Its builders had been primitive and unlettered men, yet by fashioning wood and local stone in such a manner that their work would stand long after their bones had become dust upon the wind, they had made, so it seemed to me, a magnificent affirmation of faith. I knew that all finite things must have an end, yet in this way I learned to value only those works of art or craftsmanship whose maker had endowed them with a mysterious quality of timelessness, as though they had contributed to them something of their own spirit and by that gift had transcended their mortality. Because only such things possessed for me an intrinsic value and so were truly life-enhancing, it was through this that I came to see the tragic paradox of the world in which I grew up. This was that in a society that worshipped material progress, all material things of man's creation were becoming increasingly ephemeral and therefore intrinsically valueless; ingenious certainly but, to paraphrase Traherne, 'an innumerable company of objects, rude, vulgar and worthless things'.

Besides the house itself, another source of great satisfaction to me was that it stood beside the Honeybourne–Cheltenham line of the Great Western Railway. This was then a comparatively new line, having been built as part of a determined effort made in the early years of this century to dispose of the jibe that the letters G.W.R. stood for Great Way Round. Opened throughout in August 1906, it provided the company with a new through route between Birmingham, South Wales, Bristol, and the West of England. Following the foot of the hills, the new railway passed our house in a shallow cutting, slicing diagonally through what had been a rectangular orchard with the effect that the orchard we acquired consisted of a long tapering triangle, its longest side separated from the bank of the cutting by a railway fence of posts and wire.

I made myself a comfortable wooden seat in the fork of one of the old apple trees overlooking the line and here I would sit, especially on Saturdays during the summer holidays when traffic was particularly heavy, watching the trains go by. There was a regular service of fast trains between Cardiff or Bristol and the Midlands which were then invariably hauled by locomotives of the 'Atbara' or 'Flower' classes—inside cylinder 4-4-0s with outside frames and taper boilers. But there was one train I used to look out for with particular eagerness, a through express (later to be called The Cornishman) which ran once a day in each direction between Wolverhampton and Penzance. This was invariably hauled by a locomotive of the 'County' class, a heavier and more powerful four-coupled engine with outside cylinders. I invested this train with all that romance of far journeys which we normally associate with an ocean-going steamship, for I had never been to Cornwall and Penzance seemed as foreign and remote as Pernambuco.

At first, most of the engines were in their war-time livery of unlined green, but soon they blossomed out in all their pre-war finery of elaborate lining, brass-beaded splashers and gleaming copper-capped chimneys. The trains they drew also changed as the crimson lake livery adopted for coaching stock in 1912 reverted to the familiar 'chocolate and cream' which I thought a tremendous improvement. At summer holiday week-ends, traffic to and from the west of England became so heavy that sometimes the Penzance express had to be run in as many as four parts. Hence my interest, for such traffic brought many unfamiliar locomotives to the line. Sometimes these would include a locomotive of the 'City' class that then carried a legendary aura of fame because, as I knew, one of them, *City of Truro* was said to have reached a speed of 100 m.p.h. down Wellington bank in Somerset.

One of the steps my father took as a result of the financial misfortune was to sell the Overland. This was wise for it had a voracious appetite for petrol and gave singularly little in return. He decided we must have a smaller and more economical car and purchased a new Belsize-Bradshaw, a small open two-seater with a single dickey seat to which I used to be relegated. I do not know what considerations governed this choice, but it proved singularly unfortunate. The car was an optimistic and unsuccessful bid on the part of the Belsize Company to conquer the British light car market with what was really a refined cyclecar. It was propelled by a 90° twin-cylinder oil-cooled engine designed by Granville Bradshaw which was a beautiful piece of engineering and, when running, was as smooth and silent as any four-cylinder engine of the day. Unfortunately, however, my father, who was by now advancing in years, could never succeed in starting it and this, as can be imagined, proved to be a very serious disadvantage. It was not helped by the fact that the car had no self-starter. For reasons of economy he had neglected to purchase this 'extra' in the first place, but why he did not subsequently do so is a question I cannot answer. Perhaps it was merely a stubborn refusal to admit defeat.

Stanley Pontlarge is situated upon a hill, a circumstance that has proved its value throughout my lifetime's association with peculiar and often temperamental motor-cars, but never more so than in the case of my father and his Belsize. By starting it down this hill, at least we were able to set out in the car, but once we stopped it on level ground our minds would be haunted by nagging doubt as to whether it could ever be induced to start again. I remember one such embarrassing occasion when we had stopped it outside the Lygon Arms at Broadway while we had tea. We sat in the car trying to look unconcerned, while my father applied himself to the starting handle with concentrated but unavailing fury. A succession of kindly but slightly patronising chauffeurs took pity on him ('Let me have a go, sir') and were each in turn reduced to a state of breathless apoplexy. Finally they pushed us off down the road and when, by this agency, the engine fired, the small crowd that had gathered gave us an encouraging cheer. I found such scenes most humiliating. Their cause was that the 90° angle of the twin-cylinders does not agree with the armature positions of maximum polarity on a normal magneto. This faces the mechanic with a choice of evils: either two indifferent sparks or one powerful one and one extremely weak. Presumably our car had been given the first of these two settings. I did not discover this until some years later, while it was completely beyond my father's comprehension.

From this it will be understood why normally we only used the Belsize for long journeys such as our annual Christmas visits to Chester and relied on public transport or bicycles for shopping expeditions to Cheltenham or other local outings. There were no 'buses in those days, so public transport meant the service of 'push-and-pull' local trains that served all stations and halts between Cheltenham (St James) and Honeybourne. We boarded these at Gretton Halt, a typical Great Western halt with its wooden platforms and pagoda-like shelters situated a quarter of a mile away. We were very dependent on the railway's reliable and comfortable service, a state of affairs that continued for many years. We even had our *Morning Post* delivered by rail from the bookstall at Cheltenham St James, bearing a G.W.R. newspaper stamp. The guard of the 8 a.m. 'local' was officially supposed to leave it in the up side shelter at Gretton Halt but, to save us the trouble of going to collect it, whenever the weather was fine he threw it out of the window opposite a platelayers' hut by our orchard. It would then be retrieved by a friendly lengthman who stuck it in the railings by the house.

I shall always remember one early excursion by rail to Cheltenham with my mother because, when we had boarded the train at St James to return, she opened the local evening newspaper she had just bought at the bookstall and read the astounding news that our erstwhile neighbour, Major Armstrong, had been arrested and charged with the murder of his wife. Soon we learned the whole fantastic and terrible story. When Martin, the young solicitor who had bought our old house, started practice in Hay, Armstrong had determined to rid himself of this unwelcome competitor by poisoning him with arsenic. His opening gambit was to send Martin an anonymous present of a box of chocolates through the post. This failed because neither Martin nor his wife liked chocolates, but when they subsequently handed them round at a bridge party, their guests became seriously ill. His suspicions aroused, Martin then sent the remaining chocolates to the Public Analyst who discovered that each contained arsenic which had been injected through a minute hole in the base. Martin then remembered that the box had been addressed to his house under its new name although he had only just made the change and no one outside the immediate district had been notified of it. This convinced him that the poisoner must be someone living locally.

Meanwhile, finding that his chocolates had failed to have the desired effect, Armstrong began repeatedly pressing Martin to take tea with him. Although Martin had taken a hearty dislike to the man, Armstrong was so persistent that he could no longer with good manners refuse a business colleague. So he reluctantly accepted. That night Martin was taken so seriously ill that had he not possessed a remarkably strong constitution he would have died. As he was recovering, he recalled a curious little incident at that tea party. There had been a plate of buttered scones on the table. 'Have a scone?' Armstrong had asked and, without waiting for his answer, had remarked 'Excuse fingers' as he selected one and placed it on his guest's plate.

Undaunted by this second failure, Armstrong renewed his invitations but, not unnaturally, after his previous experience, his prospective victim stolidly refused, having secretly informed Scotland Yard of the suspicious circumstances. The two plain clothes detectives who visited Hay, ostensibly travelling in cheap watches, were not only interested in Martin. In the light of his experience they were concerned to investigate the circumstances of Mrs Armstrong's sudden death. When her body was secretly exhumed in Cusop churchyard there was scarcely any need for an autopsy for even the soil around the coffin was impregnated with arsenic. Armstrong had been slowly poisoning her so that it was no wonder she made so remarkable a recovery when she was removed to a nursing home beyond his reach. No wonder, either, that the celebratory party the unfortunate woman gave on her return proved to be the last nail in her coffin where her husband was concerned. He felt that things had dragged on far too long and speedily administered the final, fatal dose.

Following these ghoulish proceedings, people recalled that the last two representatives of a respectable old firm of family solicitors in Hay named Cheese had died suddenly in recent years shortly after Armstrong had set up in business. Whether they should also be exhumed was seriously considered, but in the event this was not necessary. After a long and sensational trial in which Armstrong pleaded that the arsenic found in envelopes in his desk (each envelope containing a fatal dose) was purchased from the local chemist for the purpose of killing the dandelions on his lawn, he was sentenced to death and hanged. For many years afterwards his effigy stood in the Chamber of Horrors at Madame Tussaud, but as memories of his crime faded the sight of the little erect figure with the bright blue eyes failed to produce any *frisson* and it was either put into store or melted down.

After their first astonishment and shock, my parents' feeling was one of relief that we had left Hay when we did, because otherwise they might have been called as witnesses at the trial.

I think this unlikely because if Martin had not bought our old house, Armstrong might never have attempted his life, or at least not in such a bungling way, and the murder would still be unsuspected.

At this distance of time it is difficult to recall the precise effect that the revelation of these sensational events had upon me. I think my reaction was then, as it is now, one of sheer incredulity. I found it very hard to believe that in such a peaceful little community these things could actually have happened. I made a mental effort to recall the Major Armstrong I had known, striding over the hills or reading the lessons in Cusop church, in order to discover whether, in retrospect, there was anything sinister about him. For some reason the occasion I found I could recall most vividly was of watching him wind up the carbide container of the acetylene gas lighting plant which he had installed in an outhouse at Mayfield. This container, as I remember it, was suspended by wire cables and was actuated by some clockwork mechanism which allowed it to sink slowly into a tank of water. I could hear the clicking of the pawl on its ratchet as Armstrong wound it up. Perhaps it was some association between the white powder of the spent carbide and arsenic that made this gas generator seem in recollection a sinister infernal machine and the building which housed it a Bluebeard's chamber. But there was never any doubt in my mind that, despite the fact that he murdered 'in cold blood', Armstrong was as mad as a hatter. His story is like some monstrous black comedy. No sane man would go about his fell business in so naïve and ridiculous a manner. His conviction and execution led me in later life to question the validity of the McNaghten rules and the whole concept of capital punishment.

It is difficult nowadays to appreciate what the sudden loss of domestic help meant to my parents' generation. For my mother it was undoubtedly the consequence of 'The Misfortune' which she found the hardest to bear. Being house-proud, she took to housework happily enough while gardening was the consuming passion of her life. But she always insisted that she hated cooking although she became quite proficient at it, using a reeking paraffin cooker in the scullery in preference to the large kitchen range which was soon ousted in favour of an independent boiler. However, like some shameful secret, she was always at pains to conceal the fact that we now had no staff. Consequently friends or neighbours were seldom or never entertained and even the visits of members of the family became rarer. Mrs Peart, a dear old countrywoman, tiny and bird-like, used to arrive from time to time on an ancient bicycle to 'do the rough' for my mother. Her husband, old 'Lisha Peart, was the local pig-killer and terrier man for the hunt and they lived in a cottage at the top of Prescott Hill nearby. On the very rare occasions when we had a visitor to luncheon, Mrs Peart would be summoned to wait at table, tricked out in housemaid's uniform, and in this way honour was saved.

The move to Gloucestershire coincided with, or may have helped to bring about, a marked change in my mother's standards of taste. Edwardian furniture which we had hitherto taken for granted now suddenly looked incongruous in its new surroundings. Over the years it was gradually replaced by antiques purchased with shrewd judgement by my mother. All the bric-à-brac of the Edwardian drawing-room, precarious occasional tables, brass 'hearth furniture', art nouveau vases, family photographs and weak water-colours on wide mounts in gilt frames, was consigned to oblivion in the attic along with (I suspect to his secret regret) my father's trophies: the silver cups, the whale bone and the pelican's head. Even his gun case was relegated to an inconspicuous position under the stairs. The two ugly modern grates with glazed tiles which had been installed in the hall and drawing-room as part of the recent 'restoration' were ripped out. Patterned wallpaper was taboo and we now lived in almost monastic simplicity surrounded by white or cream washed walls and an almost complete lack of colour and ornament apart from chintz curtains and bowls of flowers. No greater contrast to our two previous homes could be imagined.

The only part of this transformation I have lived to regret was that every piece of interior woodwork, ancient or modern, was stained almost black according to the mistaken notion of the time that all old houses must be 'black and white'. Only the massive roof timbers of the older of the two wings were spared this treatment and retained the lovely pale colour of ancient seasoned oak. The whole of the first floor had once been open to this roof, forming a single great hall, originally reached by a tallet or outside staircase.[1] But the first floor had been ceiled off and partitioned

---

[1] Early references to a court house at Stanley Pontlarge have led me to suspect that this may have been the hall in which the manorial courts were held. The manor was originally given by William the Conqueror to one of his kinsmen, Robert de Pont l'Arch—hence the name.

in the seventeenth century leaving a large, chapel-like attic above which became my particular domain.

To recall this part of Gloucestershire as I knew it as a boy in the 1920s is a somewhat melancholy exercise, so great have been the changes that have come about since, not all of them for the better. Rural life in the neighbourhood has changed more profoundly in my lifetime than at any other period since this ancient house was built, the enclosures not excepted. When I was a boy, an old Gloucestershire yeoman farmer named Mr Bowl ran the neighbouring Manor Farm on traditional mixed farming lines little different from those I had known at Cusop. I can see him now as he walked down the lane, leading his sheep, crook in hand and wearing a magnificent smock, richly embroidered over the chest. The farm tractor had not then reached Stanley Pontlarge and there was a large stable of horses at the Manor Farm. The fields surrounding the farm and on the hill slopes above were all permanent pastures grazed by cattle and sheep and by a large herd of cows which filled the stalls of the long cow byre at milking time. Each morning, the bulk of the milk was despatched in brightly polished churns on a horse-drawn milk float to Winchcombe station and one of my pleasures during the holidays was to accompany the farmer's son on this errand and give him a hand with the churns. In the fresh air of sunlit summer mornings it was delightful to jog along between the green hedgerows, the iron tyres of the float rumbling over the white, dusty road. Some of the milk would be kept back for local consumption and I would go to the dairy, presided over by the farmer's daughter, Florence, to fetch our daily jug of milk. Here on slate slabs the milk stood in great flat pans so that the cream would rise to the surface to be skimmed off. Those who buy their cream in cartons will never know the richness and flavour of such cream as that.

The farm's arable fields were all on the light Cotswold brash on the top of the hill and at harvest time the heavy-laden wagons would come swaying slowly down the rough track to the big stone barn. When this barn was full, the sheaves were built into symmetrical and beautifully thatched ricks in the adjacent rickyard. Then, on some misty autumn morning, came the thrill of the threshing. A traction engine belonging to the Winchcombe Steam Ploughing Company, brass lagging bands a-twinkle, would come panting heavily up the lane past our house towing threshing drum and straw elevator and 'set up' in the rickyard. For the next few days we would hear the drone of the drum, its note rising and falling as the sheaves were fed in, while a column of steam and smoke rose over the roof of the barn.

In the orchard beyond the barn a stone-walled dam had been built to impound a small stream that came off the hill. Below this dam was a washpool where, each year at the end of May, the ritual of washing farmer Bowl's sheep flock took place. Here I would watch the men who, standing on the parapet of the pool, wielded their long dipping-hooks deftly to guide the floundering sheep and ensure that each was properly immersed. Such men were highly skilled in innumerable farming tasks and could as readily repair one of the dry-stone walls that surrounded the arable fields on the uplands as they could lay a hedge in the vale below. Yet they received little in return. One farm labourer I remember named Gregory kept a wife and nine children on 26s a week. He and his family lived in a small stone shepherd's cottage halfway up the hill which was inaccessible except on foot.

This particular district midway between hill and vale was noted for its cider, for it was said that the heavy clay land that extends to the knees of the hills hereabouts grew particularly good cider fruit. Although the drink was always referred to as cider, it was the practice to use more pears than apples in its making and many varieties of pear were grown, each of which imparted a particular flavour and quality to the cider. These pear trees grow to great size and when white with blossom in spring put on a beauty that would have ravished the eye of Samuel Palmer. There are still three such trees in our orchard and a few years ago I asked an old farmer whether he could identify them. 'Them's Malvern 'ills,' he said. 'We used 'em to make sweet cider for the ladies and them's Bucks, we used 'em to make a man's drink, sharp and strong.' But when I was a boy there used to be another tree in our orchard, now long vanished, which bore pears of a bright red colour. Like many another species, its precise use is probably now lost to memory. Such fruit is useless for any other purpose. I remember my mother, attracted by their appetising colour, attempting without success to stew those red pears. The fruit remained obstinately wooden and tasteless.

Every farm along the lower slopes of the hills not only had its cider orchard but a great stone mill for pulping the fruit which was turned by a horse. There was—and still is—the circular stone trough and roller of such a mill in our orchard; it had not been used since time out of mind though other mills of similar

type still worked at neighbouring farms. There was also a local
public 'cider house' which had its own orchard and mill.

Old farmer Bowl at the Manor Farm was a connoisseur of
cider. He used to leave the fruit heaped up in an old farm wagon
until it was rotten before making his cider and transferring the
liquor to the great wooden casks in his cellar. The result was of
superb quality, richly flavoured and bland but deceptively potent.
It was totally different from that sharp rough cider known as
scrumpy that removes the varnish from one's teeth and from
that gaseous liquid in bottles that now bears the name. In later
years after I had left school, whenever I returned on a visit to
my parents I habitually spent an evening yarning with this old
farmer. It was a ritual to which I always looked forward. His
first action after greeting me was to draw a jug of cider from his
cellar which we drank from china mugs seated one on either side
of the wood fire. The mellow liquor, the warmth and the scent of
the glowing logs and the placid voice of the old man as he spoke
of country matters past or present in his rich Gloucestershire
dialect had upon me an effect that was positively euphoric. I used
to feel delicious but indescribable sensations crawling up my
spine into the base of my neck and all the anxieties of life would
seem of no account. I have since found that, even without such
aids as a wood fire and alcohol, the talk of certain wise old
people, usually countrymen or craftsmen, can have a similarly
therapeutic effect upon me.

While most of the nearby villages depended on outside stand-
pipes, at Stanley Pontlarge we did have piped water. It flowed—
and still flows—by gravity from a spring on the hillside into
roof storage tanks. But we had no electric light or telephone and
I have to confess that it was I who first introduced the wire-
scape to Stanley Pontlarge. As a result of a judicious swop at
school I became the proud owner of a crystal wireless receiving
set. This latest marvel of science consisted of a little box of
stained and varnished deal with a couple of coils, one fixed and
one movable, sprouting from its side. In the centre of its black
vulcanite top was mounted the little glass cylinder containing
the crystal and the slender corkscrew of the 'cat's-whisker',
clamped in the adjusting arm. Also two terminals to which one
attached the headphones. I bore this magical piece of apparatus
home in triumph. My mother looked at the box as though it
contained a poisonous snake and banished it to the attic forth-
with. My father, however, was more co-operative and inquisi-
tive. He rigged up a long aerial for me, slinging it from the roof

to a branch of a nearby pear tree, bringing the lead-in through an attic window and fixing up an earth lead. Triumph! When all the connections had been made, the coils adjusted and the crystal delicately probed with the cat's-whisker, the distant voice of 2LO spoke clearly through the headphones. Despite this success, however, my mother's prejudice was not lightly over-come and for many months the wireless set was confined to the attic. My father used to go furtively aloft sometimes to listen to the news.

My mother never permitted the set in our drawing-room, but by a very gradual process of compromise she came, first to tolerate it and finally even to listen to it. The set was eventually brought down to one of the window sills in the hall where it was concealed behind a curtain. Finally, my father constructed a terminal board to which two pairs of headphones could be attached. By unwinding from the board a long length of flex, it could be conveyed into the drawing room where my parents would 'listen in', seated one on either side of the fire. Since they rarely liked the same programme, headphones had their advan-tages. This arrangement had a serious drawback, however. More often than not, no sooner was my father settled in his chair with his pipe going well than a heavy goods train would pass by and its vibration shake the cat's-whisker off the sensitive spot in the crystal. Then, muttering curses under his breath, he would have to get up from his chair and go out, paraffin lamp in hand and trailing terminal board and flex, into the dark hall to adjust the set. Nevertheless, despite such snags, this device survived until after my father's death in 1941 although by that time reception was hardly satisfactory due to the unselectivity of a crystal set in an ether becoming increasingly crowded. Often it would produce a positive babel of sound as it received at least three stations at equal strength with the Post Office transatlantic telephone beam from Hillmorton thrown in for good measure. When, in its later days, I picked up the headphones expecting to hear the news and listened instead to two voices negotiating the sale of a dog across the Atlantic, I wondered if we could boast the last crystal set still in regular use in England.

One of these listening-in sessions was more alarmingly inter-rupted than by a passing train. There was suddenly a loud report in the drawing-room. In the same instant a small round hole appeared in the ceiling above my father's head and his lap was filled with shreds of smouldering tobacco. It transpired that a round of ·22 ammunition which he was carrying in his pocket (he had been potting starlings on the roof with the Winchester) had found its way into his tobacco pouch and from thence inadvertently into his pipe.

Dramatic incidents of this kind rarely disturbed the even tenor of life at Stanley Pontlarge. Compared with life today it seems remarkably static and uneventful. My parents occupied themselves with gardening during the day and usually retired to bed at ten o'clock. Visitors were extremely rare and this unvarying domestic routine would be punctuated only by the weekly shopping expedition to Cheltenham and, during term time, by fetching me from school after morning chapel on Sundays for a few hours. In such a level plain a few experiences stand out like mountains, the highest peak being when my father took me to see the Wembley Exhibition. It was my first visit to London and we stayed at Berners Hotel. I remember gazing in awe at the *Flying Scotsman* and *Caerphilly Castle* in the Palace of Engineering; also at the ingenious 'Never-stop Railway' through the Exhibition grounds in which the cars were 'threaded' on a screw of varying pitch revolving between the rails so that they slowed to a crawl at the station platforms. But there was such an indigestible plethora of 'serious' exhibits that I soon tired of it and confess that I spent much of my time and most of my father's money ecstatically riding on the Giant Switchback, the Great Racer and the Scenic Railway in the amusement park. In the evenings my father took me to see *The Green Goddess* at the St James's Theatre, with George Arliss in Western clothes and turban playing the smooth and sinister rajah, and to 'Maskelyne's Theatre of Mysteries' at St George's Hall. I think all subsequent generations of children have been the poorer for the passing of Maskelyne's. It was, in both senses of the word, a magical entertainment with which no pantomine could compare and it held me completely enthralled.

In the autumn of 1925 my father made another of his rare trips to London to visit the Motor Show at Olympia. I do not know whether he went with the serious intention of buying another car to replace the recalcitrant Belsize—I suspect not—but he was so attracted by a Model TE sports four-seater displayed on the Alvis stand that he bought it on the spot. It was a fairly expensive car at that time and a somewhat surprising choice for an elderly man to make. What my mother thought of his extravagance I do not know. It was my father's last financial fling but, unlike previous ones, it proved a good investment. For throughout the remaining sixteen years of his life, the Alvis was an unfailing source of pleasure and pride to him. Though he was quite unmechanically minded, the car never let him down on the road and never needed any major repairs. And because it is still in my possession I have every reason to endorse the wisdom of his choice.

Such longevity is the more surprising because, although for a man of his age my father was a fast and spirited driver, he never succeeded in mastering the art of changing gear on a 'crash' gearbox. Unable to equate engine speed to road speed, he always changed down to third by pushing the lever straight through with a sickening crunch most horrible to the mechanical ear. His other besetting fault was his impatience. After following a slower vehicle for some distance along a winding road he would invariably become exasperated and, shouting 'Why can't the dam' feller get a move on?' above the high-pitched whine of the gears, storm past in third quite regardless of any lack of visibility ahead. This manœuvre caused even the most unimaginative of passengers to shut his eyes and offer up a silent prayer. It is unlikely that either my father or his Alvis could have survived for long under modern traffic conditions. One trip beside him, never to be repeated, was enough to convince my ultra-cautious uncle George that he was a serious menace. But, miraculously, he never had an accident of any kind and the recurring appearance of the Alvis outside the College chapel on Sunday mornings to take me out 'on invite' raised my stock considerably. I became an insufferable little car snob.

Over my school life at this period it were best to draw a kindly veil. Although, like every other schoolboy, I was assured that school days would give me the best time of my life, in fact my experience was the precise opposite. I have yet to meet a man who subscribes to this 'best years of your life' myth, while autobiographers of my generation agree in anathematising their school days so roundly and at such length that for me to join their chorus would be tedious. Suffice it to say that I duly passed from the Junior House into the Military and Engineering side of Cheltenham College where I fondly hoped I would learn something about engineering. I was soon disappointed. I was not an academic type, but by some fluke I did so well in Common Entrance that I passed straight in to the fourth form in the college where I remained floundering ever after like some stranded fish. I made only two friends at college. Dissimilar in character and united only in our intense dislike of 'corps', compulsory games, school meals and petty rules, customs and conventions, we were looked upon as a thoroughly disreputable trio, entirely lacking the 'college spirit'. In such a closed community I felt completely cut off from the outside world and by the end of 1925, this frustrating situation had become quite intolerable. It was the more intolerable because I was now old enough to realise that my parents could scarcely afford to pay my school fees. That they should have to make such a financial sacrifice to enable me to waste my precious time when all I wanted to do was to get out into the world struck me as an absurd situation. So I asked my father if he would take me away from school at the end of the spring term and, somewhat to my surprise, he agreed to do so.

When my father gave notice of his intention, he and I were bidden to the presence of the headmaster as though we were two errant pupils. That interview was frigid and extremely brief. We found the head seated behind the large desk in his study, elbows on the desk top and fingertips together in a stern judicial pose. 'I suppose you realise, Mr Rolt,' he intoned gravely, 'that by taking this step you are ruining your son's career.' My father was not in the least overawed. 'I think that is a matter for me to judge,' he replied smoothly and, taking me by the arm, we walked out together. I felt like cheering and clapping my father on the back so great was my sense of relief and my joy in the prospect of an early end to a prison sentence that had seemed interminable. Seven long wasted years would soon be ended. At last I could begin living and learning in a much larger school.

It was one of the red-letter days of my life when, in April 1926 at the age of sixteen, I finally turned my back on school. Nor have I ever had cause to regret this precipitate step. I suppose that by taking it I was the 1920s equivalent of today's so-called 'drop-outs'. But there was a difference. For whereas they depend on doles from an 'establishment' they affect to despise, my great ambition was to be dependent on no one but myself. It is true that during the five years of my apprenticeship my parents had to contribute towards my board and lodging but, knowing their straitened circumstances, my aim from the start was to earn my own living as soon as might be. It was going to be a much more difficult goal to achieve than I bargained for, so dark were the economic clouds that would soon gather.

# Part II

# Chapter 5

# Steam at Pitchill

Apart from that one tenuous link with James Nasmyth, my family had no connections whatever with engineering so, at this critical time, my parents and I turned for help and advice to my uncle—as I called him—Kyrle Willans, who had married my mother's great friend and my godmother, Hero Taylor, sister to my uncle George. Because no man had a greater influence upon the course of my life for several years to come than Kyrle Willans, some account of the family background and career of this most remarkable man will not be out of place at this point.

He was the son of Peter Willans, a brilliantly inventive mechanical engineer whose most famous invention was the central valve steam engine, a vertical, fully enclosed high speed unit which, in association with his friend Colonel R. E. B. Crompton, was developed for electricity generation. Willans engines of this type were employed in many of the early power stations before the advent of the steam turbine. With his partner, Mark Robinson, Peter Willans built his engines and small steam craft at the Ferry Works, Thames Ditton. Later, he removed to Rugby to a factory which is still referred to locally as the Willans Works. It was at Rugby that Peter Willans died prematurely in May 1892 as a result of a fall from a trap.

While he was at Thames Ditton, Peter Willans owned a demonstration steam launch which he fitted with one of his early engines and named *Black Angel*. About the year 1879, he made a voyage of 1,000 miles through the inland waterways in *Black Angel* from the Thames to Ripon and back. This fact is not without significance, for Kyrle Willans inherited his father's interest in inland waterways and, in turn, communicated it to me. He also inherited from his father and passed on to me views on the value of practical engineering training and experience which would be considered deplorably old-fashioned and heretical today. While it is true that British engineering has suffered in the past from too great a reliance on practice to the exclusion of theory, I wonder sometimes whether the pendulum has not now swung too far the other way. 'A pinch of practice is worth a pound of theory' was one of my uncle's favourite maxims and he would refer to 'that curse of all works, the designer without workshop experience', quoting one of his famous father's trenchant remarks: 'Any fool can tighten a nut with a pencil'. He was a brilliant mechanical engineer with much of his father's inventive talent. He was also an uncompromising individualist with no respect at all for the upper hierarchies of commerce or for the sanctities of the boardroom. Hating pomposity and pretension, he had a delightfully sardonic sense of humour which made him a past-master in the art of deflating self-esteem. When he was in a mellow mood there could be no more delightful companion, but he was self-opinionated to a degree and extremely touchy. Quick to take offence, often where none was intended, he would suddenly become inexplicably morose. He was a short, thick-set man with a square face, a firm humorous mouth down-turned at the corners and a massive jaw. I found him at once endearing and formidable and admired him enormously.

With such a character it is not surprising that Kyrle Willans was regarded askance as something of a stormy petrel by an engineering world which, to an increasing extent, was becoming dominated by the board room, the accountant and the theorist. He could seldom disguise his contempt for 'white collar men' who had no experience on the shop floor yet who sought to interfere in practical engineering matters. Consequently, for all his undoubted engineering genius, he pursued a roving career from job to job, never attaining the high position that his talent merited. I do not think he would have been happy if he had, for such a position would almost certainly have cut him off from those practical engineering activities which he loved. Owing to his peripatetic existence I would not care to count accurately the number of different houses he and his family occupied. This was hard on my godmother, 'aunt Hero' who, like my mother, was passionately fond of gardening. No sooner had she got a garden established to her liking than her husband would decide to move on and she had to begin all over again, often in a totally different part of England. Yet she never complained for she was one of the kindest and best of women whose memory I cherish with deep affection.

While I was still at school, Kyrle Willans held the post of chief engineer with a small firm of general engineers named Blackwells in Northampton and the Willans family had moved into a roomy old house of golden Northamptonshire limestone known as The Grange in the attractive village of Milton Melzor between Northampton and Blisworth. During my holidays, my mother and I paid more than one visit there, travelling from our nearest Midland Railway station at Beckford through Evesham to Broom Junction and thence via the Stratford-on-Avon and Midland Junction Railway[1] to Blisworth. At that time my uncle Kyrle was using a 1906 6 h.p. single-cylinder Rover to commute between his house and the works at Northampton, a choice of vehicle which, even in 1924, was considered a trifle eccentric since it possessed neither hood nor windscreen. It was a brilliant summer's day with a sky of cloudless blue when my uncle first invited me to accompany him to the works in the Rover. I was therefore somewhat surprised when he attired himself for so short a journey in a seaman's oilskin and sou'-wester. It was a precaution which I thought excessive, but I soon discovered the reason for it. Ascending the hill on the approach to Northampton in bottom gear, the Rover began to boil so violently that we were liberally sprayed with hot water and so enveloped in steam that it became difficult to see the road ahead. That was the first car I ever drove. In low gear and on full lock, I remember circulating proudly round and round the yard at the back of the house at Milton.

For works transport, Blackwells used an even more remarkable vehicle, a White steam lorry of indeterminate date. Outwardly, this resembled a solid-tyred petrol-engined lorry of the period, but its bonnet concealed a vertical steam engine which was supplied from a flash boiler under the seat of the cab, its 'radiator' being a condenser. On one occasion my cousin Bill Willans and I were allowed to accompany the driver of this vehicle on his rounds. I think that the paraffin burner which fired the flash boiler must have been more than usually temperamental, for the cab would sometimes fill with choking fumes and I was alarmed by the tongues of flame which occasionally

[1] The S.M.J. was rudely christened the Slow, Mouldy & Jolting. Tedious it may have been, yet I have the happiest memories of these slow journeys by this unfrequented railway byway that wandered across the breadth of the midland shires. Like most cross-country lines, it is now no more than a memory.

licked out in unexpected places. One of our ports of call was a local celluloid factory where, not unnaturally, the strictest fire precautions were enforced. Here the appearance of the White, exuding smoke and flame, occasioned considerable alarm and we were unceremoniously shooed away.

One of Blackwells' regular jobs was the repair of industrial steam locomotives from the local ironstone quarry railways. My uncle, a steam man born and bred, deplored the inefficiency of the orthodox steam locomotive for such slow-moving applications, arguing that a steam engine which could be geared down to the wheels would be far more efficient because it could be kept turning at an economic speed, avoiding unnecessary heat losses accompanied by condensation of the steam in the cylinders. When a small Manning Wardle four-coupled saddle tank locomotive named *Ancoats*, from the Isham Quarries between Kettering and Wellingborough, came into the works for repair and it was found that she needed a new boiler, my uncle, with the permission of the quarry company, was able to try out his theory. An old Sentinel steam waggon was purchased second-hand, its engine and boiler removed and mounted in the frames of *Ancoats*. The engine drove on to one axle by roller chain and a second similar chain was used to couple the two axles together. On my first visit to Blackwells, I saw this conversion in progress on the shop floor and on a subsequent visit I was able to ride the footplate of *Ancoats* when she made her first trial run over the Isham Quarry line.

So successful did *Ancoats* prove that the Sentinel Waggon Works at Shrewsbury decided to take up the manufacture of geared steam locomotives. Engine and boiler units of greater power and capacity than those used in the road vehicle were designed for the new locomotives and my uncle was appointed to take charge of a Sentinel locomotive sales office in Chester. This entailed a move from Northamptonshire and at the time I left school the Willans family were installed in a house called Deebank in the village of Farndon. This was situated on the upstream side of Farndon bridge, looking out from a high bank across the Dee which here forms the border between Cheshire and Flintshire. From the house one could see the weekly Sunday pilgrimage of thirsty Welshmen crossing the bridge from 'dry' Wales into 'wet' Cheshire. I visited Deebank on my first motorcycle, a 2¼ h.p. B.S.A., at the time of the General Strike.

With such exciting experiences during my holidays it can be imagined how eagerly I looked forward to the day when I would no longer be a passive spectator of the engineering activities of others but would be able to put on a suit of overalls and get down to the job myself. My uncle Kyrle recommended my parents to send me as a pupil for two years to his friends, the brothers Douglas, Leslie and Ernest Bomford, farmers and agricultural engineers of Pitchill, near Evesham. This was only fifteen miles away from Stanley Pontlarge, so I should be able to come home for week-ends on my motorcycle. I began my new life at Pitchill on 29th May 1926.

Pitchill is on the fringe of the Vale of Evesham near the Worcestershire–Warwickshire border and the Bomfords had been farming there for three generations. Their grandfather, Benjamin Bomford, had been a pioneer in the district of steam cultivation and there are old photographs extant showing his first set of steam cable engines—curious Savory machines with rope drum encircling the boiler barrel. Their father had been a great friend of Sir Oliver Lodge who frequently came to stay at the former's home at Bevington Hall. On one of these occasions Sir Oliver determined to try the effect of high tension, low amperage current on the growth of strawberry plants and with his friend's enthusiastic collaboration a trial plot in one of the strawberry fields was strung with a cat's-cradle of wires supported on poles. Such strange goings-on were not popular with the farm labourers whose hoes were apt to make contact with the wires with electrifying results. But apparently the strawberry plants benefited, though not to an economic extent. With the same pioneer spirit as their forebears, the three Bomford brothers not only ran a very large farm, part of it devoted to growing fruit, but also maintained a sizeable engineering workshop beside the farm at Pitchill. This, besides dealing with home farm machinery, repaired and serviced the five sets of steam cable ploughing tackle with which they undertook contract cultivation and ploughing all over the Evesham vale. Four of these sets consisted of Fowler compounds, while the fifth was a pair of compound MacLarens. A sixth set of very old single-cylinder Fowlers was kept for use on the home farm. In addition there was a Ransome traction engine and threshing drum which went out on contract and also did work on the farm. Finally, there was an old Sentinel steam waggon which did farm road haulage and a Marshall steam portable engine which was used to drive the workshop machinery. My uncle was right in thinking that working in this small shop would be a good introduction to steam engineering.

For a young apprentice straight from school it is far better that his initiation should be in a small jobbing engineering workshop of this kind rather than in some large works. Not only does he get more personal attention, but there is a much greater variety of work. Almost every day some new job comes along with its own special problems to test his aptitude, his initiative and his manual dexterity whereas, in a large production shop he is often given some menial, unskilled task to perform which may last for weeks or even months. This may be good discipline but it is a waste of his precious training time because it does not teach him his craft.

Besides myself, there were only seven on the regular strength of the Pitchill shop. They were Percy Lester, the working foreman, Will Salisbury and Alan Bloxham, fitters and machinists, a blacksmith whose name I do not remember, Ernest Cole the carpenter, Joe Bailey, an ex-steam-plough driver, and a little shop boy, younger than myself, named George Leonard. Joe Bailey finished his steam-ploughing career when he lost his forearm in the motion of his engine. He was now the shop labourer and looked after the portable engine which supplied the power. With the exception of Percy Lester, whose home was in Redditch and who came to work on a motorcycle, all were local countrymen. Humorous, wise and gentle men, they taught me much, not only about their crafts but about human nature and country ways. While the memory of many men with whom I have been associated subsequently has faded, after more than forty years I find I can recall them most clearly to mind, see their faces, their characteristic expressions and gestures, and even hear their voices.

When a set of ploughing tackle which had been out on contract work returned to its base at Pitchill for attention and overhaul, its living van would be parked in the yard and the men in charge of it then helped with the maintenance work. This meant that there were usually more than seven of us working in the shop. Because they came and went, I do not recall these 'outside' men so clearly. I remember Archie Ellison, a small, lean, gnome-like man who was in charge of the big MacLarens and Will Robbins who drove the Sentinel steam waggon and, occasionally, one of the steam ploughing engines used on the farm. Will Robbins was a tall, lugubrious man of about sixty with the expression of a sad spaniel. He wore a heavy black moustache which completely concealed his mouth so that I do not know if he ever smiled. I assumed so from the occasional twinkle that lit his steady blues eyes. But of the steam plough drivers the man I remember best of all was old Bill Smith. Over seventy years of age, he no longer went out on contract work but was in charge of the two old Fowler engines which were used on the farm. He therefore spent much more of his time in the shop than did the other drivers. Bill Smith was a rural character of a kind rarely to be met today. His notions of personal hygiene were minimal. He habitually wore a very battered and faded trilby hat, wisps of sparse white hair straying beneath its brim. Because he never wore overalls and apparently never changed his clothes he presented an appearance so filthy and so tattered that it verged upon the indecent. The humorous wrinkles that fanned from the corner of his eyes were deeply ingrained with dirt. Not surprisingly, he smelt, but fortunately this stench was usually overlaid by the reek of his incredibly strong shag tobacco. He rolled this between his grimy paws before stuffing it in an old briar pipe from which the vulcanite mouthpiece had long since broken off. Consequently, it was so short that the edge of the bowl touched the tip of his nose. He appeared to subsist entirely on thick slices of cold boiled bacon wedged between great hunks of bread. This he washed down with noisy gulps from a bottle of home-made parsnip wine of great potency. One hot noon day, Ernest Cole the carpenter incautiously accepted a swig from Bill Smith's proffered bottle, tottered back to his shop and was discovered later that afternoon stretched out insensible upon his bench. Yet Bill habitually drank a pint of the stuff at each lunchtime sitting and appeared to suffer no ill effects. Since he often ate his lunch with hands plastered in white lead after making a new joint for a steam pipe or inspection cover, he was apparently impervious alike to poison, strong drink or strong tobacco. Yet he was an engaging old man with a salty wit, experienced and wise in the ways of steam.

I lived in the farmhouse at Pitchill with Ernest Bomford, who was unmarried, and we were looked after by a middle-aged married couple. In one room of this large early Victorian house was the farm office. Ernest Bomford ran the farm and had nothing to do with the engineering side of the business which was the sole concern of his eldest brother Douglas who lived with his wife Betty at nearby Bevington Hall. Except in their voices, the two brothers were quite unlike each other. Ernest, nicknamed by his brothers 'Herx', was a massive sandy-haired, red-faced man, always very friendly and jovial towards me.

Douglas Bomford, on the other hand, was tall, slim and dark.

He walked with the aid of a stick as the result of a wound in the leg which he had received during the war when he was also badly gassed. Many years later I came to know Douglas very well as an equal and found in him, until his recent death in 1969, a most charming and delightful friend. But at this time I stood very much in awe of him. He was never so forthcoming towards me as his brother Ernest, seeming to be stern and withdrawn, never allowing me to forget that he was the boss and I his pupil, although he always treated me with scrupulous fairness. If he seemed to me moody it was, I think, because his leg frequently pained him and he suffered ill health as a result of the gassing. Like my uncle Kyrle, he was a 'natural' mechanical engineer with considerable power of invention and the ability to solve a tricky mechanical problem on the spot with a quick sketch on the back of an old envelope. Indeed the two men, though quite unlike physically, temperamentally had much in common and I soon understood the reason for their friendship.

There was a fourth and youngest brother, Dick, who resembled Ernest in appearance and whom I saw but rarely as he became a doctor and was at this time studying for his degree in London. Of the four brothers, my favourite then was Leslie. Next in age to Douglas, he was like him physically and also shared his engineering bent. I found in him, young as I was, the friend I was later to find in Douglas and we got along famously.

Leslie owned a Stanley steam car, a 1921 four-seater tourer which, unlike the earlier pre-war models, was fitted with a condenser. The Stanley's two-cylinder engine was mounted horizontally to the rear of the chassis and was in unit with the back-axle which it drove through fixed reduction gears. There was a vertical, multitubular boiler under the bonnet fired by a petrol/paraffin burner which worked on the same principle as a blowlamp, the petrol pilot burner heating the vaporiser of the main paraffin burner which resembled a greatly enlarged gas ring. From the moment of lighting the pilot burner, it took about fifteen minutes to raise a full head of steam at 600 lbs. p.s.i. In the heyday of the Stanley car in America when petrol there was very cheap, it was the practice of owners to leave the pilot burner alight all night in the garage to ensure a quick start next morning. But by 1926 steam cars of any make had become extremely rare in England and they resembled the more orthodox cars of the day so closely that if the pilot burner was left on there were apt to be embarrassing misunderstandings. Thus on one occasion Leslie Bomford parked the Stanley in Birmingham and returned to find an apprehensive crowd watching it from a safe distance, convinced that it was about to burst into flames or explode. Someone had glimpsed a flicker of flame from the pilot burner, had mistaken for smoke the wisp of steam that was drifting through the bonnet louvres and had prudently sent for the fire brigade. Leslie had some difficulty in convincing these men that their services were not required.

In my spare time in the evenings I helped Leslie overhaul the Stanley in the workshop. By the time I had explored the intricacies of the automatic fuel and water controls, I had learned that a steam car is by no means the delightfully simple affair that most people suppose it to be. When the work was done I was rewarded for my help with a trial run in the car for some miles along the road towards Redditch. At a time when such ordinary cars as I had experienced made a lot of mechanical commotion, particularly in the indirect gears, the complete silence of the Stanley, its feeling of effortless power and surging acceleration, made a profound impression upon me so that I became an enthusiastic devotee of the steam car from that moment. In fact, as I learned later, with this model Stanley it was impossible to maintain a speed much in excess of 40 m.p.h. without losing steam pressure, although, by driving judiciously, one could keep power in reserve for hill-climbing or for short bursts of speed.

I was sorry when, not long after I came to Pitchill, Leslie Bomford and his steam car removed themselves to Shrewsbury. Through the agency of my uncle Kyrle, he had obtained a post at the Sentinel Waggon Works. My uncle was himself now stationed at Shrewsbury, having removed his family yet again to a house at Dovaston on the Welsh Border some miles to the west of the town.

Work in the Pitchill shop began at seven o'clock, though I had a half-hour break at 9 a.m. when I returned to the farmhouse for breakfast. Then work continued until 5 p.m. with an hour's break for lunch at one o'clock. Throughout the summer months this timetable was pleasant enough, but on dark, frosty mornings in winter with only a quick cup of tea to warm my belly the first two hours were an ordeal. The only heat in the shops came from the blacksmith's hearth, and a malodorous acetylene gas plant, which lurked in a small shed at the back of the shop, provided the only light from bat's wing burners. The big steam ploughing engines stood side by side in a large open-sided shed in front of the workshops and to work on them in the first pallid dawnlight of a winter morning was the coldest job I have ever known. Their metal was so cold that one's fingers stuck to it.

Here, slowly and very painfully, I began to learn the rudiments of the engineer's craft: how to use a hammer and chisel; how to file a surface truly flat; how to scrape and fit a bearing brass; how to strike for the blacksmith (a welcome job on a cold day) and how to turn a screw with an odd number of threads to the inch in a lathe. When chiselling I at first had my eye fixed nervously on the chisel head while I tapped it ineffectually with the hammer, holding its shaft only about four inches below the head. This provoked amused cries of 'hit it, don't kiss it!' until, at the price of bruised and bloody knuckles, I learned to swing a hammer properly, keeping my eye on the cutting edge of the chisel the while. Moreover, because I happened to be ambidextrous, I found I could do this equally well with the hammer held in either hand. This can be a great advantage when working in a confined space. 'Didn't know you was amphibious' remarked one of my workmates admiringly on one occasion. Others, less polite, used to call me 'keg-handed'.

We had no powered hand tools, so any work on an engine or farm implement that could not be removed to the machine shop had to be done slowly and laboriously by muscle power. Many an hour I spent and many a blister I raised on my palms in the infinitely tedious task of drilling large holes in steel or iron with a ratchet drill using, not twist drills, but the old hand-forged and hardened spear-pointed drill bits. Any new rivets or stays had to be closed by hand, one man wielding a riveting hammer and the other 'holding up'. When any old rivets had to be removed, their heads were cut off by means of a chisel bar and sledge hammer. The one job I really disliked was holding the chisel bar while my mate belted it with a sledge, knowing that if I lost my nerve and failed to hold the bar true and steady he would strike it a glancing blow or miss it altogether and probably break my arm. As in the case of hammer and chisel, the golden rule was to keep one's eye on the cutting end of the bar and try to forget about the striker.

Whenever there was work to be done inside a boiler or a water tank, plates to be scaled or new rivets to be held up, the task was allotted to me or to the shop boy, George Leonard, because we were the only ones slim enough to crawl through the man-holes. The boiler man-holes on the Fowler compounds were very awkwardly placed on the top of the barrel between the two sets of motion. It was easy enough to get in by simply

1. A muster of Rolt uncles and aunts at Chester, *c*. 1902. Left to right: my father, Marjory, Wilfred, Harry, Gladys, 'Granny Garnett', Algernon, Vivian, Dorothy, Marjory's husband

2. My mother, right, with my godmother Hero Willans, *c*. 1904

3. With my mother at Cusop

4. With my father on a trip to Llangorse Lake

5. Kilvert Country: the Black Mountains from the Wye, *c.* 1916

6. Llanthony Priory, *c.* 1916. These two photographs are taken from the family album

7. A picnic, Kilvert style, on Cusop Hill. Major Armstrong is seated (in uniform) with my mother behind him, and my tutor Thomas Southwick is standing on the left

8. First family transport: the Williamson Combination

9. Hay station as I remember it

10. G.V.T. Baldwin at Glynceiriog, 1922. The locomotive on which I made my first footplate trip

11. Radnor View, Cusop, 1918

12. The Cottage, Stanley Pontlarge, 1921

13. Fowler Ploughing Engine, Pitchill, 1926–7

14. On the footplate of the first Sentinel Ploughing Engine, Pitchill, 1926–7

15. Charge-hand Ernest Lines
and the new 4–8–0 for Buenos
Aires, Kerr Stuarts, 1928–9

16. High pressure geared steam locomotive, Kerr Stuarts, 1928–9

lowering oneself down, but it was extremely difficult to get out again and more than once I got stuck. At such times the rule that one must never panic was not so easy to observe in practice.

One valuable lesson I learnt during my two years at Pitchill was that many routine jobs were by no means so simple and unskilled as they appeared to be. It was the judgement and economy of effort born of long practice with which they were performed that made them appear deceptively simple. For example, one-armed Joe Bailey's job of looking after the shop portable engine seemed as simple as stoking some domestic boiler. Joe never hurried. Occasionally he would casually throw on a shovelful of coal or, as casually, close the feed-pump by-pass cock to supply the boiler with water. And all day long the steam pressure never varied by more than 5 lb. while the water gauge showed constant half glass. Yet when I was asked to deputise for him I seemed to be constantly rushing out to fiddle with the fire or the water pump while steam and water gauges fluctuated wildly. There seemed always to be either too much steam and too little water or vice versa.

It was exactly the same with the mill. This was housed in one of the substantial brick barns on the opposite side of the yard from the shop and it was used once or twice a week to grind cattle meal. It was powered by an old Tangye hot bulb horizontal oil engine. Alan Bloxham normally took charge of the running of this mill and whenever I passed by he appeared to be casually propping up the mill doorway, enjoying the morning sunshine and puffing at his pipe, his old trilby hat pulled down over his eyes and his dirty blue overalls dusted with flour. What a pleasant, easy job I used to think until one day Alan was called away to some urgent job and I was told to deputise for him. It was simple, he said. There were only three things I had to do. First, to ensure that the wooden hoppers on the topmost floor of the mill were kept filled with grain, for to deny millstones their grain is like running an engine short of oil. Secondly, to remove the sacks from their hooks under the flour shoots when they were full, replacing them by empty ones and tying their necks with binder twine. Thirdly, to prevent the hot bulb of the engine from becoming either too hot or too cold. He showed me the small pipe and cock which achieved this temperature regulation by feeding a drip of water to the hot bulb. Ideally, he explained, it should be kept just below red heat.

There was to be no basking in the sunshine for me. No sooner had Alan, having delivered his simple-sounding instructions, strolled away, than I became the slave of the mill, a kind of demented sorcerer's apprentice. I hurried panting up to the top floor to see to the hoppers and by the time I had humped in more sacks of grain and clattered pell-mell down the wooden stairs, one of the flour sacks was overflowing and the hot bulb of the engine was glowing an ominous cherry red. Later, when I had for the second time gone aloft to feed the insatiable hoppers, I heard the engine change its steady beat and the chattering voice of the damsels that fed the grain into the centre of the runner stones became less insistent. I flew down the stairs, realising that I had now turned on too much water to the hot bulb and that it was becoming too cold in consequence. But somehow I managed to keep the mill running until Alan returned, but never was I more glad to see him. 'Well, how d'ye get on, Tom?' he asked. 'Oh, all right,' I replied casually, but he eyed me quizzically and I am afraid my red and sweating face must have betrayed me.

It was Alan Bloxham who first taught me to drive, or rather patiently allowed me to teach myself. This was on the 10 cwt. Model T Ford truck which was used for servicing ploughing engines in the field or on other outside maintenance jobs. There must be many people of my generation who learned to drive on the famous Model T because it was an ideal vehicle for the purpose. Having epicyclic gears that called for no skill, the learner could concentrate all his attention on the control of the vehicle and on acquiring road sense without having to worry about that bane of the learner-driver, the crash gearbox. Having thus graduated on the Model T, my father soon allowed me to take the wheel of his 12/50 Alvis. I then found that, having already mastered the feel of driving a car, the art of changing gear was very easily acquired.

My experience at Pitchill was by no means confined to the workshop. An old cherry orchard nearby had got past bearing and to old Bill Smith was assigned the task of grubbing it up— in other words uprooting the trees, using one of the old single-cylinder Fowler ploughing engines. One of my first outside jobs was to be sent along as his mate on this exploit. My job was simple. I had to wrap a chain sling round a tree bole, hitch the hook on the end of the engine's steel rope on to this chain and then stand back. Old Bill would first of all nudge his regulator, open a crack to take up the slack and then open it fully. One of two things happened, either the tree came crashing down or the engine, after giving one powerful snort, stuck on dead centre. In the latter event, old Bill, who always moved with the country-man's slow deliberation, would ponder the situation for a few moments, removing that foul stub of a pipe from his mouth and spitting a thin yellow stream over the side of his engine. Then sometimes he would try another pull, but more usually he would screw down the knurled brass nut on the top of the Salter safety valve. He would then adopt the classic steam-plough driver's stance, left foot up on the raised side of his footplate, left arm resting casually on bent knee while his right hand grasped the regulator. In this attitude he appeared to fall into profound meditation while steam pressure in the ancient boiler mounted far above its prescribed limit. Meanwhile my instinct for self-preservation was such that I took cover behind a tree bole at what I considered a safe distance. But no disaster occur-red and the trees all came up. I still think it was something of a miracle that Bill Smith was not blown sky high, for when the boiler of his engine was given a hydraulic test a few months later, the crown of the firebox dropped three-eighths of an inch. However, the boiler inspector was in a mellow mood and passed it. As was usual before he inspected the older engines, he had been liberally entertained at the Queen's Head during the lunch hour.

It is incredible what an old boiler will stand without failure. Once Will Salisbury and I were sent to Worcester to retube an elderly portable engine which was supplying process steam at 25 lbs. pressure for sterilising in an ice-cream factory. As we drew the old tubes they literally fell apart in our hands. Only the scale appeared to have been holding them together.

Sometimes I would be despatched on my motorcycle with a message or a small spare part for one of the steam ploughing sets that was working out on contract somewhere in the Evesham vale. I seldom had difficulty in finding them. Usually a column of steam and smoke rising above the hedgerows betrayed their presence, but if not I would stop my motorcycle and listen for the labouring beat of an engine or the unmistakable ring of the drum gearing which carried surprisingly far over the fields. Similarly, when a set was due back at Pitchill, we invariably heard it coming a mile away. As a complete set of ploughing tackle consisted of two engines, a Fowler balanced plough with two sets of five or six plough bodies, a massive cultivator, a four-wheeled living van and a water cart, it made an impressive cavalcade on the road. Perched aloft on the footplate or at the steering wheel you felt like a lord of creation for the great engines towered above all other traffic and every head would turn as they rumbled majestically through a village. Moving a set from place to place was not always easy. Although they bore a small brass plate on their smoke boxes inscribed '14T' this was a brazen lie for in fact they weighed far more than this, though exactly how much was a dark secret that no one seemed willing to divulge. Certain bridges had to be avoided. Evesham was out of bounds for this reason as the railway bridge on the only approach to the town from Pitchill, though it still stands today, was judged incapable of taking their weight. Some roads also had to be avoided because the old plough drivers knew that there was no convenient stream or pool beside them where the engines could stop to suck up water through their armoured hoses. In hot summer weather, the engines could move on the road only in the early hours of the morning. Otherwise the diagonal strakes on their driving wheels would pick up long strips of hot tarmac from the road to leave a nicely corrugated surface behind them which made the local road surveyor tear his hair.

My first experience of steering one of these steam juggernauts was terrifying. I was deputed to steer one on the old farm engines across the fields, her driver being Will Robbins. Unlike all later machines, which have irreversible worm-and-wheel steering gear, the mechanism on these old engines consisted of a vertical steering column, mounted on the side of the tank and bunker just aft of the nearside rear wheel, which operated chain and rod connections to the swivelling front axle through straight gears. The steersman stood on a little metal platform, perilously outrigged from the bunker side, grasping the huge horizontal iron steering wheel. No sooner had I assumed this precarious perch, feeling like a small monkey on the top of a very tall stick, than Will Robbins, perhaps with malicious aforethought, set off full tilt at about 3 m.p.h., driving the engine diagonally across an old pasture of deep ridge and furrow. As we lumbered over this uneven ground the front axle swung to and fro sending the steering wheel spinning uncontrollably first one way and then the other. It nearly broke my wrist and flung me off the steering platform. It was only then that I grasped the significance of the gadget on the steering column immediately below the wheel. It was a primitive form of steering damper consisting of a disc encircled by a brake band which could be tightened by a hand-screw. Under such conditions the correct thing to do was to tighten up the damper as much as possible and then leave the wheel severely alone until it became essential to alter course.

On many occasions I worked on the steam ploughing tackle in the fields, riding the plough or the cultivator, and so eventually graduated to driving the engines. These stood one at either end of the field, drawing the implement back and forth between them, the idle engine moving an implement's width along the headland while the other was pulling until the whole field had been covered. Two men rode the plough, the ploughman behind the metal wheel on its long horizontal column, guiding it along the furrow, and his mate perched on a little tip-up seat right at the tail of the plough frame. The plough was balanced like a seesaw about its central axle. When it reached the end of the furrow, its crew jumped off their seats, tipping the plough to bring the other set of plough bodies into action, and swinging it into its new position as the other engine began slowly to pull. Then both jumped on again, the mate hinging down his seat at the plough tail, hitching the trailing rope over the hook beneath it. I can only compare the unique sensation of riding a steam plough to that of sailing a ship through the earth. Under good conditions, the taut rope ahead drew the plough along at a surprising speed and as it tore through the ground with a hissing sound the brown earth billowed away from the gleaming steel mouldboards like water from the prow of a ship. It was all very exhilarating and I used to revel in the sensation of silent but irresistible power, mingled with slight misgiving as to what might happen if the steel rope broke. Would it come snaking back and cut my head off? I have never heard tell of such an accident although ropes occasionally broke harmlessly, in which case the ploughmen would splice them in the field.

The cultivator was a totally different implement from the plough. Its massive tines were set in a triangular frame mounted on three wheels, the third pivoting in a turntable and controlled by the steering wheel. This turntable also carried a Vee-shaped double drawbar to which both engine ropes were attached, one pulling while the other trailed along the side of the frame. At the end of the field, when the rope that had been trailing took the pull its effect was to swing the drawbar and the front wheel round. By means of a chain connection and linkage, this movement also lifted the whole frame of the cultivator, thus raising the tines clear of the ground. It was retained in this position by a toothed sector and pawl, the latter being part of a lever which could be pulled to drop the cultivator frame again when the turn had been completed. When turning the cultivator in this way, the engineman had to pull very slowly otherwise the implement would tilt alarmingly. The old steam plough drivers could judge to a nicety how far to make it tip without actually turning over and this was their favourite trick whenever there was a new man on the cultivator. As the tyro jumped from his seat and ran for his life (as I did when the trick was played on me) they would shake with laughter.

A good set of steam tackle could get over the ground as fast or faster than a modern tractor plough, but the snag was the great width of the headlands which were left. These amounted to the width of an engine plus half the length of the implement. Consequently when the field had been covered, the tackle had to be twice repositioned to plough or cultivate the headlands. In a small or irregularly shaped field, the speed of steam tackle was nullified by this time-consuming process of finishing off. This is why the use of steam tackle survived longest in the large flat fields of East Anglia. It was also expensive in labour, for in addition to the four men who worked the tackle, a fifth was needed to haul water and coal to the engines. While the ploughing contractor supplied a water cart, his farmer customer usually supplied a horse and man to draw it.

Another disadvantage was the great weight of the engines. When the ground was soggy 'spuds' had to be attached by bolts to the rims of the driving wheels to provide extra grip, as if the big wheels began to slip an engine very soon dug itself in. Each of these spuds must have weighed at least a quarter of a hundredweight. Of T section with one end bent over to clasp the rim of the wheel, when not in use they were hung on a bar surrounding the water tank. Putting them on was a heavy and tedious job, but taking them off again on leaving a field for the hard road when spuds, bolts and wheels were plastered in slimy mud was one of the most unpleasant tasks I have ever had to perform. By the time it was done we looked like so many mudlarks, as filthy as the wheels themselves.

One day, while waiting its turn to pick up water from a pond at Norton, near Worcester, one of the big Fowlers slowly subsided sideways into a deep ditch as the bank at the side of the road gave way under her weight. She finally assumed such an alarming angle that her driver hurriedly drew the fire in case the firebox crown sheet sustained damage. It took us two days of hard labour before, with aid of a pull from the rope of her sister engine, she finally got back on to the hard road. Fortunately, relaying had recently been done on the Worcester–Paddington line which was close by, so we were able to use many old railway sleepers. These were laid in the ditch to form, first a firm foundation for our bottle jacks, and later a platform for the wheels. But before any of this work could start part of the hedge and bank had to be dug away.

Another of my outside experiences was to serve as fireman to Will Robbins on the Sentinel steam waggon. I do not know the exact date of this vehicle except that it was an early model made before the 'Super Sentinel' was introduced. Unlike the latter, it had no windscreen but was open to the elements above the simple semi-circular apron which surrounded the vertical boiler in the front of the cab. Firing a Sentinel called for no skill whatever. One simply shovelled coal from the bunker at the back of the cab and poured it down a vertical shoot in the centre of the boiler on to the circular firegrate beneath, relying upon the vibration of the vehicle to distribute the fire evenly over the grate. When running at from 15 to 20 m.p.h. on solid tyres, this vibration had to be experienced to be believed. The designer of the Sentinel had evidently assumed that the driver's mate would be a moron, for he had placed the injector and the control valve of the alternative water pump on the driver's side of the boiler. For some reason best known to himself, Will Robbins preferred to use the injector. To get this instrument to pick up cleanly as we rattled and jolted along called for the nice and patient adjustment of the steam and water controls, a proceeding I used to find very alarming as it completely diverted Will's attention from the wheel and from the road ahead. I could not have grabbed the wheel had an accident appeared imminent because it was out of reach from where I sat. There were some disconcerting moments, too, when the safety valve suddenly blew off. Although a pipe was provided which, in theory, conducted the steam above the cab roof, in practice we were instantly enveloped in an impenetrable fog.

Although the Sentinel boiler was so unscientifically fired, it was distinctly choosy about the type of fuel it consumed. Given anything but the best Welsh steam coal it was not only a shy steamer, but it became a very fair imitation of a travelling volcano, vomiting smoke and red hot cinders to the confusion of any motorist following behind. Every ten miles or so the water would need replenishing, using the steam water-lifter to draw supplies through a hose from a convenient roadside stream or pond. Like the steam plough drivers, Will Robbins carried in his mind a map of local watering points and knew which roads had to be avoided because they were waterless.

We carried a variety of loads in the Sentinel. For example, we spent two hot summer days discharging a truckload of shoddy at Salford Priors station. Shoddy is a waste product from the Yorkshire woollen mills, then widely used in the Evesham district as a fertiliser. It was brown in colour, of a flock-like consistency, acrid smelling and extremely dusty. As, hour after hour, we shovelled the stuff, the choking dust filled our lungs and stuck to our sweating faces. But when I complained to Will he merely remarked dourly that I should thank my lucky stars it was shoddy and not blood. Dried blood from slaughter-houses was another favoured fertiliser at this time and, according to Will, smelt worse than the shoddy, besides being more difficult to handle.

On another occasion we carried a load of strawberries in wooden tubs to a jam factory in Evesham. I have always thought there is a lot of truth in the old saying that we must all eat a peck of dirt before we die, believing that too great a concern for sterilisation must inevitably lower the body's natural resistance to infection. Nevertheless, this experience put me off strawberry jam for a long time afterwards. To begin with, by the time they reached the factory, the strawberries in our tubs were reduced to a glutinous mass of purple porridge. As the Sentinel rolled into the factory yard I saw a number of women working amid the great open-topped pans in which the jam was boiling. This boiling shed was open at the sides and buzzing with eager wasps and flies. An old labourer with a wooden barrow and shovel was keeping the women supplied with sugar from a large bin at the opposite side of the yard as though it had been coal. In fact, I strongly suspected he used the same barrow and shovel to bring coal to the boiler house.

The Bomfords grew a considerable acreage of strawberries at Pitchill at this time so that I came to know something of the usages and hazards of the soft fruit trade. Each strawberry season a tatterdemalion horde from the Black Country would descend like starlings on the farm to pick the fruit. Although the Black Country was little more than thirty miles away from Pitchill it might have been on a different continent so far as the local countrymen were concerned. They habitually referred to these foreign invaders as 'the Dudleys' and regarded them with suspicion as an alien and primitive race, wild, dirty and of very questionable habits. They were certainly verminous. To house them, the lofts of two large barns on the farm had been converted into dormitories. I went into one of these barns shortly after it had been occupied and noticed a strange phenomenon. There appeared to be a slight mist hanging over a patch of the barn floor immediately below the vertical ladder and opening that led to the loft above. On closer approach I saw that this effect was produced by millions of hopping fleas. The ground was literally sizzling with them. Small wonder that cleaning up and fumigating these lofts after the Dudleys' annual visit was considered the most unenviable job on the farm. The man who benefited most from their visits was the landlord of the Queen's Head, but even to him they must have been a doubtful blessing, for each night around closing time his pub became the centre of rowdy, drunken scenes such as we associate with the old railway navvy gangs. Police frequently had to be called in to restore order and the landlord's regular customers wisely stayed at home.

The harvesting of the strawberry crop was always peculiarly subject to the vagaries of the weather. Picking into chip baskets for dessert would be in full swing when a sudden heavy shower of thundery rain, falling on dry ground, might cover the fruit with grit and enforce an immediate switch to picking into tubs for jam. This was a disaster for grower and picker alike, the former because jam fruit commanded a much lower price, the latter because picking into tubs earned proportionately less per pound. Our trip to the jam factory with the Sentinel had followed a disaster of this kind.

That old Sentinel waggon eventually suffered a spectacular mechanical disintegration. The classic Sentinel two-cylinder poppet valve engine was slung horizontally under the chassis driving the rear axle by means of sprockets and a single large roller chain. The chain sprocket on the axle incorporated the differential unit, four large pins fitting between its teeth acting as journals for the four star-wheels. Will Robbins was trundling happily through the village of Salford Priors one day with a 5 ton load of bricks on board when one of these four pins broke. As the sprocket revolved, the broken pin slid out until it came into violent contact with the lower portion of the driving chain, forcing it downwards into the road. The old waggon had never stopped so suddenly in its life; it literally took root in the road and even the phlegmatic Will Robbins was shaken. When he clambered down from his cab and peered underneath a scene of ruin met his eyes. Above a large, tell-tale pool of oil the stout cast iron crankcase was broken and the driving end of the crankshaft had been torn out of the engine. A secondhand engine was acquired to replace the wrecked unit and the waggon eventually took to the road again.

Despite such vicissitudes, the Sentinel was undoubtedly the best and the most popular of commercial steam road vehicles and just as my uncle Kyrle had been encouraged to fit a Sentinel engine and boiler into a locomotive, so now, inspired by his example, Leslie and Douglas Bomford began to consider similar agricultural applications. The fruit of Leslie's work at Shrewsbury was the Sentinel 'Rhino'. A wheeled tractor for direct cultivation designed for colonial use, it was fitted with the larger boiler and engine which had been developed for the locomotive. Later, a crawler version of this tractor was produced. The prototype Rhino with Leslie in charge came down to Pitchill for field trials, towing a cable set cultivator. I did not have anything directly to do with this tractor although I remember being very impressed by its performance.

Meanwhile we had built in the shop at Pitchill a cable plough-ing engine to Douglas Bomford's design using, as my uncle had done in the case of *Ancoats*, the engine and boiler out of a second-hand Sentinel waggon. At the age of sixteen I felt very proud to be intimately concerned with the construction and subsequent field trials of this new and novel machine. It consisted of a marriage of Sentinel and Fowler components, the only new item being a simple frame constructed from 'I' section girders. The Sentinel boiler was mounted at the extreme rear end of this new chassis, next came the Sentinel engine lying horizontally with the footplate beside it and the coal bunker on top of it, then a Fowler rope drum mounted vertically between the frame mem-bers and finally, at the front end, a Sentinel water tank. The four wheels were off an old Fowler ploughing engine. The engine drove by a short roller chain a cross-shaft arranged directly beneath it from which the drive was taken via counter-shaft gears to the rear wheels and by gears to the rope drum, these alternative final drives being engaged by sliding dog clutches operated by a lever on the footplate. The rope from the drum passed round a large diameter Vee pulley beneath the boiler, then forward to a second pulley mounted amidships from which it emerged in the orthodox manner midway between front and rear wheels. The Fowler ploughing engine has an ingenious mechanism below the drum which causes the rope guide pulleys to move up and down across the face of the drum as it rotates in order to ensure accurate coiling of the rope.

With the drum placed vertically it became impossible to use this Fowler 'coiling gear', as it was called. Douglas Bomford cudgelled his brains needlessly over this problem because we found in practice that with this arrangement of pulleys the rope coiled itself automatically and perfectly on the drum.

Although this unorthodox ploughing engine was hardly a thing of beauty it performed very satisfactorily and I cannot recall any teething troubles. But it was not capable of doing the work of a Fowler engine, as I very soon discovered when I drove it on its first serious field trial. The job was to plough a large, flat stubble field close to Pitchill. My opposite number was Bill Smith with one of the farm pair of Fowlers and it was soon obvious that he was not going to allow any quarter to this new-fangled machine and its youthful driver. When the Sentinel was pulling the plough its engine turned over at a speed so much in excess of normal that the feed pump could not be used and I had to rely entirely on the one small Penberthy injector to feed the boiler. So great was the vibration that this injector could not be worked so long as the engine was pulling and it was such a long pull that the situation became very fraught. A chronic fault of the Sentinel boiler, particularly the early model, was that it tended to lift the water, in other words, when the regulator was opened, water went out with the steam and the water gauge showed a falsely high level. I had to start each pull with the boiler three-quarters full which aggravated this trouble, for each time I opened my regulator the level in the gauge glass rose until it disappeared into the top fitting and I was deluged by the water that shot out of the chimney. Conversely, by the time I had finished the pull there would only be about half an inch of water still showing in the glass and the moment I closed the regulator this would sink out of sight. This was the most anxious moment, for I was terrified that I would 'run the plug',[1] the most ignominious mishap that can befall any engineman. I could not get that injector on quickly enough, at the same time putting the blower on to urge the fire because such a copious draught of cold water inevitably brought the steam pressure down.

In this steam raising department I was also in trouble. On the advice of the Sentinel Waggon Works we had fitted to this boiler

---

[1] A lead-filled plug inserted in the crown sheet of a firebox which melts, putting out the fire, if the water is low and no longer covers the firebox crown.

a new design of firegrate which was slightly conical in shape, thus encouraging the coal that was fed down the chute to distribute itself evenly. The theory had been that when the engine was standing and pulling the plough rope there would be insufficient vibration to spread the fire over a flat grate of the kind used on the waggon. In fact, of course, there was more than enough vibration with the effect that all the coal immediately ran to the perimeter of the grate, leaving a large hole in the middle. Through this hole the fierce draught drew quantities of cold air. Not only did this seriously impair steam raising but, in its free passage through the grate, the air made a penetrating humming sound which could be heard half a mile away, thus advertising to the knowledgeable the fact that I had a hole in my fire, a shame-making circumstance for any conscientious fireman.

Meanwhile, from the clouds of smoke and steam erupting from the Fowler at the opposite end of the field it was clear that Bill Smith was not prepared to show me any mercy. He would whip that plough across so that, in no time at all it seemed, it was my turn to pull again. Such an unequal contest could have only one ending and the plough was soon at a standstill while I 'waited for steam' to the accompaniment of derisive toots on the Fowler whistle.

It was obvious from this experiment that, compared with a Fowler, the Sentinel ploughing engine was underpowered, but its performance and economy were sufficiently promising to justify building a sister engine. This was not completed until after I had left Pitchill. Finally, both engines were rebuilt with larger engines and boilers and fitted with special, lighter, round-spoked wheels of welded construction. In this form they gave good service on contract work until some time in the 1930s when the firm gave up cable ploughing engines in favour of Fowler Gyrotillers propelled by oil engines.

The field where this first experiment took place was also the scene of my only venture on horseback. I was with a set of ploughing tackle there one day when Douglas Bomford rode up on his bay mare Tina. He became so deeply involved in some technical problem that he eventually turned to me and said: 'Tom, take my horse back to Pitchill'. After my childhood's experience with Meg, my Shetland pony, I regarded all members of the species with the gravest suspicion. If I had been ordered into a cage with a tiger I could hardly have been more apprehensive as I began dutifully leading Tina away by the bridle. Before me stretched the wide field of stubble and the long straight drive up to Pitchill, while the mare followed me in so docile a fashion that, as I plodded on, I began to feel a cowardly fool. I imagined Douglas and the other men regarding with contempt the fact that that I continued to walk when I could ride. So, greatly daring, I hoisted myself clumsily and with difficulty into the saddle while the mare stood perfectly still. Once aloft, I did not dare to trot but allowed Tina to walk sedately home. Arrived at Pitchill, I swung myself down from the saddle and led her into a loose-box, chewing an imaginary straw and feeling a thoroughly horsey fellow. The point of this story is that I was totally unaware of the fact that Tina was a very mettlesome creature who would allow no one but Douglas to ride her. She could invariably unseat the most experienced horsemen who attempted to do so. I can only conclude that she sensed a complete tyro and took pity on him. This incident appealed strongly to Douglas's sense of humour, but it was many years before he shared the joke with me.

While I was at Pitchill, Douglas Bomford, like many another inventive engineer before and since, became afflicted by the desire to make an infinitely variable speed gear. Like the alchemist's dream of turning base metal into gold, the pursuit of this ideal form of transmission, like the perpetual motion machine, can become an obsession. The test bed for these experiments was a basic wooden chassis powered by a Villiers two-stroke engine and carried on motorcycle wheels. This was kept in a corner of the shop and periodically dusted off and wheeled out of retirement to try out some fresh idea such as a rubber ring moving between tapering wooden rollers. The last experiment in which I participated consisted in using an adaptation of the classic Stephenson's link valve motion. The engine oscillated the vertical link while the equivalent of the valve rod on a steam engine actuated the pawl of a ratchet-and-pawl on the back axle. This meant that 'mid-gear' position became neutral and 'full-gear' top speed, the pawl taking several teeth of the ratchet at each bite. The results of a single test run down the Pitchill drive were not encouraging. A maximum speed of about 6 m.p.h. was achieved for I remember that I and its other anxious attendants had to walk very fast to keep up, but owing to the intermittent torque produced by the prodding of the pawl, progress was by fits and starts. Meanwhile, the engine roared, the transmission became a blur of fast moving rods like some demented knitting machine and the vibration was appalling. Not surprisingly, the little chassis was wheeled back into its dark corner from which it did not emerge again in my time.

Those two years I spent at Pitchill are fragrant in memory. They were also rich in experience and so more useful to me than the previous six I had spent at school. For not only did they give me a valuable grounding in the rudiments of the engineer's craft but they also taught me much about farming, about country ways and country men. In that small country workshop, engineering seemed to have been grafted on to the older country crafts of blacksmith, wheelwright and carpenter and to have grown naturally out of these ancient roots. The steam plough drivers regarded their elephantine charges with the same affection and pride that the old waggoners had felt for their horses. They groomed them with oily waste and polished their brass lagging bands till they shone. It was easy to understand and to share this pathetic fallacy, for those engines indeed resembled lovable elephants, slow moving and ponderous yet proud and powerful, warm and mysteriously alive when fire was in their bellies and steam was simmering or when they sucked up water through their armoured trunks to quench their thirst. Small wonder that their drivers habitually referred to them as 'her' or 'she'. It is a strange paradox that as machines grow more complex and able to usurp more human functions, this pathetic fallacy becomes much more difficult to sustain. No one, so far as I know, refers to a computer as 'she'.

I learned to admire and respect my workmates for their versatility in tackling the practical problems of some new job almost every day and for the calm, unhurried, dryly humorous way these countrymen set about such tasks. In trying to emulate them I was introduced to the kind of freemasonry that exists between all men who share the discipline of exacting manual work. It was through this freemasonry that I so soon found myself on terms of such easy and understanding friendship with these men, some of whom, in the words of Edmund Blunden, 'scarce could read or hold a quill'. For an unsociable boy who, at school, had found it impossible to come to terms with my masters or with boys of my own age and upbringing, I think this was the most valuable lesson of all.

# Chapter 6

# Stoke-on-Trent

On 11th June 1928, at the age of eighteen, I began a three years' premium apprenticeship at the California Works of Kerr, Stuart and Co. Ltd, Locomotive Engineers, of Stoke-on-Trent, finding lodgings for myself in a small terrace house, No. 439, London Road, Stoke. Under the terms of my apprenticeship indenture, the premium of £100 which my parents had paid would be returned to them at the end of three years, always assuming I behaved myself and worked diligently. The firm also undertook to pay me the princely weekly wage of 10s. for the first year, 15s. for the second and £1 for the final year. This, the first money I had ever earned, was my pocket money, my parents paying the 30s. a week for my lodgings.

So far I had spent my life in a country setting and it was a rural world that I had come to know and to love. If I had occasionally visited or travelled through industrial areas, I had had but fleeting glimpses of them from the outside which left only the most superficial impressions. Now, however, I experienced life in an industrial city from the inside which was quite a different matter. My reactions to this new environment were complex. I felt oppressed by the all-pervading dirt and squalor of the endless cobbled street lined by terrace houses of soot-blackened brick; by the smouldering waste tips, pit mounds and heaps of furnace slag. This sombre man-made landscape in which even the occasional tree or patch of grass was soiled with soot and struggled to survive was overlaid by a perpetual pall of smoke. Although Arnold Bennett's Five Towns (the locals always pointed out that the author was wrong in forgetting Fenton and that there should have been six) had then only recently combined to form the City of Stoke-on-Trent, the name had no reality; signposts in all the country round pointed simply to 'The Potteries' and one was never allowed to forget that the making of pottery was the district's chief preoccupation. All the wares it produced were then fired with coal in bottle ovens.[1] The whole area was peppered with their characteristic shapes; they would appear in serried ranks, like a row of gigantic nine-pins, above the rooftops of the terrace houses. And because each oven, when it was being fired up, belched dense black smoke, the effect on the atmosphere and on all surrounding objects below may be imagined. Yet, because this smoke was the out-ward and visible sign of prosperity, the people of the Potteries were proud of it. Little general stores on street corners sold shiny picture postcards showing typical 'smokescapes' of Hanley, Burslem or Tunstall. But, living in such sulphurous surroundings I thought of my childhood under the clear skies of the Welsh Border and felt like some fallen angel recalling lost paradise.

But there were compensations. In contrast to the mild-man-nered countrymen I had hitherto known, the people of the Potteries at first seemed coarse and hard; they spoke in a broad, harsh dialect; their wit was sharper and liberally salted with profanities and obscene four-letter words. But I soon discovered that this rough exterior was only an outer shell which they had grown to protect them from the buffets of a pitiless environment. In reality they were the most genuine, friendly and kindly people I have ever known. Honest and forthright themselves, the only thing they cordially detested was the lack of such qualities in others. They could detect the false pride and affectation of social climbers infallibly and deal with it unmercifully. They would refer contemptuously to the inhabitants of the smug suburbs on the fringes of the city as 'Them as wears plus fours and only 'as porridge for breakfast'. One of my fellow apprentices was the son of a wealthy local man in the pottery trade who had sent him to a public school. Unfortunately he could never forget the superior notions he had thereby acquired and was incapable of mixing unselfconsciously with his workmates. Whenever he walked through the shops he would be greeted by a ringing of hammers on metal and men would call after him in exagger-ated mimicry of a public school accent: 'Good morning, Charles, and how are we getting on today?' Charles always struck me as a sad and lonely figure. I had my two years at Pitchill to thank for the fact that I escaped his fate, partly because my new work-mates realised that I had already learned the rudiments of my

[1] For some reason they were always called ovens locally. Only those used to fire enamels were referred to as kilns.

trade and respected me accordingly, and partly because I knew that in any workshop there is only one true entitlement to superiority and that is to excel in one's craft. I can only feel humble in the presence of a man who is doing his job superlatively well and in 1928, there was no lack of such craftsmen at the California Works.

I used often to reflect how I should feel if I knew I was condemned to spend the rest of my days in this sombre environment beneath a smoke-filled sky, my life monotonously ruled by the daily summons of a steam hooter, braying into the raw dark of winter mornings, until I became too old and worn out to work any more. I shrank from such a prospect and this made me admire all the more the courage and the good-humoured stoicism of my companions. As I worked beside them, I soon realised that what made their lives tolerable was, above all, their satisfaction in their skill. That skill was a precious thing which had taken years to acquire and which no one could take away—or so I thought then.

Although the industrial scene of man-made desolation appalled me, at the same time it had an intensely dramatic quality which I found fascinating. Evening after evening I spent exploring the Five Towns, travelling by bus, on foot or on my motorcycle. Because they are situated in a hilly region near the headwaters of the Trent, the townscape of the Potteries was made the more dramatic. A street would suddenly fall away or end in a rickety fence on the edge of some steep bank to reveal an unexpected vista of bottle ovens, tall chimneys, pit-head gears and smouldering spoil banks as arid and desolate as moon mountains. My favourite viewpoint of all was on the heights of Basford which commanded the district of Etruria in the valley below and the slopes of Hanley opposite. To the right, ranged beside the Trent and Mersey Canal, was the most famous pottery of all—Josiah Wedgwood's Etruria. Its ovens still smoked then, for Wedgwood's new pottery at Barlaston with its electric kilns was still in the future. To the left, the canal snaked away to lose itself amidst a medley of mountainous tips, railway lines, blast furnaces and rolling mills that was the Shelton Iron and Steel Company or, as the locals always called it 'Shelton Bar'.[1] This prospect was spectacular at any time but never more so than at night when

[1] H. G. Wells made this works the scene of his horrifying short story *The Cone*.

the fume that rose from the valley beneath my feet made the streetlights of Hanley that climbed the slope opposite appear like stars glimpsed through cloud wrack. Under the arc-lights of Shelton Bar, dark shunting engines moved like shuttles over a web of gleaming rails with a recurrent clashing of buffers. At such a time the steel works made a very fair representation of the mouth of hell in some medieval Last Judgement. The works seemed to be perpetually shrouded in a cloud of smoke and steam which fumed or jetted upward from innumerable chimneys and pipes, a cloud reddened here and there by reflected furnace light. Occasionally a shunting locomotive would labour up to the top of one of the tips pushing before it a ladle of molten slag. When it reached the summit, for a few moments the tip would resemble a volcano in eruption as the molten stream coursed downwards, its vivid glare lighting up the night sky. At last I was seeing the source of that glow that I had glimpsed beyond my mountains as a child. The sight was accompanied by an appropriate cacophony of confused sounds: the crash of a sudden torrent of coke falling from the hoppers of the coking plant; the thunder of the rolling mills.

I found this fierce and violent drama of the steel works at night so hypnotically fascinating that I visited it repeatedly, viewing the spectacle from every angle; from the top of the towering tips, seamed with veins of fire and hot beneath my feet; from the towpath of the steaming canal which afforded me a glimpse into the rolling mill where huge white-hot billets of steel were flattened like pastry under a rolling pin. So this was the heart of the matter; this was what the Industrial Revolution was all about. It was a lesson I had never been taught at school. When first seen, this prospect made as profound an impression upon me as had that first childish glimpse of the Vale of Ewyas, though for a very different reason. If that prospect had seemed like paradise, this was pandemonium. It excited me, yet at the same time it filled me with a strange sense of apocalyptic foreboding. But if anyone had asked me then the source of this disquiet I should have been at a loss to explain it.

No. 439 London Road where I lodged was a step above the meanest of the terraced houses. It boasted a bay window in front and was set back from the pavement to the extent of a yard's width of blackened earth enclosed by cast-iron railings. Nevertheless, these pretensions to respectability were merely a façade offered to the main street. From the alley at the back,

the house, with its narrow yard, outside lavatory, coal store
and drooping clothes line, resembled a thousand others. Inside,
its rooms were very small and cramped, the staircase narrow
and vertiginously steep. So it did give me a very fair first-hand
experience of how the average inhabitant of the district lived.

We always used the back door which opened into a tiny
kitchen/scullery built on to the back of the house. This gave
into the back room proper which was a general living and
dining room for six days of the week. It contained table
and chairs, an old Victorian horsehair-stuffed chaise longue
covered in shiny black leathercloth under its single window
that looked down the backyard and a tuneless upright piano
against the opposite wall. These bulky objects left little space
to move around. On either side of the black mock-marble
mantelshelf were two large cast ornaments, also black. These
depicted rearing horses whose classically draped attendants
struggled to control them with reins made of brass wire.
Between them stood a black clock with a brass face, which
rarely kept time, and two prized pieces of Wedgwood 'black
basalt' ware. As the walls were covered with densely patterned
wall paper and the window admitted little light, the general
effect was sombre in the extreme. Nor was it much better after
dark by the light of a single pendant gas mantle with glass globe.
Even this light was intermittent because it was the invariable
custom to feed only one coin at a time into the penny-in-the-
slot meter on the assumption, I can only suppose, that otherwise you would not get your money's worth. Whenever the
light dimmed, my landlady would be heard calling frantically
from the back-kitchen: 'Anyone got a penny for the gas?'
and as the meter was inconveniently situated in a diminutive
cellar reached by a flight of steep and narrow steps littered
with extraneous objects, this cry would be followed by a
prolonged period of confusion before light was restored.

In the front of the house and behind the bay window was
that holy of holies, the front room which was occupied only
on Sundays when I was usually out of the house. On weekdays
it struck dank and chilly, its carpet-patterned linoleum smelling
strongly of floor polish. It was also dark, for the lace curtains
over the bay window were kept three parts drawn and the
space between them almost filled by a luxuriant aspidistra
in a large pot of livid green and yellow standing on a precarious
bamboo table. China Alsatian dogs or cherry boys had not yet
usurped the traditional aspidistra's pride of place at No. 439.

My bedroom was directly above this front room. I had imported a large and comfortable basket chair which converted it into a bed-sitter except in winter when it became much too cold. My mother had made me a present of a brocade dressing gown of which I was very proud and on spring or summer evenings I would don this resplendent garment, put a contemporary jazz record on my portable gramophone ('O where is Sahara, far across the western sea') and loll in the basket chair smoking a cheap Turkish cigarette in a long holder. The prospect from my window, however, made my fancied resemblance to Noel Coward completely incongruous. It looked across the road to the black, rubbish-strewn waters of the disused Newcastle-under-Lyme branch of the Trent and Mersey Canal. Beyond this was the high, blank boundary wall of the Michelin Tyre Works, then the only large new factory to be established in Stoke for many years.

My landlord at No. 439 was William Rock, a carter at a local pottery, a slight, lean man with a face drawn into lines of perpetual tiredness. I can see him now seated in the back kitchen in his collarless shirt sleeves, elbows on the table, one hand supporting his head while in the other he held a Woodbine between his middle fingers, his thumb flicking the ash from its glowing end which was cupped within his palm. He would often sit like this by the hour and I used to wonder what, if anything, he was thinking about. His wife was a brisk Shropshire countrywoman who had been 'in service' in her youth and fancied herself superior on this account. Her ideas of refinement sometimes took peculiar form. Thus on Saturdays when I was changing for the week-end she would call up the stairs: 'D'you want yer clean linings, Mr Tom?' I could not at first conceive what she meant by this until I realised that she could not bring herself to say 'vest and pants' or even 'underclothes' out loud.

For most of the time, I was their only lodger, but there was a third small bedroom in the house which was occasionally occupied by short term lodgers of whom I only recall two. One was a young man who worked as a clerk. He had sleek black hair which he brushed back and oiled copiously. He wore cheap, flashy suits and vivid ties and fancied himself as a lady-killer. He even prevailed on Mrs Rock to allow him to use her sacred front room and its sofa for his frequent dalliances. I cordially disliked him. The other lodger I remember was a much more endearing character. He was a massive, muscled man of middle age, beginning to run to seed. A racy conversationalist, he worked for 'the Tarmac', breaking up furnace slag for road metal. He had a fine set of false teeth of which he was so proud that he would never eat with them. Before each meal he took them out, laid them reverently on the table beside him, and then champed away heartily with his bare gums, his nose and chin almost meeting like a pair of pincers.

Each weekday morning I got up in time to eat a hurried breakfast and reach the works before the steam hooter sounded at eight o'clock. Usually, I walked to work, but if I was late I took my motorcycle from the backyard. In summer, I found this routine easy enough but cold dark mornings in winter were a different matter and I had the utmost difficulty in dragging myself out of bed. To overcome this I converted an old alarm clock so that when it went off its clapper closed a contact and rang a battery operated electric bell close beside my ear. This continued to ring so that I had to get out of bed to break the contact. During the works lunch hour I just had time to return to No. 439 for my main meal of the day, though it had to be rather a hurried affair. In the evening there was a high tea and if I subsequently went off on one of my exploratory rambles or to the cinema there was usually cocoa and biscuits for me when I got back.

Many of the cinemas in the Potteries in those days were converted theatres or music halls. The local name of the 'Blood Tub', by which the Hippodrome at Stoke was universally known, recalled the many turgid melodramas that had been played on its boards. Despite their conversion, such theatres had remained substantially unchanged, and for a young man with a girl on his arm and the money to spare the great thing to do was to take a box and thus ensure undisturbed privacy. This assumed a preoccupation with matters other than the film, for the penalty for this dearly bought privilege was that, owing to the extreme angle of vision, all the characters on the screen appeared to be preternaturally elongated. At this time the screen was still silent and it was while I was in the Potteries that it at last found a voice, albeit a somewhat unnatural and unpredictable one at first. There were then two sound systems, sound-on-film, which eventually triumphed, and sound-on-disc where the sound was produced by long-playing records that were apt to get out of synchronisation. A cinema in Hanley was equipped with the latter system and I remember how the audience rocked with mirth when, in a tender scene, a beautiful Hollywood blonde suddenly began to speak in a rich baritone.

At this point I should explain how I came to be translated from a small workshop in the Vale of Evesham into what was to me an alien and, in some ways, hostile urban environment. Once again it was through the agency of my uncle, Kyrle Willans. His work on Sentinel locomotives had made him very conscious of the shortcomings of the Sentinel boiler, faults of which I, too, had become well aware through my experience with the Sentinel ploughing engine at Pitchill. He was a great admirer of the work of Loftus Perkins, the pioneer of ultra high-pressure steam, and he conceived the idea of a high pressure water tube boiler on Perkins' principles for a geared steam locomotive which would have a large grate area, a very large heating surface and thus steam freely on any fuel with the lightest of draughts. At about the same time, although he was a dedicated steam man, he became attracted to the idea of using one of the new high-speed oil engines, which were then just coming on to the scene, as an alternative power unit for an industrial locomotive. Failing to interest the Sentinel Waggon Works in these new ideas, he decided to try the nearest locomotive builders with the result that he joined Kerr Stuart and Co. as what would now be called their chief development engineer and was presently joined there by Leslie Bomford. At the time I arrived in Stoke and for many months after that, my uncle lodged in a cottage at Trentham during the week, trundling off each week-end in his Model T Ford sedan to rejoin his family at Dovaston House in Shropshire.

The firm of Kerr Stuart was originally founded in Glasgow in 1881 as factors of locomotives and railway equipment. In 1892, however, the firm decided to launch out as manufacturers and bought out one of their sub-contractors, Messrs Hartley, Arnoux and Fanning, general engineers catering especially for the pottery trade, of California Works, Stoke-on-Trent. The original works of brick and slate with iron-framed windows still survived as the offices and machine shop, but between the years 1894 and 1912 a whole series of large new shops had been built to house the Erecting Shop, the Tool Room with canteen over, the Foundry, Heavy Forge, Boiler Shop and Wagon Shop and finally the Joinery and Paint Shop. From the office entrance in Whieldon Road the works extended for over a quarter of a mile along a narrow site bounded on one side by the main line of the old North Staffordshire Railway and on the other by the Trent and Mersey Canal. When working at full pressure, this plant could employ over a thousand men and at the time I came to Stoke, Kerr Stuart had recently completed an order for fifty standard 0–6–0 goods locomotives of Midland design for the L.M.S. Railway.

As soon as I joined the firm I was handed a brass disc with a hole at the top and a number stamped below. This was my 'check'. Each morning as I came to work I handed it in through the window of the small 'check office' by the main gates to be hung on an appropriately numbered pin on the large blackboard within. During the morning, the gatekeeper's assistant, the 'check boy', would return these discs to their owners. I was first set to work in the Wagon Shop assembling bogies for a series of eight-wheeled wagon underframes which were destined for an Indian railway. This was in the northern end of a huge steel-framed building divided by columns into three equal bays. Two of these were floored with railway sleepers laid edge to edge and were shared by the Wagon Shop and Boiler Shop. The third bay on the east side housed the heavy forge at its northern end followed, at the Boiler Shop end, by hydraulic presses and rolls for shaping boiler plates. Overhead, high under the roof trusses, electric cranes moaned and rumbled to and fro emitting occasional vivid arcs of blue fire from their conductor wires. From where I worked, the view of the far end of this shop appeared indistinct in the shimmer of heat rising from the coke-fired riveting hearths of the boiler makers. Men seemed to be everywhere and their diverse and purposeful activity filled the whole building with a torrent of urgent sound. Pneumatic hammers closed stays and rivets with a deafening clamour like sudden bursts of machine-gun fire; tall steam hammers pounded and every now and again a heavy hot stamping press opposite my place of work rose creaking, hung poised for a moment, and then plummeted downwards with a crash that shook the ground under my feet. After the quiet of the little workshop at Pitchill it was like Bedlam and at first I found it bewildering and a little alarming. But I soon became used to it, which was just as well because I worked for six months or more in that building, progressing first to the Boiler Shop and then to the Forge.

The universal friendliness, kindness and helpfulness that was shown to me by the men soon made me feel at home. My bungling efforts sometimes provoked them to ridicule or coarse jokes, but never to anger. For my part, so much did I admire their skill that I felt secretly flattered by the fact that such men could accept me as an equal. For one lesson I speedily learned was the prodigious amount of human skill that went into the building of a steam locomotive. Despite the formidable array of powerful machinery, steam, hydraulic and pneumatic, there was never any doubt in this shop as to which was the servant and which the master. Sometimes the skill involved was obvious to the merest onlooker, but sometimes it was not until you tried for yourself. For example, I thought the drivers of the overhead travelling cranes had the cushiest jobs in the shop, sitting comfortably in their little cabins aloof from the turmoil on the floor below. I had to scale a vertical steel ladder, clamber into one of these cabins and take over the crane controls to discover that the job was not so pleasant and simple as I had thought and that the lives of the men below often depended on the crane driver's skill and judgement. It was by no means easy to see from this high vantage point whether the crane hook was directly above the point of balance of some heavy and awkwardly shaped load. If it was not, the load would swing dangerously when it was lifted, perhaps knocking a man down or crushing him against a column. Nor was it easy to check that such a load had been correctly and safely slung or to ensure that it did not swing when it was traversed. Yet in the hands of these men flexible chains and steel cables seemed to become rigid, such was the effortless precision with which they lifted their unwieldy loads aloft, moved them swiftly along and across the shop, both traverses working simultaneously, and then lowered them in the exact spot required. I also discovered that the atmosphere under the roof in which the crane driver had to work was often scarcely breathable. They certainly earned their frequent billy cans of sweet tea which the shop boys delivered by hanging them on the crane hooks. Needless to say, they never spilled a drop.

The making of a locomotive boiler began in the oil-fired furnaces where the plates were heated. Every now and again one of these furnaces would yawn like the mouth of hell as its counterbalanced door was lifted so that a red hot plate could be grappled with long tongs and drawn forth over rollers to the bending rolls or on to the table of the big hydraulic press. In times past, the flanges that had to be turned on tube plates, back plate and throat plate (so that the boiler barrel and the side plates of the inner and outer fireboxes could be united to them by riveted joints) were formed by men with sledge hammers beating them over blocks. Now, however, the red hot plates were squeezed between massive cast-iron formers, male and female, held in the jaws of the press. The most dramatic of these operations on the press was the making of a throat plate. This must have a flange formed in one direction to receive the firebox wrapper plate and a second, smaller, circular flange formed in the opposite direction in the centre of the plate to receive the barrel. For the latter purpose a pilot hole was cut in the flat plate before it was heated. In the shaping of these throat plates, speed was of the essence because two operations had to be performed while the plate was still red hot. In an inferno of heat, glare and smoke, each man in the gang had to move with the well rehearsed speed and precision of a ballet dancer, the men manœuvring the almost white hot plate precisely into position under the press while the charge hand stood tensely watchful behind the row of levers that controlled it. When he judged its position correct he signalled with one hand to the men to lower their tongs and stand back, while with the other he pulled the lever which raised the platform of the press to form the outer flange and to hold the glowing plate firmly between the two blocks. Then at the bidding of a second lever the centre ram of the press rose and forced a third, dome-shaped block through the central hole in the plate, thus forming the second flange. It was a spectacular demonstration of skilled manual team work and of hydraulic power.

Equally impressive was the sight of three strikers swinging their seven-pound sledge hammers in perfect rhythm, the master smith keeping the time with his hammer, as they scarf welded the white hot ends of a foundation ring. This ring would form the bottom of the water space between the inner and outer fireboxes. Rectangular in shape and formed of steel bar up to four inches square in section, it was forged in two halves and then welded together.

In one corner of the Boiler Shop there was a huge hydraulic gap riveter, its bulk partly sunk in a pit. The function of this machine was to rivet the seams of boiler barrels which were lowered between its jaws by crane. Unlike its pneumatic counterparts, it made no noise, squeezing down the hot rivets into neat heads by sheer silent power. By contrast, the supreme noise maker in the whole works was a device known as 'Happy Sam'. This was shaped like a gigantic horseshoe. Two pneumatic hammers could be firmly housed in its opposed ends. When hung from a crane it was lowered over an upturned firebox and used to pean the heads of the many screwed stays that passed through the water space to unite the inner and outer fireboxes. Because these stays, unlike rivets, were hammered cold and the boiler acted as a sound-box, the noise of Happy Sam in full cry was almost intolerable and the men claimed that his devilish chatter could be heard two miles away. The noise in that boiler shop certainly left me slightly deaf for the rest of my life. Nor was there any question, in this shop at any rate, of boiler makers whispering to each other and lip reading as is frequently alleged. We communicated by bawling into each other's ears at close range.

My spell in the Forge provided me with another example of craftsmanship in the highly skilled team work of the steam hammer gangs. I soon learnt that the making of a heavy forging called for perfect co-ordination between the master smith, who was in charge of the operation, his hammer driver who stood behind the hammer and worked the steam valve handle which caused the hammer to strike a hard or a soft blow, and the men who, clinging to long chain-supported tongs, manipulated the glowing billet on the anvil as the smith directed. One mistake on the part of any of them might cause the hammer to strike a false blow, springing the tongs like the arm of a Roman catapult, perhaps with lethal results. Yet I never saw a single accident of this kind occur.

A typical hammer smith was a heavily built man who wore his collarless shirt open to the midriff. His fleshy, pallid face was seamed with dirt-encrusted wrinkles. The working of each heat would leave him pouring with sweat and he would mop his face and neck on a filthy piece of coarse towelling. Long experience in his craft had given him powers of judgement that seemed almost uncanny. After a quick glance at the forging drawing of a cranked axle, a coupling or connecting rod, he would potter out into the steel yard to choose a suitable billet, followed by a labourer trundling a lifting bogie. Whereas all other men in the works carried a two-foot steel rule tucked in the rule pocket of their overalls, for some reason that I never discovered, the smith's rule was invariably of brass and usually the scale and figures on it had long since worn away. In the yard he would wave this rule as cursorily as a wand over likely billets, finally striking one with it to indicate to the labourer that he had made his choice. It measured, shall we say, a foot square by two feet long and when he had forged it into a connecting rod some six feet long there would be only a small fraction of waste metal to spare.

The smith was dwarfed by his great hammer. It towered above him like some crouching prehistoric monster. Yet for all their size and brute strength, steam-hammers are surprisingly tetchy things and he tended it as meticulously as every true craftsman cares for his tools. On cold winter mornings steam was turned on to the hammer and it was slowly warmed through to rid it of the water that condensed in the cold cylinder. The great hammer head or 'tup', as it was called, was gently lowered on to the anvil and warmed by surrounding it with pieces of red hot scrap metal. I thought this ritual an unnecessary and time-wasting precaution until I saw the piston rod of a hammer—a shaft of solid steel seven inches in diameter—shear off just above the tup as cleanly as if it had been cut with a knife. Then I learned what fatigue and frost between them could do to metal.

I was thankful that I served my stint in the Forge during the dark months of the year, for in summer the heat there became almost intolerable to anyone unused to it. With a big oil-fired furnace roaring away beside each of the eight hammers and the drop-stamp, this was inevitable. Also in the Forge was a large Thomson water-tube boiler for supplying steam to the hammers and also to the steam operated hydraulic pumps which raised an accumulator that stood just outside the building beside the tall chimney stack. It was the boilerman's job to summon us to work and send us home by sounding the steam hooter that projected through the roof above this boiler. Most of the pottery works called their workers by steam sirens similar to those used on the old steam roundabouts. Each morning these would break into a frenzy of excited whoops to which Kerr Stuarts added a deep, mournful and slightly hoarse ground bass, like the voice of a liner lost in a fog.

From the Forge I moved into the Machine Shop. Whereas the plant in the more recently built shops was contemporary with the buildings and was thus comparatively modern in the 1920s, the Machine Shop was already outdated. Not only was it housed in part of the original factory, but I suspect that many of the machine tools dated from the nineteenth century and had been taken over with the building. The shop would have seemed low roofed and dark even without the line shafting and the forest of flapping belts with which it was cluttered.

Such was the reputation of the Forge and Foundry that they secured a lot of sub-contract work which helped to tide them over periods when locomotives orders fell slack. But the Machine Shop was nothing to be proud of. Modern tungsten-carbide tipped tools were still in the future, but some of the machines still used the old carbon steel tools which were already archaic. I remember being sent to the tool smith in the Forge to get them tempered. However, the machines, though slow, were adequate for their purpose, for tolerance on the machined parts of locomotives were generous by modern standards because they assumed a great deal of skilled hand fitting. Nevertheless, like many another apprentice before me, I perpetrated the occasional 'waster'. The time-honoured procedure then was to conceal the spoiled part beneath one's overalls and consign it to the waters of the Trent and Mersey Canal. I used to wonder just how many guilty secrets would be revealed if ever that particular pound were drained. I now suspect that foremen and staff must have turned a blind eye to this practice for, on espying a young apprentice heading across the yard for the canal, they must surely have pondered on the reason why he had acquired a pot belly or a stiff leg, depending on the dimensions of the object concealed.

The Foundry was situated at low level directly alongside the canal, a convenient arrangement because it enabled the tall cupolas to be charged with coke, pig-iron and scrap at yard level. I never worked there, but I welcomed any excuse to walk through it, particularly in the late afternoon when the sand-moulds were being filled with molten metal so that the castings would have a chance to cool down overnight. For if a casting is broken out of its mould too soon it becomes chilled, making its metal hard and difficult to machine. The larger the casting the longer it must remain in the sand. The Foundry was the quietest place in the works, for here there were no noisy machines but only men, moving silently over the floor of soft black sand or stooping or kneeling beside their mould-boxes, working with the rapt concentration of a child making a sand castle. Although his hands were black, a skilled moulder used them with the precision and deftness of a surgeon. He would ease a wooden pattern from the sand with extreme care and then make good any slight damage that the edges of the fragile mould might have sustained, using little gleaming tools which the sand had burnished.

But at casting time, when the draught roared in the bellies

of the cupolas, the Foundry became a highly dramatic place. Wielding his long pricker like a lance, the furnaceman broke through the bung of fireclay that had stopped the mouth of the tapping hole and amid a dazzle of sizzling sparks a stream of white hot metal would gush out into the waiting ladle. He had a new clay bung formed ready on the end of a rod so that he could stop the flow when the ladle was full. The biggest and most complicated casting produced by this Foundry comprised the two cylinders and valve chests for a large inside cylinder locomotive. To cast this a huge ladle containing anything up to five tons of metal was needed. When it had been filled it was raised aloft by the overhead crane, traversed and then lowered gently into position in front of the mould, the crane driver leaning forward out of his cabin, his face lit by the glare from the ladle as the charge-hand below signalled to him with the palm of his hand. For the ladle had to be positioned very precisely so that when it was tilted the stream of metal would be directed precisely into the mouth of the mould runner. Then the pouring began, two men manning the hand-wheels that tipped the ladle, a third, armed with a long skimmer, holding back the dross that formed on the surface of the molten metal to prevent it falling into the mould and a fourth igniting the gas that issued from the mould vents while the charge-hand kept a vigilant eye on the whole operation. For, to be successful, it had to be carried out promptly and speedily but without haste and flurry. Otherwise, either the casting would be spoiled or there would be an accident. Molten metal is deadly stuff.

The Erecting Shop at Kerr Stuarts was as lofty as a cathedral. This was to enable the two Royce cranes to lift one locomotive over another if the need arose. Such an operation was impossible in the older erecting shops where locomotives were built in line ahead and if anything delayed completion of the engine at the head of the line, the rest were imprisoned. This new shop had been built alongside the original Erecting Shop of Hartley, Arnoux and Fanning, one wall of which had been demolished so that it now formed a kind of side aisle with a lower roof than the main building. In this aisle a variety of machine and hand operations were performed in the production of locomotive frames, wheels, axles, axle boxes and motion. At the time I came to the works there was no flame cutting and main frame plates were cut to shape by an incredibly laborious method. The plates, each an inch or more thick, were dealt with in batches of six, the top plate of each batch being white-washed and marked out with a scriber to indicate the exact form in which it was to be cut. This batch was then moved to the tables of a row of Archdale radial drilling machines whose operators proceeded to drill closely spaced holes all round the scribed outline. The metal between these holes was next cut through by hammer and chisel. This left an extremely ragged edge, so finally the batch was transferred to the table of a very large vertical milling machine to be milled all round.

Here also a giant lathe turned pairs of wheels and axles and tyres were shrunk on to wheels by a method very similar to that used by a village wheelwright to tyre wagon wheels. Safety screws were then fitted as a precaution although I have never heard of a tyre working loose. There was also a row of fitters' benches where a great deal of highly skilled and patient hand fitting of valve motion parts was done. I worked for a time at one of these benches with file, scraper and surface plate bedding the two halves of eccentric sheaves together. I found this a particularly tricky job because the two surfaces were not flat but stepped which meant that three faces, one of them vertical, had to bed accurately. Moreover, this had to be done so that, when drawn together by bolts, the sheave would 'pinch' on the axle and its keys, otherwise it would soon work loose when running. However, I persevered, knowing that with my next move I should achieve the summit of my ambition —to work in the Erecting Shop.

The men in the Erecting Shop were divided into gangs, each working as a team under a charge-hand. Each of these gangs was responsible for building a locomotive from the time the bare frame plates were set up until it left the shop under its own steam. I joined a gang led by Ernest Lines ('Ernie'), a splendid character, short, stocky and humorous with a lantern jaw who looked as though he liked his beer but was absolute master of his trade. It was particularly fortunate for me that at this time the shop was building six of the largest locomotives ever to be turned out by the firm. These were 4–8–0 mixed traffic engines destined for the Buenos Aires Central Railway (F.C.C.B.A.). Although of standard gauge, they were too big to travel over British metals to Birkenhead for shipment but had to be partially dismantled. Compared with the average British locomotive of the day, their cabs seemed vast and positively palatial with their sliding teak shutters, tip-up seats for the crew and flexibly mounted electric lights to illuminate steam and water gauges. These lights, and the big headlamps mounted fore and aft,[1] were supplied with current by a turbo-generator mounted on top of the firebox. Their tenders were so big that on one occasion, while waiting for some part to arrive, an erecting gang settled down in the water tank to play a quiet game of halfpenny nap by the light of tallow dips. They imagined they were secure from prying eyes until a member of a rival gang dropped a handful of smouldering cotton waste down through the tank filler and smoked them out.

There was much good-natured horse-play of this kind in the Erecting Shop, for the men were the aristocrats of their trade and management treated them indulgently. Perennial works jokes were played on simple apprentices. They would be sent to the stores to fetch a left-handed hammer or a long stand. On asking for the latter, the innocent youth would be kept waiting interminably until, on repeating his request, the grinning store-keeper replied 'You've had it'. The joke dated back at least a hundred years. Once, when a gang had got behind with their locomotive, they returned after the lunch break to find grass apparently growing luxuriantly out of the top of the funnel. 'Yockerton Hall' was their invariable reply to any query as to the whereabouts of an individual, a missing part or a tool. And to the obvious question that this provoked they would reply in mock surprise: 'What, yo' never 'eard o' Yockerton! It's where there's neither land nor water and they walk about on planks.' The exploits of a legendary driver named Gluepot were another feature of works mythology. He was so-called because he was said on one occasion to have filled his cylinder lubricator up with glue in mistake for hot cylinder oil with very surprising results. On another occasion he was alleged to have driven a train from Shrewsbury into Crewe with the shattered remains of Nantwich level crossing gates dangling from his front buffers, much to the dismay of station officials. These are typical examples of my workmates' humour.

For me it was a rich experience to work with such men on such a locomotive and to watch the monster grow in power and majesty from day to day. When the frames had been completed, the outside cylinders and smoke-box saddle could be bolted up. Next, the boiler was propelled into the shop on a bogie flat wagon by the works shunting engine and dropped into place

[1] Evidently they did a lot of tender-first running in Argentina.

on the frames. A big moment came when the locomotive was lifted bodily by both cranes and lowered gently on to its wheels. Additional hands were needed for this operation because a man had to guide each axle box between the cheeks of the horn-blocks on the frames. Then, after valve gear and connecting rods had been fitted up and set, the engine was gently pulled forwards by the works shunter until its driving wheels rested precisely on two rollers at track level near the shop doors. Now the time had come to raise steam. With the regulator opened a crack, the engine was allowed to run herself in for an hour or so. As she stood thus, driving wheels revolving slowly on the rollers, the men who had built her fussed about her like anxious midwives. Grimy hands felt the temperature of bearings and, as the cross-head swept to and fro, Ernie Lines passed a rapid finger across the oily surface of the slide bars before and behind it to ensure that its bronze slippers were bedding properly.

Only when this test had been passed satisfactorily was it time to fit the coupling rods and then give the locomotive its first run under steam. There was a multi-gauge track in the Erecting Shop, the gauges ranging from 2 ft. up to 5 ft. 6 in. Most of these ended at the first turnout of the works railway about fifty yards outside the shop, but the 3 ft. gauge and, of course, the 4 ft. 8½ in., continued to provide a long straight test track that ran beside the main railway boundary fence to a terminus in the paint shop at the far end of the works. So we could give our monster quite a respectable run and that Ernie Lines allowed me to handle her was more than ample reward for all the hard work that had gone before. It was the first time in my life that I had driven a locomotive and it gave me an indescribable thrill, when I nudged the regulator cautiously open, to hear the first deep exhaust beat and to feel the great machine suddenly come alive under my hand and begin to roll obediently forward. After we had progressed majestically to and fro for some time, I stopped her and took a photograph to record the great occasion, Ernie Lines posing proudly on the front buffer beam.

Locomotives intended for export as this one was were usually finished in flat 'shop grey', much to the disappointment of the paint shop, although the first of any new type was lined black and white solely for photographic purposes. But, about this time, one of the large and handsome tank engines which the firm had built just after the war for the Aylesbury line of the Metropolitan Railway came back to the works for a complete overhaul and when this was finished she received 'the full treatment' in the paint shop. After laborious de-scaling of the plates followed by seemingly endless coats of paint, each rubbed down by hand with bath-brick and water and after repeated varnishings, she emerged wearing that gleaming, lustrous livery such as one can now admire only in old photographs. Her side-tanks were like the surface of a mirror. Look how you would, you could not detect the slightest wave in the plate or the faintest suggestion of a countersunk rivet. I am glad that I saw her, for she was certainly the last locomotive to be painted in the traditional style at the California Works and probably one of the last in the country. By contrast, when twenty-five new six-coupled pannier tank locomotives were built later for the Great Western Railway, the poor standard of finish that was specified caused a lot of head-shaking in the Paint Shop. This was by no means the only dictate to cause dismay among the craftsmen at Kerr Stuarts, but there could be no argument for throughout the contract a Great Western resident inspector was on the prowl to ensure that all the work was carried out precisely to Swindon specification.

In this case the firm became virtually a sub-contractor to Swindon. Normally, the procedure was very different. Once the outline design and specification of a new type of locomotive for an overseas railway company had been approved in principle by the consulting engineers, the drawing office would produce the detail drawings and issue them to the foremen of the shops—boiler drawings to the foreman of the Boiler Shop and so on. These drawings were the basis of a tender and when they were issued everyone in the works knew that a new contract was in the wind because the foremen (each wearing the bowler hat which was his permanent badge of office) would be seen filing into the canteen for a meeting. From this each man would return, drawings under arm, to his own office where he would call a similar meeting of his charge-hands who, in their turn, would discuss matters with their gangs. Under this hierarchical system, each shop agreed upon its price for a particular part of the job and it was upon this basis that the final tender was submitted. Compared with other industries in Britain where the rate-fixer with his stop-watch had already made his appearance, this method was already obsolete, yet in human terms it possessed incalculable advantages not to be measured in terms of economics or business efficiency. For it made every skilled man in the works feel he was a responsible member of a team and the news that a tender had been accepted caused general jubilation in the shops.

I have set down in some detail the way steam locomotives were built at the California Works because the whole process has now become as much a thing of the past as the making of a farm wagon in George Sturt's wheelwright's shop at Farnham. The men I was privileged to work beside were craftsmen as surely as were Sturt's wheelwrights. If they erred it was on the side of conservatism. Occasionally they might adopt a stubborn 'nothing like leather' mentality. But in the main they resisted the changes that were coming about in engineering methods, not because they threatened their pay packets, but because they involved a lowering of the standards of workmanship in which they took such pride and satisfaction and so menaced the future of those traditional skills which were their only real assets. In short, they were of the species *homo faber* and it is as well to emphasise this now that all social or economic studies are based on the facile Marxist assumption that man is merely an economic animal, and all talk of craftsmanship or pride in work dismissed as merely romantic sentimentality. On the contrary, having worked beside such men I know that, although they had had little formal education, because they were craftsmen their general standards were exacting. Take away that craftsmanship and standards inevitably fall, only the weight of the pay packet counts, and man becomes indeed an economic animal.

# Chapter 7

# Shropshire Railways
# and Canals

On week-days I found the demonic energy of the Pottery towns, all those belching chimneys and ovens, the jostling crowds and traffic—much of it still horse-drawn—in the streets, strangely exhilarating. It fascinated me in spite of myself in the same way that Milton was obviously attracted by the activities of Satan. But on Sundays the Potteries became anathema to me. For then innumerable furnace fires were banked allowing its skies to clear so that, in summer, the pitiless eye of the sun revealed with unfamiliar clarity the sordidness of the cobbled streets with their rows of terraced houses, their blackness unrelieved by any green thing. Apart from occasional figures squatting aimlessly on raddled front doorsteps, or the footfalls of some miner exercising his whippet, these streets were silent and deserted at such a time. The smell of roasting Sunday joints mingled with a stale smell of beer from street corner pubs, this last a hangover, like the pieces of vinegar stained newspaper that the wind stirred in the gutters, of previous Saturday night orgies. Now they were sleeping it off. Not until afternoon did the Potteries begin to show signs of life as buses began to churn down London Road carrying loads of young couples to their love-making amid the bracken of Trentham Park.

I found these Sundays so depressing that I could not wait to get out of the Potteries at week-ends. As soon as work was over at midday on Saturday and I had my 'dinner' at No. 439, I would change and head off into the country on my motorcycle. Fortunately, unlike some industrial areas, the Pottery towns are easy to get out of. Strung along the headwaters of the Trent, they form a long, narrow industrial belt with unspoiled country upon either side. Strangely enough, the northern side towards the Peak District where Staffordshire soon merges into Derbyshire never appealed to me and it was south-westwards into Shropshire that I usually turned, often to spend the weekend with the Willans family at their home near the Welsh Border.

Dovaston was one of those pleasant, roomy, four-square early nineteenth-century houses of stone-faced mellow brick with a low-pitched slate roof such as one finds in the countryside of Shropshire and Cheshire. It had only one snag; its water supply had to be pumped by hand, using an antiquated green-painted pump that stood outside the back door in a small cobbled yard surrounded by a low range of outbuildings. In my recollection of the various Willans' houses, water supply problems persistently dogged the family but were usually solved by my uncle with improvisations remarkable for their ingenuity and economy. Dovaston House was no exception. He had purchased an old horizontal 'hit-and-miss' petrol/paraffin engine. By means of a flat belt, this drove a cranked countershaft which actuated the pump handle by a long connecting rod. In action, this novel arrangement reminded me of one of Heath Robinson's crazy inventions. Quivering with animation and slopping water from its steaming cooling hopper, the engine coughed and wheezed, the driving belt slapped, while the old pump, finding its handle gripped by a tireless iron arm, rocked on its foundation and made loud groaning complaints. But it worked.

The house stood on rising ground and the tall windows of the drawing room commanded a magnificent view over a wide expanse of flood plain, the meeting place of rivers Vyrnwy and Severn, to the dramatic shapes of the Briedden Hills beyond. Although they were of modest height, as such outliers are apt to do, the Brieddens looked impressively steep and mountainous. In any season of the year, they caught and held the eye. In autumn they would look like some volcanic islands of the Pacific above a ghostly sea of mist. More than once when I was at Dovaston I looked out of my bedroom window on a Sunday morning to see their bold shapes mirrored in a real sea when heavy overnight rain over the Welsh mountains had caused both rivers to rise with astonishing speed, drowning all the land below. Where so lately there had been green fields, now only trees and hedgerows stood darkly out of an expanse of silver waters. In the midst of this plain lay the little village of Melverley, ancient and remote, where even the graveyard surrounding the little timbered church has to be protected lest Severn wash away its dead. 'God help Melverley!' was a saying in those parts whenever the floods were out, and at such times I would repeat it to myself, wondering the while why ever a village came to be built there. It seemed as improbable as that mythical Yockerton Hall.

Although it is forty years since I was last at Dovaston, I find that memory can still re-create in all its details that landscape as I saw it then. Such loveliness, so indelibly imprinted on the mind by the sensitive lens of youth is, I find, as great a solace and as evocative of the past as an old tune or remembered voices. But because we now treat our country, not as a paradise garden but as a squalid and neglected backyard, if the image is not to be shattered forever, it is usually wiser not to revisit the scenes of our youth.

I thought this Shropshire landscape like, and yet at the same time strangely unlike, that other country of the Herefordshire marches further to the south which I had come to know so well as a child. Despite its great natural beauty, however, I felt then—as I still feel—that there is something indefinably melancholy about western Shropshire. Instead of seeming to transcend time and lift the heart as did the country of my childhood, it seemed to speak of time passing and to evoke race memories of old, unhappy, far off things. I had not read Housman at this time, but when I did so, some of his poems seemed to me to be loaded with the burden of this profound sadness.

The contrast between Dovaston House and my dingy lodgings in Stoke-on-Trent was so extreme that I was loath to leave it. Rather than depart on Sunday evening, I preferred to rise at 6 a.m. the following day, creep out of the house and ride back to Stoke in time for work, even in the darkness and cold of a winter's morning. Once on such a morning I struck an unsuspected patch of black ice on a corner near Shrewsbury and skidded into a wet ditch with the bike on top of me. But I had become inured to spills of this kind, sorted myself out and was soon pressing on again through the darkness though my teeth were chattering with the cold.

By this time, my cousin Bill Willans, who was slightly younger than I was and had just left school at Stowe, was living at home. Acting on the same principle that had sent me to Pitchill—that a small shop makes the best primary school for a budding engineer—his father had arranged for him to work in the shops at nearby Kinnerley Junction. Kinnerley was the Swindon of that most endearing rural byway, the Shropshire and Montgomeryshire Railway. It had only received its title in this century from a remarkable character named Colonel H. F. Stephens who made it his precarious business to buy up moribund railways and attempt to re-animate them, using cast-off locomotives and rolling stock purchased cheap from other, grander railways. The S. & M.R. was thus the railway equivalent of some of the smaller and poorer South American airlines today and its shops at Kinnerley resembled a graveyard where old locomotives, like so many old elephants, came to die. The railway owed its existence to a crazy speculation of the 1860s aiming to provide a direct rail link between the Potteries and Portmadoc on the coast of North Wales, and Shropshire countrymen, who have long memories, habitually referred to it as 'the Pots'. Its main line set off boldly from Shrewsbury but petered out tamely at Llanymynech, just over the Welsh Border, as though the speculators had taken fright at the sight of the Welsh hills ahead. From Kinnerley a branch line curved away to the southward, crossing the Severn and its flood plain to end at Criggion at the foot of the Briedden Hills. Here there was a large granite quarry which employed a Sentinel locomotive and provided most of the S. & M.R.'s meagre freight traffic.

I will not describe this railway in detail, its ageing locomotives or the eccentric manner in which it was operated, because I have already done so fully in an earlier book.[1] But at least I should explain that although it could boast a stud of eight locomotives, there was seldom more than one of them which was capable of being steamed at any one time. The resourceful owner, however, had triumphantly overcome this deficiency by purchasing four old Model T Ford buses, mounting them on railway wheels and running them in pairs coupled back to back. To equip them for this new role, only the minimum of alteration was done. For example, steering wheels were retained. Perhaps they helped the driver to feel at home. They offered the maximum of discomfort ever achieved in rail travel, while on account of the clangour of their hollow steel wheels, which could be heard miles away in still weather, they were nicknamed 'the rattlers' by the locals.

[1] *Lines of Character* (Constable, 1952).

Bill had entered into the life of the railway wholeheartedly. No doubt he found the change from school as refreshing as I did. He was already playing for the village cricket team which was captained by Mr Funnel, the stationmaster at Kinnerley Junction, a red-faced portly man who always employed a runner because of his bad heart. Kinnerley was within walking distance of Dovaston House, and although Bill had worked on the railway all the week, it seemed as though he could never have enough of it. Whenever I arrived for the week-end we usually made a bee-line for the loco shed and repair shop which was situated at right angles to the station beside the Criggion Branch. Ancient locomotives in various stages of disrepair lay slumbering in the sunshine on the grassgrown tracks outside the shed. Here, for example, stood the rusting wreck of the locomotive *Hesperus*, patiently awaiting a new boiler which never seemed to come. (Curiously enough, to the amazement of all at Kinnerley, that new boiler did eventually arrive and *Hesperus* was rebuilt. As her sister engine *Pyramus* presently expired, it was not before time.) Equipment and facilities for repair were either non-existent or so primitive that even the most minor repair job entailed a major feat of improvisation. But, remembering that great engineer Frederick Lanchester's terse comment: 'Too much apparatus, not enough brains' on being shown round a modern research laboratory, it was obviously an ideal training school for Bill. To one who had come straight from the fiery tumult of the California Works, the contrast of this little quiet shop, dozing in the depths of the country, was extreme. I felt I had indeed come to the end of the line.

In the yard at Kinnerley there was kept one of those plate-layer's trolleys which two men can propel by means of a central seesaw handle connected to its cranked axle. By energetic pumping of the handle, this device was capable of quite a fair turn of speed and on fine Sundays Bill and I used to explore the railway. On more than one occasion we trundled off down the branch line towards Criggion. This crossed the Severn near Melverley by a timber bridge that looked as frail as an early American trestle viaduct and I used to marvel that it could ever withstand the weight of a locomotive. To cross this bridge was the thrilling highlight of the journey, for there was no decking, the rails being fixed to longitudinal baulks supported by cross beams. One could look down between these timbers to the swirling brown waters of the Severn below.

On another occasion we set out to cover the 4½ miles of main line between Kinnerley and Llanymynech in the scheduled running time of the passenger service, including making the regulation intermediate pauses at Wern Las halt and Maesbrook station en route. That we achieved this does not say much for the celerity of passenger trains on the S. & M.R. Breathless and pumping furiously on the handles, we swung round the curve leading into the old Cambrian station at Llanymynech, coming to rest in the bay platform exactly on time.

The Shropshire and Montgomeryshire Railway was not the only thing that attracted me to Dovaston House at this time. Inspired no doubt by memories of his father's steam launch *Black Angel*, my uncle Kyrle conceived the idea of building a roomy steam boat in which the Willans family and their friends could go for leisurely holidays on the canals. Only a few miles away from Dovaston was the Llangollen branch of the Shropshire Union Canal and also the canal line to Welshpool and Newtown (the old Montgomeryshire Canal) which joined the former at Frankton Junction. The Shropshire Union Railways and Canal Company and its associate, the Shropshire Union Canal Carrying Company, were both controlled by the London and North Western Railway which, because the canal passed through rival railway territory, traded vigorously on it, having a fleet of over two hundred boats in action as late as 1920. In the following year, however, the railway unions insisted that the boatmen and their families who manned these craft should in future only work an eight-hour day like the railwaymen. This typically obtuse egalitarian move, betraying a total ignorance of the very different working conditions on canals, could only have one result: the entire Shropshire Union fleet was disbanded and the boats either broken up or sold to local traders and small carrying concerns. In 1929, some of the latter were still trading on the western branches of the system though upon a much diminished scale. Among these by-traders were the Peate family who used their boats to carry grain from Ellesmere Port on the Mersey to their own mill beside the canal at Maesbury, fifteen miles north of Welshpool. It was from them that Kyrle Willans purchased *Cressy*. She had been built for the Shropshire Union Canal Carrying Company during the Great War in a dockyard at the northern end of Telford's great aqueduct at Pont Cysyllte.[1]

---

[1] She was named after a battle cruiser of the first world war.

Although they must all conform to approximately the same general dimensions (70 ft. long by 7 ft. beam), canal narrow boats vary so much in build that it is possible for the know-ledgeable to spot the different types at a glance. Of these, in my opinion, the Shropshire Union boats were easily the most graceful. They were smaller and of lighter burthen (they were a plank lower in the side than other wooden boats), and, whereas most narrow boats are virtually elongated floating boxes with very bluff bows and sterns, the sides of the typical Shropshire Union hull were built with considerable sheer which led into a beautiful tapering and up-curving bow and stern. In boatman's parlance they were good swimmers. This, then, was the boat that, on my uncle's instructions, was brought from Maesbury to Mr Beech's dock beside the locks at Frankton Junction to be converted into a comfortable house-boat. So far as I know, there were then only two similar narrow boat conversions in existence. A trip over to Frankton Dock to inspect progress on *Cressy* thereafter became a regular feature of my visits to Dovaston House.

*Cressy* had been a horse-drawn boat and to propel her my uncle acquired a small vertical compound steam engine by Plentys of Newbury which had previously powered an Admiralty pinnace. In order to install this it was necessary to bore and otherwise modify the stern post to take a shaft and propeller and to fit a new rudder and tiller of motor boat type. Acting on one of his favourite maxims that 'there's no such thing as too big a boiler', my uncle bought a second-hand boiler out of a Yorkshire steam wagon to supply the little Plenty engine with steam. This was a T-shaped boiler of double-ended return tube type. Two short barrels terminating in smoke-boxes extended from either side of a central firebox, the chimney being directly above the firedoor. The boiler exactly fitted into *Cressy*, the two smoke boxes being just inboard of the gunwhales. This meant that sweeping the tubes on the water side of the boat was something of an acrobatic feat and after Bill had fallen backwards into the canal still clutching a tube brush, we usually swept the tubes while the boat was lying in a narrow lock.

*Cressy's* original living accommodation, a cabin at the stern and a smaller raised fore-cabin in the bow, were retained. The steam plant was installed in an engine room immediately ahead of the stern cabin and, apart from a small open deck just aft of the fore-cabin, the remainder of her hold was cabined over to provide extra accommodation.

When all this work had been completed, *Cressy* was floated out of Mr Beech's dock and a steam trial was held up the canal in the direction of Llangollen one Sunday afternoon. I remember thinking how wonderful it would be to steam over the tall aqueduct across the Vale of Llangollen at Pontcysyllte, but since our speed was only three miles an hour and the aqueduct was eleven miles away, this was manifestly impossible in the short time available and we had to turn *Cressy* about in the first convenient 'winding hole'. Exactly twenty years were to pass before I finally achieved this ambition by taking *Cressy* over Pontcysyllte.

It was at this juncture that the Willans family left Dovaston House and moved to an old house at Barlaston to the south of the Potteries. Selfishly, I welcomed this move for obvious reasons though I was saddened to think I would never see Dovaston again. Although the village of Barlaston was much more countrified then than it is today, the outskirts of the Potteries must have seemed to my long-suffering Aunt Hero a very poor exchange for west Shropshire. But, kindly and cheerful as ever, she appeared to take it in her stride and it is only now, as I look back, that I realise what a wrench it must have been to her to leave that beautiful house. This move led to a decision to steam *Cressy* from Frankton to a mooring on the Trent and Mersey Canal at the tail of Trentham lock where she would be only the breadth of a gently sloping meadow away from the new house. This would be her maiden voyage as a powered craft, and as we planned to complete it in two days, there was little room for mishap or mechanical failure. So to simplify the operation *Cressy* was moved, a week beforehand, from Frankton to a more convenient and accessible mooring at Ellesmere. For this momentous voyage there was to be an all male crew of four, my uncle Kyrle, my cousin Bill, a youth named Frank from Kinnerley, who had done odd jobs about the house at Dovaston, and myself. I took the Saturday morning off by special dispensation so that we could all sleep on board on the Friday night and make an early start the following morning.

As this was to be very much of a working trip, we were all in our overalls and slept in the old cabins fore and aft to avoid sullying the pristine accommodation amidships. It was the first night I had ever spent afloat and it was a short one. On that March morning of 1930 two of us got up while it was still quite dark to light up the boiler and to oil round.

Then, after a scratch breakfast washed down with mugs of scalding tea to fortify us against the cold while steam was making, we cast off and slipped away in the first faint light of dawn.

The long level pound of canal that we first traversed passes through a country strangely remote and of a mysterious beauty. It first runs close beside two of the Shropshire meres, Colemere and Blakemere, winds about for a space by Hampton Bank and Bettisfield, and then suddenly broadens into a wider and deeper channel that cuts straight across Whixall Moss, a great expanse of peat bog more reminiscent of Ireland than England. That morning dawned dry but cold and still with an overcast sky of a uniform pearly grey. My recollection is of the black interlacement of bare branches silhouetted against this colourless sky, of a thin white mist lying waist high over the dark waters. Tree-encircled and veiled in this mist, Blake-mere might have been that magic lake of Arthurian legend into which Sir Bedivere had flung the sword Excalibur. In memory it has become the still and silent landscape of a dream and through it *Cressy* glided smoothly and quietly along, her little compound engine ticking over with no more noise than a well-oiled sewing machine. She did not intrude upon the landscape; she became a part of it like the canal itself. As I realised this, my consuming interest in engineering and my feeling for the natural world, which, since I had come to Stoke-on-Trent had begun disturbingly to conflict with each other, were suddenly reconciled and before we had covered many miles I had fallen head-over-heels in love with canals. This is it, I thought; this is what travel ought to be like.

We took turn and turn about, one at the tiller and one in the engine room, while the other two crew members worked the locks or snatched a bite of food. The engine continued to run perfectly, the boiler steamed freely and, as darkness fell, we tied up below Wardle Lock, Middlewich, at the junction of the Trent and Mersey Canal having covered 37 miles and worked through 23 locks. This may not sound much to anyone unacquainted with canal travelling but it was a pretty good day's journey for an inexperienced crew with an untried boat. This performance reflects, not so much on the ability of the crew as on the deterioration in the state of the canals between then and now.

Next morning we were up betimes as a long hard day's work lay ahead of us if we were to reach Barlaston by nightfall.

First we had to scale the thirty-four Cheshire Locks which lay between us and the northern end of the long summit tunnel at Harecastle. And after we had passed through that tunnel there would still be a further nine miles to go with five falling locks before we reached our destination. We had climbed the locks and reached the mouth of the tunnel when an unexpected hitch occurred. Knowledgeable heads were shaken over the height of *Cressy's* new cabinwork. The headroom in the tunnel had been greatly reduced owing to mining subsidence, we were told, and because, according to regulations, we would have to be towed through by an unstoppable electric tug, the new cabin would certainly be torn off in the process. There was only one thing to be done—bring her down in the water by loading up the fore-end with some suitable ballast. This put an end to our hopes of reaching Barlaston that evening. *Cressy* was moored up where she lay and left in charge of Frank. So ended my ever-memorable first canal voyage, for I had to be back at work in the morning. Next day, *Cressy* was loaded with bricks, off-loaded again when she had successfully passed through the tunnel, and worked down to Barlaston by the other three crew members.

On this first trip, *Cressy* had worked as a 'puffer', that is to say, steam from the engine exhausted up her funnel. This produced steam in such embarrassing volume that it was difficult to prevent the boiler blowing off and enveloping the steerer in a cloud of steam. Consequently, my uncle decided that she would steam quite adequately on natural draught, so he had a small jet condenser built to his design in the Boiler Shop at Kerr Stuarts. When this was finished, *Cressy* was steamed up to Stoke and moored beside the Foundry where the condenser and the necessary pipe-work were installed, the men thoroughly enjoying this unusual 'foreign order', as they termed it. After this, we made two week-end trips to Great Haywood and back before, in August 1930, I joined *Cressy* for the first week of a long fortnight's cruise.

We steamed down the canal to the Trent, turned up the Soar through Loughborough and Leicester, passed through the Leicester Section of the Grand Union and thence down the main line of that canal as far as Blisworth. There I and another member of the crew were replaced by others, leaving the boat to return to Barlaston by a different route. I remember that my cousin Bill and I had to bow-haul the boat through dense weed for a distance of a mile or more north of Alrewas on the

Trent and Mersey, but this was exceptional; over most of the route the going was much better than it is today. Once again, the steam plant performed perfectly, its silence was a delight and we made use of it to do much of our cooking. In the early evening my aunt Hero and my cousin Barbara, assisted by other spare members of the crew, would prepare the ingredients for a king-sized stew. These were put into a massive steam-jacketed pot which was placed on the cabin roof aft with a sack thrown over it. The engine room hand would couple it up to the boiler, turn on steam and in a short while the hungry steerer was regaled by the most delectable smell of cooking.

But there were snags to steam. It took up a lot of space; two men were needed to work the boat and although an electric bell was rigged up to act as an engine room telegraph, reaction in emergency was not always quick enough. Having rung 'full astern' the unfortunate steerer was apt to find the boat steaming towards some immovable obstruction because the engine room attendant was preoccupied in oiling the engine or coaxing the injector. Another source of friction between steerer and engineer was the smoke. Although *Cressy* ran more silently than before and steamed well enough with the condenser fitted, there was now not enough draught to lift the smoke over the steerer's head. Too preoccupied to see the canal ahead, the engineer often unwittingly chose to fire up the moment before *Cressy* dived into a long tunnel. This provoked bitter recriminations and these were echoed at the bow if the unfortunate steerer, blinded by smoke, bumped the side wall violently, disrupting cooking operations in the galley. Nor was it always easy to obtain supplies of suitable coal. I remember Bill and I sweating profusely one hot August afternoon as we humped hundredweight sacks from a neighbouring coalyard along the towing path at Loughborough.

After the move to Barlaston, Bill was apprenticed for a time in the maintenance shop of the North Staffordshire Coal and Iron Company, whose pits and furnaces (the latter long since gone) were situated beside the canal to the south of Kerr Stuarts. This work took him frequently below ground to repair compressed-air haulage engines and other equipment. Although this was exacting work carried out under difficult conditions, the men at Kerr Stuarts referred to the 'pit fitter' scathingly and regarded him as a figure of fun. They often referred to a hand-hammer as a pit-fitter's spanner, claiming that it was the only tool he ever used. But I learnt to appreciate his work better after, at Bill's instigation, I had been down one of the 'North Stafford' pits to the 800 yard level. The experience of our descent of the shaft in the cage came as no surprise to me because I had been warned that when the cage started I should feel as though I had left most of my insides behind on the surface. The fastest express lift was nothing to it. The surprising thing was to discover that the 800 yard level was a level only in name. Because the North Staffordshire coal seams are extravagantly buckled and because the miner naturally follows the seam, the main haulage-way leading from the pit bottom to the working face resembled an underground switchback railway. At the pit bottom I could hear the draught whistling through chinks in the airlock doors between the downcast and upcast shafts, yet the atmosphere seemed stale and hot, the pit dry and dusty underfoot. As we plodded along for what seemed an interminable distance, now toiling up a steep ascent, now back on our heels as we faced an equally steep descent, I became increasingly conscious of the vast weight of earth and rock directly above my head. It was not a pleasant feeling. Coal mines are definitely not for the claustrophobic. No wooden props here; the tunnel was arched with steel sections some of which had buckled under the immense weight to such an extent that we had to stoop as we passed beneath them. We must have walked the best part of two miles before we reached the coal face where the compressed air coal-cutting machines were running and I was reminded that a miner's working day began and ended at the face.[1] I had admired the way my workmates at Kerr Stuarts faced their working lives, but after this experience I admired the coal miner very much more.

Life at Stoke was very much more enjoyable now that I had the company of Bill Willans in the evenings and at week-ends. But there was one serious snag. His parents absolutely forbade him to ride pillion on the 2¾ h.p. A.J.S. motorcycle which I had bought to replace my old B.S.A. It is true that my motorcycling career had been one long chapter of accidents. I could never manage the acetylene headlamp on my B.S.A. for one thing. Either it went up in flames and became red-hot, or it burnt with only a dim blue glow. It was on one of the latter

[1] The company were at this time sinking a new shaft at Hem Heath, near Trentham, to reduce this distance, but this had not yet come into operation.

occasions that I had run into the back of a Sentinel Wagon at night on the road from Pitchill to Evesham with such force that the driver noticed it and stopped to investigate. If the top of my front forks had not made contact with the tail of the Sentinel but had run underneath it, I might not have survived. As it was I merely fell over on to a heap of stones by the side of the road, dislocating my shoulder. Nevertheless, somehow or other I managed to ride the damaged bike back to the farm. On another occasion at Pitchill I rode straight through a barn door, making myself decidedly unpopular in the process. I had arrived in the farmyard at speed only to find the footbrake rod had broken. Since the handbrake was useless in such circumstances I instantly chose the barn door as a more resilient form of energency stop than the brick walls which offered the only alternative. Twice I had flown over the handlebars and miraculously landed in the road on my bottom instead of on my head, once when I collided with a suicidal sheep on a Welsh mountain pass, and again when someone, unknown to me, had slackened the front fork shock-absorbers right off and I experienced a monumental steering wobble. Only a week after I had acquired my new A.J.S. I had set off from Stoke on a week-end visit to Gloucestershire which ended in disaster in Wolverhampton on my return journey. I collided violently with a Model T Ford Post Office delivery van when, as I was about to pass, its driver suddenly turned across my bows without making any signal. My new machine was practically written off and all my friends were very gloomy about the outcome. 'You'll never get anything out of the Post Office', they said. But, after much correspondence, the G.P.O. did pay for the damage in full. Although, apart from the first one, all these were pure accidents, I was certainly accident-prone and could scarcely blame my uncle and aunt for their embargo, indeed in the light of events I have reason to be grateful for it.

Faced with this transport problem, Bill concluded that if we switched from two wheels to four, his family could not possibly object and we agreed to purchase a car between us. Because our means were slender we scanned the second-hand columns of the local *Sentinel* anxiously and finally agreed to purchase a 1922 G.N. 'Popular' model from its owner in Longton for £6. I had envisaged that we should only use this car locally and that for long journeys solo I would continue to use my motorcycle, but I was so delighted with the G.N. that I soon repaid Bill his share, sold the A.J.S., and thereafter used a car exclusively. Strange to say I never enjoyed motorcycling, never grew fond of my motorcycles but used them solely as a means to an end. Occasionally, I went to the works in the G.N., but although it was hardly a luxury vehicle I found it somewhat embarrassing. For I was the only employee to come to work in a car; all the rest came either on foot or by bicycle.

The G.N. was in the state that dealers describe tersely as 'good runner', which meant that it looked dilapidated and needed quite a lot of mechanical attention. However, some friends in Trentham to whom we had been introduced, and who had three beautiful daughters, very kindly agreed to let us use their garage. Here we worked in the evenings and at week-ends restoring and repainting the car, our work enlivened by the interest of the three graces. I suspect that Bill had a soft spot for the youngest, while I fancied myself madly in love with the eldest. It was she who had been indirectly responsible for our introduction, since she had attended the same finishing school in Paris as my cousin Rosemary. Tall, golden-haired and graceful, I thought her the most ravishing creature I had ever set eyes on. But I sadly concluded that such a rare mortal was far beyond the reach of a dirty-handed, scruffy apprentice with no prospects, an assumption that was probably correct. I imagined her father (a kindly and charming man) asking in solemn Victorian tones: 'And what are your prospects, young man?', and thereafter decided it would be wiser to nurse my passion in secret, like some medieval troubadour. Painful though it may be at the time, for a romantic, unrequited and hopeless love has certain advantages. The imagined possesses an immortal perfection not attainable in reality.

On one never-to-be-forgotten occasion, this goddess actually agreed to accompany me to a cinema in Hanley, riding on the pillion of my motorcycle. Never did I negotiate the cobbles and treacherous tramlines of Stoke with greater care. Later, since we had both received invitations to my cousin Rosemary's wedding, it was agreed that we should travel down to Gloucestershire in the G.N. to spend the week-end with my parents, going with them in my father's Alvis to the wedding in Hertfordshire. This, so far as I can recall, was the first long journey I had attempted in the G.N. I looked forward to the trip with a mixture of expectation and trepidation (what if the car should break down?) and spent hours checking and re-checking everything.

As anyone acquainted with the marque will know, a G.N. is hardly the most appropriate mode of conveyance for goddesses. The big air-cooled twin-cylinder engine creates an immense amount of mechanical commotion and enough vibration to set the whole frail chassis rocking on its springs. When the great day came at last, it poured with rain from leaden skies all the way down to Gloucestershire, causing steam to rise from the exposed cylinders. Rain leaked through the hood and blew in through the gap between hood and windscreen. It also leaked through the dickey seat lid, soaking the suitcase containing my passenger's wedding finery. Occasionally worse would befall. The G.N. hood was held up by two straps secured to vestigial hooks on the pillars of the one-piece screen. Every now and again the effect of a bad bump was to free the straps from their hooks, whereupon the hood, helped by the wind, would instantly furl itself. By the time we had stopped and re-erected it we were decidedly damp. But at least, throughout the round trip the engine kept happily hammering away and all the transmission chains stayed on. The fact that she was able to endure the rigours of such a journey without any complaint makes me wonder whether my fair passenger was quite so remote as I thought she was.

# Chapter 8

# The First Diesel Lorry

The period I spent at Stoke-on-Trent was, in retrospect, undoubtedly the 'time of my life'. So crowded was it with incident and experience that now, looking back, I find it almost impossible to believe that so much could have been crammed into little more than two years of my life. Those years not only taught me a great deal about engineering but a lot about life as well, much of it disquieting and thought-provoking, but all of it intensely stimulating. That the attempt to recapture the sum of this experience should occupy so large a space in this book faithfully reflects the fact that the human clock that ticks away our time within us is not regulated by the arbitrary measure of any mechanical clock or calendar. That mysterious internal clock runs much faster when we are young, making the ordered passing of days, months and years seem the slower by contrast.

While I was living through the experiences I have described in the last two chapters, my uncle's designs for new steam and diesel[1] locomotives and—more significant in the light of the future—a new diesel lorry, were taking shape at the California Works. Following my orthodox passage through the shops, I became increasingly concerned with them and found their technical novelty and the sense they gave that one was pioneering in new fields very exciting and challenging.

As has already been said, my uncle was a disciple of Loftus Perkins and the boiler he designed for the new geared steam locomotive was designed on Perkins' principles. I will not describe it in detail here except to say that it consisted entirely of machined components and was assembled and tested in the

[1] The term 'diesel' is not technically correct in this context, but as it is the popular usage I have used it throughout in this book.

Fitting Shop, a fact which caused some headshaking among the boiler makers and would doubtless have provoked a demarcation dispute today. For its size, the boiler had an immense grate area and heating surface. Steam could be raised to its working pressure of 300 lb. p.s.i. in fifteen minutes and, in striking contrast to the Sentinel boiler, it would steam freely with the gentlest of draughts. For example, in response to an inquiry from the West Indies as to whether the new locomotive would burn bagasse,[1] I spent an afternoon firing it on wood shavings from the joinery as it ran to and fro on the test track with a full load. It was one of the hottest and most exhausting afternoons I have ever known because I had to shovel the stuff on to the fire continuously. But it was all burnt and the locomotive steamed like a witch. In any other locomotive those shavings would have been sucked straight off the shovel to emerge unburnt out of the chimney.

In January 1929, my cousin Bill and I heard my uncle read a paper on this locomotive to the Junior Institution of Mechanical Engineers in London. Present in the audience was Colonel R. E. B. Crompton, then the doyen of engineers. He had come along out of affection for the memory of his friend and one-time associate, Peter Willans, my uncle's father. Afterwards we were introduced to him. It was the only occasion when I have met a truly great engineer and I felt very overawed and very privileged. I found it difficult to believe that he had been born when George Stephenson was still alive, he appeared so hale and hearty. In fact he still had eleven more years of life ahead of him.

My uncle's new diesel locomotive used the same design of chassis as the steam locomotive and came in three sizes fitted with MacLaren-Benz engines of two, four and six cylinders delivering 30, 60 and 90 h.p. respectively. J.A.P. engines had to be used to start the two larger engines. The first to be built was of 60 h.p. and I accompanied this locomotive when it was sent to North Wales for preliminary tests on the Welsh Highland Railway at Dinas Junction. The little 30 h.p. locomotive appeared next and in the summer of 1929 I spent a week driving the prototype on a short track on the Kerr Stuart stand at the Royal Show at Harrogate. It was fitted with a multi-variable speed gear which worked magically on the stand when

[1] The waste sugar cane after the sugar has been extracted at the mill.

running light, but when the locomotive returned to the works and we put a load behind it, the gear dissolved in clouds of blue smoke from burning friction material. It was seen no more, being quickly replaced by a more conventional transmission. Last to emerge of these diesel locomotives was the 90 h.p. type of standard gauge. I spent a morning driving this engine to and fro on our works line before it was delivered to the Ravenglass and Eskdale Railway in Cumberland where it had a surprisingly long life.

But although it was the fascination of the steam locomotive that had drawn me into engineering and so to Kerr Stuarts, I must confess that it was the diesel lorry that I found in many ways the most exciting of all these new designs. I think this was because I sensed that here was a vehicle of an entirely new species. It was, after all, the first diesel lorry to be designed and built in this country and it was thrilling to feel that we were pioneering in a completely novel field. Although, like many another pioneering attempt, this one was ultimately doomed to failure, where we failed, others soon succeeded. At that time, long distance heavy road haulage could not compete seriously with railways because of the extravagant thirst of the petrol engine. The advent of the oil engine on the road revolutionised the economics of road haulage and brought about the greatest revolution in transport since the coming of the motor-car at the beginning of the century. It is ironical that I, so passionately drawn to railways and steam locomotives, should have become concerned with a vehicle and with a source of power destined so soon to supplant them, though just how soon I did not then realize.

Construction of the new lorry began during the winter of 1928-29 and by March it was ready for its first run. It was originally designed round the 60 h.p. MacLaren-Benz engine, but over the winter MacLarens had strongly recommended us to try their new six-cylinder Helios engine. At 45 h.p. it would be down on power, but a six should be smoother than a four, it was governed to 1,000 r.p.m. instead of 800 and, most important of all, it could be started by hand. Although I think we should have been warned by the fact that the German makers of the Helios engine had gone into liquidation and that the engine offered to us was part of the bankrupt stock that MacLarens had bought cheaply, we accepted their advice and the design was modified to receive the new engine. I do not doubt that MacLarens acted in good faith. It was not in their

own interest to sell us a pup and the new engine certainly
looked good. In those days none of us knew much about
high-speed oil engines and we were all feeling our way.[1]

The prototype lorry was of the semi-forward control type
with the rear portion of the engine under an internal bonnet
in the cab. It was fitted with a flat platform body and the design
was conventional; in fact, in the adoption of a final drive by
chain to a dead axle it was already archaic. As a test vehicle,
however, this arrangement had the advantage that the gear
ratios could very easily be altered by fitting larger or smaller
driving sprockets. It also meant that the unsprung weight of the
back axle was much lower than a live one would have been.
Suspension at the rear was by two transverse semi-elliptic leaf
springs, mounted side by side in a special cast-steel cradle at the
midpoint of the chassis. This relieved the chassis of all bending
moments and the lorry rode remarkably well.

A fitter named Jack Hodgkinson and I were appointed to
carry out the extensive road testing of this novel vehicle
on a selection of routes, usually carrying a six-ton test load of
cast iron blocks on the lorry's flat bed. I was issued with a
series of elaborate log sheets on which I was to record every
detail of each run. I still have my original master copies of these
sheets. They are filled in in shaky pencil and some are covered
with the imprints of my oily fingers, betokening trouble on the
road. From these I see that our first historic run was to Lichfield
and back on 18th March 1929, 69 miles in 3 hrs. 40 m., our
greatest speed on the level being 29 m.p.h. The journey
involved a total of 151 gear changes, each no mean undertaking
as we shall see. Our eighth trip on 9th April was to Manchester
and back, 79 miles, and I can remember the interest aroused
when we stopped en route for lunch at a transport café. Most of
the heavy haulage on the Manchester–Stafford road at that
time was handled by articulated Scammels running on solid

---

[1] I did not know then, but have since learned, that Messrs
Garretts of Leiston had two diesel lorries, one four- and the other
six-wheeled, on the road a month or two before ours. They were
fitted with MacLaren-Benz engines of 30 and 60 h.p. respectively and, from my experience, the smaller of the two must
have been woefully underpowered. In any case, these were purely
experimental vehicles with oil engines fitted in adapted steam
wagon chassis, whereas our K.S. lorry was a production prototype.

tyres and their drivers could scarcely have displayed greater interest in our vehicle if it had been a space ship.

We very soon found out the snags of the Helios engine. True it could be started by hand, but only just on a cold morning. Two of us would wind the enormous starting handle until, when our arms were almost in a blur, at the breathless cry of 'Right', a third would throw over the decompression lever whereupon our arms would receive a frightful jerk as the engine came onto full compression. Sometimes the engine would fire, sometimes it would not and sometimes the compression would bring us up all standing with results almost as painful as a back-fire. To lighten this labour we resorted to the barbarous practice of pouring petrol into the air inlet manifold. This used to do the trick, but the engine started with such an anvil chorus of hideous clonks, that it is a wonder the cylinder heads were not blown off. I remember on one occasion when we had just performed this priming operation, Mr Jubb, a mild-mannered, bespectacled individual from the drawing office who was responsible for lorry design, clambered up into the cab and began measuring and sketching. We wound the starting handle; there was a loud report, a long tongue of flame licked out of the mouth of the inlet manifold and the cab filled with smoke. Mr Jubb tumbled out of that cab and made off down the shop like a startled rabbit.

The Helios engine had a separate injection pump for each cylinder. These pumps were made in unit with the injectors, were of the variable stroke type, and were actuated by the same camshaft as the valves. Their behaviour was erratic and not always sensible to the control of the governor. Consequently engine speed was apt to be equally erratic, in other words it 'hunted' badly and did not always respond to the throttle. If, on taking his foot off the accelerator, engine revolutions continue to mount, it can be very disconcerting for the driver, besides making gear changing extremely tricky. This was the cause of our first serious breakdown in Stone on our way back from a test trip to Lichfield. Jack accelerated in third gear, then released the clutch and accelerator and slipped the gear lever into neutral for the change to top. This he did not succeed in achieving because the engine continued to race. We used to run without the internal bonnet fitted, and it was somewhat disconcerting to sit helpless in close proximity to such a large engine while its speed built up far in excess of its permitted maximum. Suddenly, with an alarming sound of mechanical disintegration, the engine stopped abruptly. We found that one of the overhead valves had seized solid in its guide, breaking its rocker and punching a hole in a piston.

The engine was repaired after this mishap, but it was not long after, on our ninth test run, when we had covered a total of just over 400 miles, that the end came. We were ascending a hill into the little town of Tutbury when disaster struck. Something hit me a stinging blow on the ankle. Looking down, I saw that this was a large fragment of cast-iron and that the jagged end of a broken connecting rod was menacing me through the large hole it had knocked in the side of the crankcase. We managed with difficulty to remove the big-end of the broken rod and then made for home, running on five cylinders. On the way back there was another shattering noise as the sixth piston and the small end of the connecting rod, which we had tried in vain to get out, suddenly fell down on to the whirling crankshaft. But we did get home under our own power.

After this second disaster, it was decided to revert to the original plan by fitting the 60 h.p. four-cylinder MacLaren-Benz engine. At least we knew that it was reliable. Yet, in retrospect, I can see that in some ways this was a retrograde step, that of the two power units the Helios was the more promising. It was smaller, lighter and faster running and, on its day, more flexible than the other. Despite its higher power, we never obtained with the MacLaren so high an average speed. The besetting fault of the Helios was its fuel injection system and if this could have been replaced by something less wayward, all might have been well. The Bosch fuel injection system which supplied the real answer to such problems had not yet appeared, but I have often wondered whether the reliable pump fitted to the 90 h.p. MacLaren-Benz engine might not have been adapted to the Helios.

The installation of the MacLaren-Benz engine did not take long, for on 26th April we took to the road again with this new power unit. In this form, the lorry weighed no less than 12 cwt. more than it had done before. Governed to 800 r.p.m. its maximum speed was only 20 m.p.h., unless we 'put the stick out' and coasted down hills as we frequently did. There was one major difficulty; the engine could not be started by hand. As on the locomotives, a J.A.P. auxiliary engine was needed for this. Unlike the roomy cab of a locomotive, it required a lot of ingenuity to fit this bulky starting equipment into the very restricted space of the lorry cab. While Mr Jubb was mulling over this problem at his drawing board, we were instructed to carry on with the test runs, knowing that if the engine stopped while we were out on the road we would be unable to start it except by the aid of gravity or a tow. For this reason, Market Drayton and back, $36\frac{1}{2}$ miles, became our regular test route. There were plenty of hills and on one of them there was situated an excellent country pub, the Mainwaring Arms at Whitmore, where we could—and did—frequently stop for lunch.

There was one extremely embarrassing moment, however, when the engine stalled in the middle of the small square in Market Drayton. It happened to be market day and the square thronged with booths and crowds. In the midst of this animated scene stood our lorry, completely immovable, causing what in those days was regarded as a major traffic block. To market traders who shouted to us to 'get on out of it' or to the law who ordered us to 'move along there' it was shame-making to admit that we had no means of starting our strange vehicle. Amid cheers, an enterprising local garage proprietor suddenly appeared on the scene with a Model T Ford breakdown truck, waving a tow rope. Since our lorry, with its test load, weighed $12\frac{1}{2}$ tons, the Ford simply made groaning noises from its sorely tried transmission and entirely failed to move us. This was tantalising because, only fifty yards away at the end of the square, there was a suitable declivity. But we espied in the back of that Ford a long crow-bar and this proved to be our salvation. Now by levering with such a bar between wheel and rail you can, once you get the knack, move the heaviest locomotive. But try moving a $12\frac{1}{2}$ ton lorry with pneumatic tyres along a tarmac road in the same fashion. Red-faced and sweating, cheered and jeered at by the crowd, Jack and I took turns to bar that lorry across the square. It seemed the longest fifty yards ever.

Sometimes in order to give him a break, I passed the log sheet over to Jack and took a trick at the wheel. This was the first and last time I have driven a 'heavy', and my goodness how heavy it was! Neither steering nor brakes were servo-assisted and the clutch was extremely heavy. Consequently one soon developed bulging biceps and calf muscles. Gear changing also called for considerable physical strength and was very slow and difficult, not because the engine ran erratically like the Helios, but simply because, with its massive crankshaft and flywheel revolving at not more than 800 r.p.m., it was so slow

to respond to the movements of the accelerator pedal. To drive
for any distance at a stretch was no mean feat of physical
stamina. Once on arriving back at the works I jumped down
from the driving seat and was immediately doubled up with
acute cramp of the stomach muscles. I had to be massaged by
the nurse in the ambulance room before I managed to stand
upright.

Steering called for continual concentration, for with so wide
a vehicle on the narrow roads of those days you had to keep
the nearside front-wheel within a foot of the side of the road.
Moreover, you could never for a moment relax, for owing to the
steep camber the lorry tended to run off which meant that you
were ditched, for once you had put a wheel on the grass verge,
no power on earth could get it off again. I experienced this
happening later when the lorry had gone into production. A
driver had come over from Belfast to take delivery of a new
vehicle and I had accompanied him on a trial run so that he
could get used to it. From my seat at the nearside of the cab,
I could see that he was heading for disaster and called out,
but it was too late. We came to rest in a deep ditch at an angle
of 45°. The new lorry was quite undamaged, but it took some
getting out.

The most unfortunate thing I ever did while I was driving
the prototype lorry was to carry away a shop awning in the
narrow main street of Lichfield. I had not reckoned with the
effect of a steep camber with the result that the nearside
top corner of the cab connected with the wooden edge of the
awning which fell in flapping ruin to the pavement. The owner
of the shop was not at all pleased. Although the modern
heavy diesel road vehicle is infinitely easier and less tiring
to drive than was this crude forerunner, this experience has
given me a lasting admiration and respect for all drivers of
'heavies'.

According to my log sheets, we had covered 756 miles in
the prototype before it was decided to put the lorry into
production. Fuel consumption had averaged 10 m.p.g. with a
full load, and this with fuel which then cost only 4d a gallon.
The driver of a comparable petrol-engined lorry would be
lucky to average 6 m.p.g. with fuel costing four times as much.
These were the facts on which our production hopes were
based. The production lorry was an improvement on the
prototype in many respects. It was substantially reduced in
weight, notably by replacing iron castings by welded fabrica-

tions. The exterior details were tidied up and an imposing cast aluminium radiator was fitted in conjunction with an aluminium panelled cab and bonnet sheets. In my reports on the test runs I had repeatedly stressed the amount of black smoke produced when the lorry was working hard against the gradient, much to the annoyance of following traffic. We were unable to cure this, but on the production vehicle we mitigated the nuisance by mounting the silencer on the cab roof, the gases exhausting through a short vertical stub pipe and the exhaust pipe from the engine passing up one rear corner of the cab. I have often wondered since why this example was never subsequently followed. The J.A.P. starting engine was directly behind the main engine and between the seats. It was mounted in a rocking frame by means of which a friction wheel could engage the rim of the flywheel.

The first production model to be built went to a firm of haulage contractors in Belfast and other vehicles were sold to J. Beresford and Sons Ltd, of Tunstall, a local contractor, the Stroud Brewery, Greenall Whitley and Co., Brewers, of St Helens, and F. W. Lougher and Co., Pontalln Quarries, Bridgend, this last being fitted with an hydraulic three-way tipping body.

To put this novel vehicle into production in a locomotive works meant engaging new staff with the necessary know-how. A sales manager named Greenberg arrived on the scene and so did a production engineer named Gratrex. Greenberg was an ebullient individual of immense energy and gusto. He would talk endlessly, rocking to and fro on his feet and emphasising his points with stabbing motions made with the stem of his pipe. He fervently believed his own sales talk, a prime virtue in any salesman. He seized upon our method of transverse rear suspension with great enthusiasm although it seemed perfectly normal and logical engineering to us. He christened it 'enharmonic' springing and made great play with the word in his sales literature where it was accompanied by graphs to prove how the action of one spring was damped out by the other. Next door to the works was a pottery named Winkles which specialised in the manufacture of chamber pots and other sanitary wear. Greenberg prevailed on Winkles to allow one of our lorries to be loaded with chamber pots, roughly packed in open-sided crates without straw. He then took a photograph which appeared with the caption: 'Thanks to enharmonic springing, fragile loads can be carried in safety without special packing.' When he first arrived, there were no production vehicles for Greenberg to photograph. Nothing daunted, he had sides fitted to the flat platform of the old prototype and had it driven out on the Leek road where he photographed it against the background of a steep rock cutting. It seemed an unpromising background and we could not understand what he was driving at. But when we saw in the finished photograph our old lorry ascending a steep gradient with a vast load of rock and earth on board we understood. Who says the camera cannot lie?

When road testing came to an end, I was made assistant to the new production engineer, who had come to us from David Browns from whom we bought our gears. Gratrex was a very short, stocky man with a huge, determined, jutting jaw. He was always in a hurry and, despite his short stature, contrived to walk very fast, taking (for him) immensely long strides, his bowler hat crammed down over his ears. He was what might be called a new broom and as a result he made himself decidedly unpopular in certain quarters. He brought with him a set of Swedish Johannsen gauges which were then, like Maudslay's famous micrometer in the nineteenth century, the final arbiter of accuracy in workshop measurement. With these he was able to prove to his entire satisfaction that nearly all the jigs and gauges in the tool room stores were inaccurate. On which the outraged tool room foreman was heard to growl: 'If that Mr Gratrex doesn't watch out he'll get that chin of his put back where it ought to be.'

At sight of our machine shop, Gratrex could hardly be restrained from throwing his bowler hat on the ground and jumping on it. New machines were introduced, most notably a big Kerns boring machine for the in-line boring of the shaft bearing housings of the lorry gearbox. Parallel with the wagon and boiler shop was a very long and narrow shed with a single line of rails running through it which had once been used to assemble a large contract for wagons. This was the one feature of the works that seemed to please Gratrex. He rubbed his hands together and almost smiled, declaring it would make a good lorry assembly shop. He had it marked out into divisions where the various components and sub-assemblies could be stored and then put into their appointed places as the lorries, starting as bare chassis frames, moved down the shop on a travelling gantry. Meanwhile I worked beside Gratrex in his office, preparing, under his instructions, a huge progress chart which was hung on the wall. I then began to oversee what progress the shops were making with the lorry parts, in other words I became a 'progress chaser'.

Exciting though it would be to see the first production lorries roll out, I did not particularly care for my job with Gratrex and I was mightily relieved when, in July 1930, Jack Hodgkinson and I were ordered to load a 30 h.p. diesel locomotive on to the old prototype lorry and head north to Scarborough where I was to drive the locomotive for a fortnight at a Quarry Managers' and Road Surveyors' Exhibition. Apparently these gentry were holding a conference in Scarborough; most of them had their wives with them and, since the exhibition was mounted in a field some distance from the town, hardly any of them took the trouble to visit it, preferring the pleasures of the promenade, the pier and the bathing beach when they were not conferring together. Quite a few holiday makers found their way to our showground, however, so we decided to convert the exhibition into an impromptu fun-fair. I had at my disposal a much longer length of track than I had had at Harrogate the previous year, so I trundled to and fro with wagon loads of passengers, while the driver of the Ruston Bucyrus Excavator which formed the centre-piece of the show lifted people up in his bucket and then whirled them round and round. I don't think our respective firms would have been amused by this spectacle, but at least it gave a lot of pleasure and helped us to pass the time.

I have said that the 30 h.p. MacLaren-Benz engine could be started by hand. This could only be accomplished by the judicious movement of the decompression lever, first into the half compression position and then on to full. One morning at the showground when Jack and I were swinging the big starting handle for all we were worth, the helpful bystander who was manning the decompression lever, misunderstanding our instructions, pushed it straight through to full compression. The next instant we were both lying flat on the ground. I was quickly on my feet again, but Jack had fared much worse for the starting handle had caught him full in the chest, completely winding him. Dazed, I suddenly realised that despite this immensely powerful kick back the engine was running. I wondered how this could possibly be until I saw exhaust smoke pouring from the air filter on the inlet manifold. Believe it or not, that engine was running backwards! I helped Jack to a doctor, fearing broken ribs, but fortunately he was only badly bruised although the doctor insisted on strapping him up and told him he must take things easily for a week or so. This meant that I had to drive the lorry most of the way back to Stoke. It was a long haul, for the locomotive had been sold and on the way we had to deliver it to its new owners, Boan's Sandpit near King's Lynn.

I had never been to East Anglia before and I cannot now remember where this sandpit was except that it was in very deep country reached by narrow and winding lanes somewhere to the east of Sandringham. In these lanes we met an elderly lady in black riding a motor scooter. I remember this encounter very vividly because it was such a rarity at that time. Several makes of motor scooter had appeared just after the Great War but they died an early death and it was to be nearly thirty years before the motor scooter suddenly caught on. In this country anything seemed possible for it appeared to me incredibly remote and foreign. When we had unloaded the locomotive at the sandpit, we spent the night at a small country pub called 'The Royal Oak' and found the dialect of the locals in the bar so broad that we had difficulty in understanding more than one word in ten. No doubt they had equal difficulty in understanding us, for the influence of the B.B.C. had not yet ironed out such regional distinctions. They gave us a splendid meal, I remember, which we ate with wooden-handled steel knives and 'prongs', as they called them, with two needle-sharp points. Then we retired to our room with its double feather bed. Jack happily slept in his shirt which made me selfconscious of my pyjamas.

When we finally drove into the works yard after this long journey and the old engine gave a final 'clonk' as I swung down from the cab, I little thought that it was to be my last journey in a Kerr Stuart diesel lorry and that in a few weeks' time I should leave the familiar works for ever. For although the economic outlook was bleak and England was heading fast into the great slump, at Kerr Stuarts everything, including my own prospects, looked rosy. The new locomotives that my uncle had designed were a success, while with the lorry we were 'in on the ground floor' and there appeared to me to be a great future before it. On the conventional locomotive side, the works were busy building twenty-five pannier tank engines for the Great Western Railway with the prospect of a further twenty-five to come. Then, without any warning, out of this seemingly clear sky, the bolt fell.

*131*

I remember I was standing in the new lorry assembly shop one morning, idly glancing through the *Daily Mail*. I usually skipped the financial page, but for some reason my eye was caught by a small paragraph at the foot of a column. 'The Midland Bank Ltd,' it said, 'have petitioned for the compulsory winding up of Kerr, Stuart and Co. Ltd. of Stoke-on-Trent.' I showed it to the men in the shop but they only shook their heads in frank bewilderment. I motored out to Barlaston that evening and showed it to my uncle. 'Nonsense,' he replied reassuringly, 'the Midland Bank are not our bankers, there must be some mistake; no one has heard of anything.' But, alas, it was no mistake and what follows next reads like some Victorian melodrama.

The only member of the Kerr Stuart management who did not live in the district was the chairman of the company who was 'something in the City'. I remember him as a tall man in a pin-striped suit who used to visit the works occasionally (I suppose for board meetings) in a chauffeur-driven Rolls-Royce. I only saw him on these occasions because he used to walk very rapidly through the shops, looking neither to right nor left, on what was ostensibly a tour of inspection. It was true that the Midland were not our bankers, but they had acted as bankers for a company called Evos Sliding Doorways, Ltd which this precious chairman had floated, illegally, with Kerr Stuart's money. This company had failed and the Midland Bank had come back to us for money that no longer existed. There was to be no redress. When they broke into the chairman's private office in London, it was to find his secretary dead with a bullet through his brain and the hearth choked with burnt papers. But the chairman himself had disappeared and, so far as I know, he has never been heard of again from that day to this.

My uncle Kyrle made frantic efforts to save the works, but all to no avail. In the hope of invoking Government aid, he went to see the Labour M.P. for Stoke-on-Trent and found the titled lady who then held the seat reclining elegantly upon a sofa smoking a cigarette in a long holder. She did not appear in the least concerned and merely murmured soothing platitudes. I have never known my uncle so angry and so bitter as when he returned from that interview.

Meanwhile, back at the works we had no credit. We could not even purchase coal without cash, but somehow we had to complete our existing orders. So we tore up the sleeper floors of the shops and flung them into the furnace of the big Thomson boiler so that we could keep steam on the hammers and so keep the forge alive. But, as we completed our orders men began to drift away and machines to stop. No more thunder of steam hammers from the forge; no more noise like machine-gun fire from the boiler shop. The piston rods of the hammers or the hand controls of machines that had once gleamed brightly from constant use grew, first dull and then rusty. Finally, the shops fell silent. You could hear sparrows quarrelling under the roof trusses. So quiet was it in those long aisles that you tended to speak in a whisper as in the stillness of some cathedral.

So, in a mere matter of weeks, Kerr Stuarts died. It never came to life again. The plant was sold at auction by order of the receiver, but much of it, the hydraulic press, the heavy hammers, the hydraulic riveter, was considered not worth the labour of moving and was cut up on the spot. Today, only the foundry is still active. The rest of the shops, rusty and dilapidated, with water pouring through the roofs, are used as an untidy dump for scrap metal. So is the once trim and tidy yard. To me, who had known it in full work, the place is forever haunted by memories and lost hopes, indescribably forlorn.

Some nine months after the death of the works, I unwisely motored north to spend a week-end with my friends at Trentham. As I passed through the streets of Stoke I saw many of the men whom I had worked beside, admiring their skill and proud to think of them as my friends, leaning against the walls of street-corner pubs or crouching on the steps of terrace houses. Cheap mufflers were crossed about their throats, their faces and hands looked unnaturally white and clean and their eyes did not appear to focus on anything. There was no work for them. Somehow I could not bring myself to attract their attention, still less to stop and speak to them, for I felt ashamed. I did not visit Stoke-on-Trent again.

# Chapter 9

# Dursley Days

In the course of our brief and troubled passage through life we build little cocoons spun from our hopes and ambitions, familiar faces, places, habits and routines, and in these we curl up snugly, fancying ourselves warm and secure from the large, cold world outside. It sometimes happens, however, that we are suddenly and ruthlessly stripped of this protective clothing to be left naked and shivering in a world that seems to have become strange and hostile.

This is how I felt after the tragedy of Kerr Stuarts. It was an event that made a very deep impression on my youthful mind—for remember, I was still under 21. I had not believed that such things could happen, but now my career was gone, my friends scattered and there was nothing to do but to return home and try, with as much resolution as I could, to pick up the pieces and begin again. I even lost that £100 apprenticeship premium which my parents had promised me at the end of the three-year term, for there was nothing left over from the wreck.

What of the others? For my uncle Kyrle it was the bitterest blow of his career. He obtained a post with the National Gas Engine Company at Ashton-under-Lyne, sold the house at Barlaston, went into lodgings in Ashton and bought a cottage at Patterdale, in the Lake District near the head of Ullswater, for his family. This arrangement was shortlived, however. Within a year he had moved to Petters at Yeovil and the Willans family were then installed at Boleyn House, Ash near Martock in Somerset. I paid one visit to Patterdale—I remember climbing Helvellyn and, at Bill's instigation, spending an afternoon in the engine room of one of the elderly lake steamers. Later, I spent one week-end at Boleyn House, but inevitably I gradually lost touch with the Willans family. They were no longer closely linked with my life. *Cressy* was sold to a newspaper reporter named Fortune at Leicester who had just married and intended to live on her on the river Soar. But before he sold her, my uncle had removed the steam plant and installed a petrol engine in its stead.

As for Leslie Bomford, after the Kerr Stuart débâcle he decided to have done with engineering and he bought a farm in Hampshire. Nevertheless, it was he who was responsible for the next brief phase in my career. When the works closed, I still had about seven months of my five years' apprenticeship to serve. Leslie Bomford knew Robert Lister and it was agreed between them that I could complete my 'time' by a year's apprenticeship in the works of R. A. Lister and Co. Ltd of Dursley, Gloucestershire. This I began in January 1931.

Old Sir Ashton Lister had started his career as a blacksmith in the small town of Dursley and R. A. Lister and Co. was one of those country works which had expanded and flourished as the result of the enterprise of a rural craftsman. Ashton Lister had teamed up with two ingenious Swedes named Petersen and Mellerup who had invented a bicycle and a milk separator. Although when I went to Dursley there were still a few 'Dursley Petersen' bicycles around with their unusual frames and hammock seats, it was the milk separator and a sheep-shearing machine that had founded the fortunes of the firm. Later, they had begun making a range of small petrol engines for farm and general use and to these, at the time I joined the firm, a range of diesel engines and a small petrol-engined 'autotruck' had recently been added. It was to the engine assembly and test shops that I was assigned and, apart from a short spell on outside engine service, I remained there throughout my year at Dursley.

There were then five Lister brothers in the firm. Percy, a man of immense energy, personality and drive who was managing director, Robert who was in charge of auto-truck production, Frank who was in charge of buying, George, who today would be described as personnel manager, and Cecil, the youngest, who was on the sales side. I lodged at 'The Towers', a large house that old Sir Ashton had built for himself when he became affluent. Constructed of bright red brick with white painted woodwork and rising to a tower at one front corner, it was the kind of Edwardian mansion that would not have looked out of place amid the pines of Surrey or in the lower Thames Valley, but in the Cotswolds it looked utterly incongruous. Reached by a steep drive, it stood on a commanding site, looking over the saw-toothed roofs of the shops directly below to the old grey town that climbed the opposite slope. After Sir Ashton's death, his sons had turned it into a hostel for apprentices or students, many of whom were the sons of Listers' overseas agents, sent to England for a short spell of practical instruction in the works. It was also used to accommodate visitors to the works, while on week-days the Lister brothers habitually lunched there. This establishment was in the charge of a charming and vivacious widow in early middle age named Mrs Van der Gucht.

Soon after I came to the Towers, the number of resident students rose to ten and to provide extra accommodation, the rooms over the large garage were adapted and redecorated to provide two extra bedrooms and a bathroom. There I and an Australian of my own age named Malloch, who became my particular friend, took up our quarters. As we nearly all owned second-hand cars, mostly bought very cheaply, the garage below and the covered forecourt outside it housed a motley collection of vehicles. I suppose their total value then would not have amounted to more than £500 whereas today, in equivalent order, they would fetch around £10,000 at auction. There was Mrs Van der Gucht's little Standard 9 open two-seater and a larger Standard 14 with a similar body which had been purchased from a scrap merchant in Gloucester. There was a Ruston-Hornsby with four-seater body and a disappearing hood, very slow, cumbersome and lorry-like. There was a six-cylinder Belsize four-seater touring car of immense length, one of the last models to be built by that defunct firm, and a standard model Riley 'Redwing', the only car of the bunch to have front-wheel brakes. At 1922, my G.N. was the oldest car present, while my friend Malloch owned an early six-cylinder AC with two-seater drophead coupé body. We regarded the Redwing as the only sports car in the stable and undeniably the fastest, but the AC could give it a run for its money and was certainly the most silent and comfortable.

With a group of young men all of about my own age and all with more money to spend than I had, existence at the Towers was apt to be somewhat hectic and nothing could have been in greater contrast to the life I had led in Stoke-on-Trent. I look back on this period as others do to their undergraduate days—as a time when I sowed my wild oats. Most of my companions struck me as somewhat adolescent and immature in their high spirits because they had come to Listers' straight from school or university whereas I had over four years' experience at Pitchill and Stoke-on-Trent behind me. This may sound somewhat priggish and I hope that if any of these bygone companions chance to read this they will not take it amiss. I doubt if they will because I joined wholeheartedly in the fun and games and, indeed, my boon companion, the Australian Malloch, was the most ungovernable of the bunch, a kind of 'wild colonial boy'. In retrospect, I think that to be plunged into the social whirl of this little community was the best possible antidote to the recent disaster at Stoke-on-Trent. I could never forget it; it had made far too deep an impression on my mind for that and, inevitably, it made me regard life at the Towers with a certain detachment. Yet this new milieu did enable me to 'snap out of it' which is an essential preliminary to starting life over again. For the first time in my life I found myself basking in the reassuring warmth that comes from friendship with a group of people of my own age. Had I been left alone, either in lodgings or at home, to brood over past experience and lost opportunities at the age of only twenty-one I shudder to think what the result might have been.

The local 'county' of south Gloucestershire evidently regarded the Towers as a useful reservoir for eligible young men, so there was no lack of social engagements. These re-introduced me to a world which observed the customs and conventions which my public school had attempted without success to instil into me and which I now found utterly alien and unreal. It might once have been real but, like my Rolt uncles and aunts, it seemed to me to belong wholly to the past. For me life at Stoke-on-Trent represented the raw reality, not necessarily good but something I had got to come to terms with, whereas now, when I mixed with these 'county' families, I felt as if I had strayed on to a stage where some outdated comedy of manners was going on. Failing to find any point of contact or communication, I must have seemed an extremely gauche and unmannerly young man. Dancing with some elegantly groomed young woman, her almost invariable opening gambit would be: 'Do you hunt?' and on the reply 'No' the dialogue would either fail altogether or lapse into the usual flat platitudes about the state of the floor or the merits of the band. Similarly, when introduced to her parents they would invariably ask: 'Hah! Any relation to old "Totty" Rolt?' and receive a similar negative response. I had never heard of the man. I gathered that 'old Totty' had lived at Ozleworth

Park, near Wootton-under-Edge and was regarded locally as a bit of a character, but to this day I have not discovered anything more about him or whether he had any connection with my family.

To Malloch, fresh from Australia, the conventions of English 'county' society seemed totally incomprehensible and impossibly 'stuffed shirt'. I think this was the basis of our somewhat improbable friendship. He had an impish sense of humour and used to take advantage of the fact that he was a colonial from down under by doing and saying things that were considered quite outrageous. Having no such excuse, I could only envy him this freedom and enjoy its consequences with well concealed amusement. To the despair of good Mrs Van der Gucht, who considered it part of her mission in life to introduce her young men to polite society, Malloch and I often used to avoid such social obligations, pleading an engagement elsewhere. These 'engagements' usually consisted in seeking out the toughest pubs in the neighbourhood where we found the company a refreshing change after the polite society of Dursley and district. Two that I recall particularly were the Monk's Retreat at Gloucester and the Llandogo Trow at Bristol. Both are now completely reformed (and transformed), but in those days they were very tough indeed with an authentic low-life Rabelaisian quality about them. As for the customers, they were reminiscent of some of the more sordid or sinister characters in Dickens. Such an underworld has ceased to exist today. The wide-boy or the drug-taking drop-out may be just as seamy, violent or depraved but he is neither so racy, so entertaining or so picturesque. We found such company stimulating and exciting; sometimes too exciting, for liquor tended to make Malloch argumentative and quarrelsome. I had more experience of rough company but there were times, notably when two seamen drew knives one night in the Llandogo Trow, when it required all my tact to ensure a strategic withdrawal and so avoid an ugly brawl.

The Monk's Retreat in those days consisted of a crypt-like cellar with a medieval groined roof. Facing the long bar that occupied the whole of one side were a number of little alcoves each containing three bent-wood chairs and an up-ended barrel which served as a table. There was sawdust on the floor and a mechanical organ which, when fed with pennies, ground out old music-hall tunes. It would be a collector's piece today.

The proximity of Bristol's Old Theatre Royal has now

transformed the Llandogo Trow into a smart pub, which, like the theatre, has been preserved. At least they have not, like so much of old Bristol, been sacrificed to the motor car, but in 1931 both had a very different character. The theatre was then the lowest of low music halls where bad performers became cockshys for the audience and the night's performance was apt to end prematurely, as was the case on one occasion when we were present. Performers, members of the orchestra and their patrons became locked in conflict in the stalls and the police had to be called in to clear the house. As for the Llandogo Trow it was then, as I suppose it had always been, the haunt of seamen, the twentieth-century equivalent of that 'Admiral Benbow' in *Treasure Island* where the sinister Blind Pew put the black spot on Captain Flint. Its landlord in his younger days had been a professional strong man 'on the Halls'. He still looked the part, but just in case his customers contemplated any rough stuff, his photograph hung in a prominent position above the bar as a deterrent. This depicted him at the height of his glory, striking a defiant pose, crinkly hair, waxed moustachios, bulging, richly tattooed biceps, leopard skin and all.

We were returning to Dursley from Gloucester late one night in the AC after one of these excursions when I experienced my first serious car crash. But for sheer luck, it might have proved disastrous for us both. I was driving because Malloch was suffering from a suspected hernia and had been forbidden by his doctor to do so. I remember remarking that the steering felt curiously 'lumpy', but as it was dark we did not stop to investigate and, as things turned out, even if we had, an examination would have revealed nothing. Approaching a fairly fast right hand bend by Cam Mills at about 45 m.p.h., the steering suddenly locked solid. To be thus instantly reduced to utter helplessness was the most frightening sensation I have ever experienced while driving a motor-car. We went into that bend with both of us tugging fruitlessly at a completely immovable steering wheel. The AC mounted the bank on the nearside, was deflected, shot across the road and turned upside down on the inside of the corner. The folding head was up but afforded us little protection in such circumstances. Fortunately for us, however, the car came to rest bridging a deep and very wet ditch into which we both fell. By the mercy of providence neither of us was smoking for we were instantly subjected to a spray of petrol leaking from the filler of the scuttle tank which, on this model AC, protruded through the dashboard. When we had disentangled ourselves from each other and from the flapping ruins of the folding head, the seat cushions and the floorboards which had accompanied us into the ditch, we crawled out quite unhurt. Surveying the pitiful wreck in the moonlight we agreed that at such a time of night there was nothing we could do but leave it where it was and walk back to the Towers. As we tramped along the road, my clothing, particularly my flannel trousers, steadily began to disintegrate until I was scarcely decent, a happening that completely restored our sense of humour. I realised that my clothes had been soaked in acid from the battery which was cradled under the driving seat.

Such an accident, occurring in such circumstances, can bear, in most people's minds, only one interpretation so I was relieved to be able to demonstrate to a suspicious local policeman, who was on the scene when we recovered the car next morning, that the steering box really was locked up solid. As we later learned, this particularly nasty habit of early ACs is easy to cure,[1] but in this case the knowledge came too late, for although we had been unscathed, the unfortunate AC was a complete write-off. To replace it, Malloch purchased a second-hand 14/40 Vauxhall. It was my first experience of a marque with which I was later to have much to do. This 14/40 was a good reliable car once its disconcerting habit of suddenly shedding the crowns of its split-skirt pistons had been cured by fitting a set of different type.

We were in this Vauxhall one night when we were the helpless witnesses of an accident that alarmed us almost more than our own had done. It might indeed have had much more serious results had not the element of luck once again played a part. Malloch and I, with T. H. Edye, the owner of the Belsize, were taking three girls to a dance in Cheltenham one cold and frosty night in December. Incidentally, how many girls today would relish the prospect of being driven 25 miles to a dance on such a night in an open touring car, wearing evening dress? And how many young men would even dare to

---

[1] The steering gear was of the worm-and-wheel type and the teeth on the used arc of the worm-wheel can (as had happened in our case) become so worn that the worm rides up on them and becomes locked. At the first sign of 'lumpiness' in the steering, the wise AC owner dismantled the steering box and repositioned the worm-wheel so that an arc of unworn teeth was brought into play.

suggest such a thing? But in 1931 such rigours were still
accepted as a matter of course by both sexes. Because of the
threat of fog in the vale we decided to avoid the main road
via Gloucester by keeping to the hills through Uley, Stroud
and Painswick. Accordingly we set off, Edye and his girl friend
leading in the Belsize while Malloch, myself and our two
companions followed in the Vauxhall. We were travelling
through thin fog and had reached a point near the village of
Nympsfield where the road (then unfenced) clings to the
extreme edge of the Cotswold scarp which hereabouts is
extremely steep and almost cliff-like. Edye must have become
confused by the mist, lost his sense of direction, applied his
brakes and skidded on a patch of black ice. To our horror we
saw the long white touring car swing broadside across the
narrow road and then head straight for the edge of the hill,
its long bonnet rearing for the plunge, its headlight beams
shooting into the sky like searchlights. We expected the kind
of frightful disaster such as one only sees in sensational films
where a car plunges down, down, down in a series of sickening
crashes, coming to rest a mangled wreck which usually bursts
into flames. However, fortunately the bank beside the road was
sufficiently high and the chassis of the Belsize was sufficiently
long and low for it to ground firmly just before the mid-point
and it came to a very abrupt halt. In spite of the ice on the
road, Malloch had managed to stop the Vauxhall safely just
short of the accident and we ran forward to find Edye and his
passenger sitting, petrified with fright suspended in space.
It was just as well they were petrified, for we found that the
car was literally 'on the rock' and any precipitate move on
their part might have sent it toppling over. Malloch and I hung
our weight on the back of the car and instructed its occupants
to clamber cautiously out and edge their way along the running
boards back on to the road. The Belsize was immovable by our
combined man-power, so, as we had not got a tow rope, we
decided to abandon it till the morning. We all squeezed into
the Vauxhall and continued, somewhat shaken, on our way to
Cheltenham. Next morning the Belsize presented an extraordinary spectacle, visible from far away in the plain below,
sticking up above the skyline of the edge like some new and
curious landmark. We soon recovered it from this perilous
position to find that, unlike the AC, it had sustained only
superficial damage, mainly to running boards and their supporting brackets.

Meanwhile I was still running my G.N. in the face of much good-natured ridicule, for, in addition to certain built-in foibles, it was beginning to show increasing signs of infirmity, having obviously led a hard life before I acquired it. Owing to the fact that the carburettor was positioned above the magneto with the effect that petrol dripped directly on to the contact breaker, it had the alarming habit of catching fire at frequent intervals. For example, I was cruising happily along the Gloucester–Bristol road one Sunday after a week-end visit home when two men on a motorcycle pulled out and rode abreast of me. It became clear from their contorted faces that they were attempting to communicate something urgent, but as I could not hear a word they said above our combined mechanical uproar I merely smiled at them and waved. They began to gesticulate, pointing vigorously astern, whereupon, looking back, I observed that, like some destroyer on exercise, I was leaving behind me a long screen of thick black smoke. As soon as I took my foot off the throttle and applied the brakes, two large orange flames appeared with a *woosh* from beneath the cowlings over the cylinders. I stopped, turned off the petrol, tore off the bonnet and endeavoured to smother the flames with the hairy floor mat. As the scuttle petrol tank was mounted just behind the wooden bulkhead, the situation was a bit fraught, especially as a healthy little fire was burning inaccessibly in the oily undertray that ran the length of the car. I noticed my motorcycle friends had not stayed to help and when I looked up momentarily from my fire-fighting I saw a queue of cars standing well clear in both directions, their owners evidently waiting prudently for the big bang before venturing past. However, the situation was saved by the conductor of a passing Bristol bus who gave the blaze the *coup de grâce* with a fire-extinguisher as though such tasks were a matter of everyday routine. After melted pipe joints had solidified again and I had bound naked wires with insulation tape, I was able to continue on my way to Dursley as though nothing had happened.

Another foible of the G.N. was its tendency to drift its front wheels outwards on corners, particularly on a loose surface, due to the absence of a differential. I discovered this the hard way one day when turning into the Towers drive at speed. I bent my front axle and took a sizeable chip out of the corner of one of the imposing brick gate pillars. I have no doubt the scar remains to this day.

As time went on, the G.N. broke or shed its driving chains with increasing frequency as the teeth of the sprockets wore down. If I was lucky, these remained embedded in the thick oily mess in the undertray, but more often they fell in the road. I had a girl friend who lived with two much older spinster sisters in a cottage high on the flank of Stinchcombe Hill. As this cottage was only accessible by a very steep narrow and muddy lane ascending through beech woods, visiting her was always rather a challenge to the G.N.'s failing powers. On one occasion when I had been invited to dinner I was ascending the hill in fine style only to discover that I had lost the bottom gear chain. Not wishing to be late I decided to coast back to the bottom and try to take the hill by storm in second gear. Unfortunately, this gallant effort failed by a few tantalising yards. It was very dark under the trees and the chain was not in the undertray. I walked back down the hill, striking matches at intervals, trying to find it. In a lane freshly covered with autumn beech leaves, this was not easy. However, after much groping I eventually retrieved it. Replacing a chain on a G.N. is not the cleanest of tasks, so by the time I arrived at the cottage I was not only very late but looked as though I had come straight from the works.

By a happy coincidence, the man responsible for putting an end to such troubles was that same village policeman from Cam whom Malloch and I had found regarding the wreck of the AC so suspiciously. We had arrived on the scene that morning in the G.N., followed by a breakdown outfit from the Dursley garage, and when the law had satisfied himself that it was a pure accident, he strolled over to my car and began inspecting it with critical interest. I had begun to wonder uneasily in what way I was transgressing (was my licence out of date?) when: 'Like it?' he asked laconically. 'Yes, very much,' I replied, mightily relieved. 'I got one just like that,' he volunteered. 'Wouldn't like to buy it, I suppose?' And that was how I became the proud owner of G.N. HT5057, an identical 'Popular' model. I had to pay the policeman £8 for it which I though a hard bargain although it was obviously in much better condition than poor old EH3566 had ever been. More than this, I now had a complete car to cannibalise for spares and I drove my new car back to the Towers in triumph.

It was in this second G.N. that I paid my ill-advised week-end visit to Stoke-on-Trent. On my return journey I broke an exhaust valve in Wolverhampton and found I had no spare. In response to my distress call, a gallant rescue party from Dursley, bearing a spare valve, set out for Wolverhampton in the Riley Redwing. They stood by while I fitted that valve by the light of a street lamp in windy, deserted Wolverhampton in the small hours of the morning. Then we drove in convoy back to Dursley, arriving as dawn was breaking and it was almost time to go to work. Such are the things we do when we are young.

In November 1931, Mrs Van der Gucht and the Lister brothers agreed that, in return for the hospitality we had received from the local 'county', we should hold a supper dance at the Towers. The occasion was a riot. I was never fond of dancing and have found such occasions more boring than anything I can remember. This was the only one I thoroughly enjoyed, which is why the memory of it is still green. Mrs Van der Gucht asked us which particular girls we would like to invite as our partners and we all complied except Malloch who only smiled mysteriously, raised his eyes aloft and murmured 'Wait and see!'

The afternoon of the Saturday in question saw us all in a fever of preparation. One of our number named McClure, a very handsome and charming young man who was Mrs Van der Gucht's particular favourite (he was later to marry her) innocently inquired whether she would like him to prepare the fruit cup. Since he had a special reputation for his knowledge of alcoholic liquors she might have suspected the motive behind this thoughtful suggestion, but was so dazzled by his charm that she enthusiastically agreed. McClure thereupon shut himself in the butler's pantry surrounded by bottles like some alchemist in his cell. The result was a masterpiece, though he would never divulge the recipe. It both looked and tasted like a perfectly innocuous fruit cup, a fruit salad afloat in a red liquid which might have been equally suitable for a children's Christmas party. Such was McClure's ingenuity, however, that beneath this bland exterior lurked a liquor that was powerfully alcoholic. When mixed with other drinks, of which we had plenty available, it had a kick like a mule.

Included in the interior décor of the Towers were certain useless ornamental objects with which old Sir Ashton Lister had evidently thought it appropriate for a knight to surround himself. I could never understand why the huge hornet's nest under a glass dome which occupied a place of honour in the drawing room should ever have been looked upon as a status symbol, but the big black marble statue of a dying gladiator in the hall was obviously one. This gladiator had a hole drilled in his private parts into which a wire, soldered to a crudely shaped brass fig-leaf, was inserted. I used to weave fantasies about this statue. I would imagine Sir Ashton announcing 'I must 'ave a statue in the 'all' and then when it arrived, born aloft by a number of perspiring workmen he would observe its shameless nudity and exclaim 'That'll never do!' Then a tinsmith from the works would be sent for accompanied by a man with a hand drill. . . . At this point I used to speculate on the precise wording of their instructions and what these obedient servants had to say to each other and to their mates afterwards. Anyway, I am ashamed to confess that Malloch's and my sole contribution to the preparations was to remove and conceal that fig-leaf. We felt it would add an appropriate, symbolic saturnalian touch to the coming festivities. Mrs Van der Gucht only noticed its loss as she was greeting the guests in the hall. In between polite smiles and greetings she blushed and threw an accusing glance at me, but I feigned incomprehension and merely shrugged my shoulders.

Some time before the guests were due to arrive, Malloch had disappeared and we heard the sound of his Vauxhall departing down the drive. He had not let even me into his secret and, as he had shown no particular liking for any of the young women who lived locally, speculation was rife as to who his chosen partner would turn out to be. Most of the guests had already arrived before we heard his car returning and presently the door opened and Malloch made a dramatic entry. He was accompanied by a stunning young woman of radiant charm, perfectly groomed and beautifully dressed, whom he introduced to the assembled company as Lady Margaret Harcourt-Masters, whereupon his partner, with perfect poise treated us to a flashing smile and gracefully inclined her head. That Malloch had undoubtedly produced the belle of the ball was generally agreed, but who was she? The county wrinkled their brows, muttering to themselves pensively 'Harcourt-Masters? . . . Harcourt-Masters?' as they strove to recollect a name that surely must be familiar. The object of their curiosity gave them no clue, for although she continued to behave with perfect aplomb, she spoke very little except to Malloch with whom she danced the whole of the evening.

Meanwhile we began to observe the demoralising effect

of McClure's fruit cup on the young ladies of the county. With flushed faces and sparkling eyes, with wisps of hair escaping from their once impeccable hair-dos, they began to abandon their conventions. It was like watching a naturally beautiful figure emerging from the straight-lacing of a corset and the effect was as amusing as it was charming. Soon, only Lady Harcourt-Masters remained cool and collected. I reflected that either Malloch had warned her about the potency of the fruit cup or she must have a very much stronger head for drink than the others. Anyway, Malloch departed to drive her home well before the party ended.

The next morning, Mrs Van der Gucht noticed with dismay that the hornet's nest had unaccountably vanished from its accustomed place. In the general conviviality of the night before, no one had observed its loss. However, a young lady whose coy and mincing ways particularly irritated Malloch and myself rang up in a state of some embarrassment to say that to the astonishment of her parents and herself, a strange object had been found in the back of her car. So the hornet's nest was returned to its place and no one could explain the mystery although I think Malloch and I fell under grave, and not unjustified suspicion. Pressed to tell us about Lady Margaret Harcourt-Masters, Malloch confessed that this was a name which he had invented and that, in fact, the bearer of it was a barmaid from Cheltenham. I fear that Mrs Van der Gucht did not appreciate the joke, considering it a prank such as only an ill-mannered colonial could play, but she kept the secret. She could scarcely do otherwise without damaging her reputation as a hostess.

When I recall these Dursley days, it is the leisure side of them that predominates. For, on the whole, the work bored me and it has left few memorable impressions. There were a variety of reasons for this dissatisfaction, most of them due to the contrast between Kerr Stuarts and Listers. Inevitably, but unfairly, I tended to judge the Lister works by the engineering standards I had formed at the California Works whereas, in fact, the two were not strictly comparable. While locomotive building had been a craft industry, Listers were already beginning to apply mass-production methods to the manufacture of their standard ranges of small petrol and diesel engines. They were built by semi-skilled labour on an assembly line and altogether, throughout the Lister works, the proportion of unskilled or semi-skilled men was far higher and there was no aristocracy of highly skilled and independent craftsmen on the shop floor such as I had known at Stoke-on-Trent. In any case, in the rural Gloucestershire of 1931, there was no long tradition of engineering skill upon which Listers could draw. And because it is mastery of a craft that builds character in a man, I must confess that I found my workmates at Dursley less likeable than the men I had known at the California Works. They were more class-conscious, more inclined to judge their fellow men by appearance and material possessions than by innate ability. It was as though, in their concern for material things, they lost sight of the real man inside.

Although I was paid an apprentice's wage, because I was so nearly 'out of my time', I was regarded as a skilled man. Consequently I did not move through the shops but did only two jobs while I was at Listers. The first of these was in the Engine Assembly Shop, building up the larger type of diesel engine, an 18 h.p. twin cylinder. This was considered too big and too complex to put down the assembly line so each engine was the responsibility of an individual fitter. From this work I moved to the Test House where I was responsible for running engines on the dynamometer and correcting any faults.

Both jobs were not without interest and satisfaction, yet I found them irksome because I felt that I was in a blind alley so far as my future engineering career was concerned. It was very different from the exciting pioneer work on which I had been engaged at Stoke-on-Trent. Because I had been under the impression that Leslie Bomford had told Robert Lister something about my work on the Kerr Stuart lorry, I had gone to Dursley in the fond hope that I would be able to continue this work there. But although one prototype experimental Lister diesel lorry engine was, in fact, built while I was with the firm, I was never concerned with it and this promising project was allowed to die.

In January 1932, when I was nearly 22 years of age, I completed a year's work at Dursley. As this first anniversary passed completely without remark and I continued to work as usual for some weeks after, I decided that it was high time I did something about it. After all, for a year I had been working as a skilled employee for an apprentice's meagre wages. I had assumed that, after completing that year, some action would automatically follow and since it had not it was up to me to take the initiative. So I pointed out that I was 'out of my time' and what did 'they' intend to do? The response was immediate: 'We are sorry but we cannot offer you a job here.' This hit me like a blow in the face. The lesson of it was plain. So long as I was prepared to work for an apprentice's wage, all well and good, but so soon as I asked for a man's wage it was a very different matter. I felt that the firm had treated me unfairly at the time, but over the next three years I was to learn that this was just one of the harsh facts of life in England during the years of the great trade depression.

So I packed up my belongings, bade a sad farewell to all my friends at the Towers and headed for home in the G.N., wondering gloomily what the future held for me now. All that I had left behind me was the carcass of my first G.N. from which I had removed everything of value. Later, I received a bill from the firm for the cost of removing it to a scrap heap. Yet I felt that we were quits because, as a rather futile final act of defiance, I had again removed that fig leaf from the statue in the hall and this time buried it, like Prospero's staff, 'certain fathoms in the earth'. It was over thirty years before I next crossed the threshold of the Towers as the guest of the R. A. Lister Engineering Society. The old place looked very much the same. I glanced curiously at the dying gladiator. He was still unashamedly naked.

# Part III

# Chapter 10

# The Journeyman

WHEN I left Dursley in the early spring of 1932 at the age of 22, there began a somewhat confused and unhappy period of my life which was to last for two years. True there were memorable moments in these years and I emerged from them wiser and richer in experience, but my life seemed to have lost the sense of direction and purpose it had while I was an apprentice. Then, I had been preparing myself for a future that seemed full of exciting opportunities. Now, I found myself foot-loose in the England of the great trade slump in which such opportunities had ceased to exist. The skill which it had taken me five years to acquire was no longer a marketable commodity. In this situation I became a journeyman in the most literal sense of the word. It was not, however, a purposeful journey but one governed entirely by expediency. I applied hopefully for innumerable jobs, but whenever I was lucky enough to obtain one it did not last long. For, on the principle of 'last to come, first to go', the firm would hand me my cards as soon as it became necessary to lay off men. It is because of this roving existence that I was forced to lead that I find the precise chronology of my life during this period more difficult to recall than any other.

From April 1932 until August of the following year I worked for two small firms of agricultural engineers in the south of England, first I. A. Bennett of the Tractor Stores, Hungerford and then the Aldbourne Engineering Company of the Foundry at the nearby village of Aldbourne in the Wiltshire Downs. Although, after my high aspirations, it seemed rather an unsatisfactory dead end, my work at the Tractor Stores was varied and interesting. It consisted in overhauling the tractors that I. A. Bennett took in part exchange for new ones and refurbishing them for resale. Bennett had been distributor for the British Rushton tractor and although that ill-starred attempt to challenge the American monopoly of the British tractor market had failed, there were still a number of Rushtons around. The Rushton was a copy of the Fordson and its faults, which were serious, were entirely confined to those features that departed from the well-tried Fordson design. Much of our time was spent in devising modifications to overcome these defects.

Whenever Bennett had completed a part exchange deal, we would be sent out to deliver the new tractor and bring back the old one. For this purpose we used an ancient American International lorry with solid tyres, wooden wheels and totally ineffective brakes. It had, I remember, a curious final reduction gear incorporated in the rear wheel hubs. With this vehicle, descending steep hills off the chalk downs, such as that into the village of Shalbourne, was always something of a heart-in-mouth undertaking. At such times one became all too conscious of the size and weight of the tractor behind, its front wheels nudging the back of the rickety wooden cab. Having no brakes, the only thing to do was to go down very slowly in bottom gear, keeping close to the bank so as to be ready to turn into it the moment anything broke.

We also possessed a Rushton industrial tractor on solid rubber tyres which we used to tow in any tractor too large to load on the International. One such was an ancient American Overtime tractor which had to be towed in from a remote downland farm on Chute Causeway, and it was my unfortunate lot to steer this primitive monster. It belonged to days before the farm tractor had acquired a conventional form of its own, and it resembled a steam traction engine with a huge, crude horizontal petrol/paraffin motor where one would expect to see the boiler. It gave me one of the roughest and most uncomfortable rides I have ever had. Because the road was rough and the old tractor, with its steel-straked wheels, was towed faster than it had ever travelled in its life before, the vibration was appalling. Our progress sounded like a company of clog dancers performing on a tin roof and my loudest shouts were unheard by the driver of the towing tractor. Consequently, the many intimate bits and pieces which dropped off, some of them quite large, were never recovered. What remained of the Overtime when we finally reached Hungerford was optimistically dismantled and put in store for spares. But I very much doubt if those spares were ever needed.

It was in the spring of the following year that I moved to the Foundry, Aldbourne, lodging with the manager and his family in a cottage at the back of the little works. I found this much more to my taste. Though the present business was comparatively new, it had taken over a very old country engineering business that had previously been known as Loveday and Co. and no one knew precisely when a foundry had first been established on the site. Although the pay was low, I enjoyed the work enormously because of its great variety. For this was essentially a jobbing shop in which the six employees, of whom I was one, had to be maids-of-all-work, ready to tackle any job that came along, now fitting, now doing a bit of blacksmith's work at the forge or using the drilling machine or the very ancient and inaccurate lathe. Most of the fitting was on farm tractors, but occasionally there was other work to be done such as fitting a set of new beaters to the drum of a threshing machine. A threshing machine is far less crude than most agricultural machinery and, when the new beaters had been fitted, the drum, which is quite a large and massive affair and revolves at high speed, had to be most carefully and precisely balanced. Otherwise the machine would soon shake itself to pieces.

Once a week there was a casting day when we all went into the foundry to lend a hand with pouring the moulds. This was a small, low, ancient place which was screened from the village street by our larger and loftier general shop. Except for the inimitable smell and the carpet of black sand on the floor, nothing could have been less like that only other foundry I had known at Kerr Stuarts. A panting Lister engine drove by belt the blower that supplied the blast to the small cupola. The products of this foundry were simple and prosaic. Ploughshares, mostly, which we pulled out of their moulds while they were still smoking hot in order to chill them and so make them hard and wear resistant. Rings and end brackets for land rollers were also cast, for these rollers were the one new 'production' implement to be made at Aldbourne. When assembled, they were proudly painted in a bright 'implement blue'. Occasionally, to special order, we would cast a new fireback from one of two ancient patterns found on the site. It so happened that at this time my parents needed a fireback for their new open fireplace in the hall of our house at Stanley Pontlarge. So I bespoke one, helped to cast it, and then bore it home in triumph in the back of my G.N. It still stands in our hall today to remind me of the vanished village foundry where I once worked.

In the early 'thirties, few farms of the chalk downs had mains electricity or water supply and it was our job to service or repair the many small engines, some of them very old and primitive, which were then in use on local farms, generating current, pumping water or driving barn machinery. Deepening bore-holes for water, or sinking new ones, was another job the little firm undertook. This last was a fairly regular source of employment because the level of the water table below the chalk was constantly falling. Ten to one the deepening of a bore hole for one farmer would lead sooner or later to similar requests from his neighbours. When we were required to sink a new bore hole on a farm our first step was to engage the local dowser, who lived in the neighbouring village of Baydon, to come down to the farm with us to find with his divining rod the best place to bore. There is considerable scientific scepticism about water-divining, but I can only say that we regarded the services of this dowser in a completely matter-of-fact light and that his predictions always proved remarkably accurate. For this reason, it did not occur to me to question his mysterious gift and it was many years before I did so and became interested in the subject.

My work frequently took me out of the shop into the surrounding countryside. When I had repaired a tractor on a farm, I would drive it in the field for a time so as to be sure it was up to its work. It might be pulling a plough, a seed-drill, a mowing machine or a reaper-and-binder depending on the season and in this way I gained a brief practical experience of most farming operations. Like the farmer's boy in the old song, I knew what it was to plough, to sow, to reap and to mow. Often my primitive workshop would be some lonely thatched and weather-boarded barn or cart-hovel high upon the downs and reached only by a steep, deep-rutted track. In such remote places I sometimes worked all day, with only a brief break for a lunch of bread and cheese, trying to complete a repair on some piece of agricultural machinery before the light failed while the impatient downland wind rattled at the doors of the barn.

I soon came to know the Wiltshire Downs intimately from Wanborough in the north to Stanton St Bernard in the south. I naturally became very familiar with their topography, but I use the word intimate in a more subtle sense than this. For experience has taught me that it is only by working in a particular countryside that you acquire a sense of its *genius loci* or true character, something that nature and man between them have combined to create. By working in its fields and barns in every kind of weather, the nature of the chalk down-land revealed itself to me fortuitously in a way that it would not have done had I been merely a passive spectator, viewing the landscape objectively as though it were some romantic picture. To put it in another way, I learnt that, however beautiful a landscape may be aesthetically, without the sustenance of continuing life it becomes starved, dead and forlorn. Langland's 'fair field full of folk' was only made fair by the work that was going on in it, a fact which cannot be appreciated except by those who are prepared to endure the hardship, the sweat or the bitter cold, that such work may involve.

In geological terms the chalk landscape is still young. Time may have moulded its firm flesh but it has not succeeded in weathering it to the bone. It is a spacious country of lovely, youthful curves and folds, sensuous and shamelessly bare. Yet it conveyed to me a sense of the distant past more eloquently than any landscape I had encountered before. Everything about it seemed to me suggestive of remote antiquity; the clumps of trees, planted like look-outs, silhouetted on the high sky-lines; those great stones, so aptly named the grey wethers, dropped by a melting glacier to litter the floor of the dry valley it had scoured; solitary thorns, twisted by the wind; flint nodules, turned up by the plough, of more significant and suggestive forms than any abstract sculptor could conceive.

Because all human history is so brief compared with that of this youthful landscape, in ghostly standing stone, burial mound, strip field, trackway and fortification, early man had left his imperishable marks upon it everywhere. Of all the features of the chalk downland I found these traces of civilisations long forgotten the most potently evocative. The mere fact that I was working on the Downs for this brief second in their history gave me a sense of continuity, of kinship, with these my ancient predecessors.

Through my work I became acquainted with many ancient, living men of the Wiltshire downland, an experience that was equally rewarding. Whenever I think of such men it is old Mark Palmer who first springs to my mind. Not that he was in any way unique as a country character at that time, but simply because he worked beside me at the Aldbourne foundry and I therefore came to know him best. In his younger days, Mark

Palmer had worked for Wallis and Steevens, makers of traction engines and other agricultural machinery at Basingstoke, and he possessed an inexhaustible store of amusing anecdotes about that firm to which he remained passionately loyal despite the fact that he had long since returned to his native village. Whenever I heard the familiar words: 'I recollec' one time when I were wi' Wallis and Steevens . . .' I knew the moment had come to down tools, lean comfortably against bench or machine and listen. It was a far more soothing and relaxing experience than any tea break.

Old Mark was short and thickset but surprisingly nimble for his age. Despite the fact that his fingers resembled bunches of bananas, he was a first class fitter, patient, deft and precise. He habitually wore a collarless flannel shirt with sleeves rolled back above the elbow and an ancient pair of bib-and-brace overalls that had once been brown but had faded with age and many washings to the palest khaki colour. Over his long but sparse white hair he wore a shapeless trilby hat of the same neutral colour. An untidy white moustache partly concealed his upper lip and on his large, slightly bulbous nose was perched a pair of steel-rimmed spectacles through which his grey eyes twinkled mischievously. He was the gayest old man I have ever known. On a fine sunny morning, or when work was going well and he was feeling particularly pleased with life, I would catch him humming some indecipherable tune to himself, sometimes executing a few steps of a dance in time to the music in his head. That head was stored with memories, some drawn from his own lifetime, but others going back much further in time which must have been passed on by his forebears. He would tell tales of events that had happened in Aldbourne a century or more ago so vividly and racily that they seemed to become personal recollections. It was from Mark I learned that Aldbourne had once been a centre for the making of straw hats and that, at an earlier date still, church bells had been cast in the village, perhaps, who knows, in that same foundry where I now worked.

It often happens in rural England that neighbouring villages become traditional rivals, their respective inhabitants each targets for the other's wit. So it was with Aldbourne and Ramsbury, and Mark had a wealth of stories to illustrate the fabled follies of the Ramsbury men. He stoutly maintained that it was they who had tried to dredge the moon out of the village pond at Aldbourne, thus giving a local connotation to the perennial Wiltshire story of the moonrakers. It was also the Ramsbury men, of course, who 'set the pig upon the wall to hear the band play'. Whenever Mark was asked some question about the past which he was unable to answer he would pause for a moment in silent meditation before replying slowly: 'Ah! that were a long time ago afore Adam were a boy-chap.' His tales and his graphic turns of phrase were those that Shakespeare knew and which he put into the mouths of his English countrymen. It is sad that nowadays such characters are usually played for laughs, as the townsman's idea of a village idiot, by those who have never known such men as Mark Palmer.

I have always relished the company of men like Mark Palmer. When I was at Hungerford, rich memories of past voyages on *Cressy* led me to explore the Kennet and Avon canal from the towpath and in this way I soon discovered the canal pumping station at Crofton on the edge of Savernake Forest. This station contained the first early beam pumping engines I had ever seen and I marvelled alike at their workman-ship and at the poetry of their motion. Needless to say, I soon made friends with the old engineman who lived in a solitary cottage beside the pump-house. I used to visit Crofton fre-quently on summer evenings or at week-ends to share the old man's vigil in the engine house while the massive beam nodded in the gloom under the rafters high overhead. I used to find the sounds of the engine as hypnotic as my companion's conversation: the rhythmical clicking as the highly polished detents of the valve gear alternately engaged and released; the heavy sigh of steam exhausting into the condenser beneath our feet; the sound of a great gush of water pouring into the open feeder channel each time the pump bucket came up.

This period was enlivened and made memorable for me because I acquired two more cars. In case this should convey a false impression of affluence, I hasten to add that they cost me two pounds a-piece, discounting the labour I expended on them. I found that I was using my G.N. far more now and decided, on the belt-and-braces principle, that I ought to have a second car as reserve in case of emergency. So I bought near my home a 1922 Belsize-Bradshaw. It had a big-end gone —a defect I soon remedied—but was otherwise in excellent order. In view of the chronic starting trouble that my father had experienced with this marque, it may seem a strange choice, but this one not only boasted a self-starter but also an impulse starter[1] on its magneto. These ensured that I never had any starting troubles. I drove the Belsize some thousands of miles, but although it was a nice little car for its date and never let me down on the road, it lacked the sporting character of the G.N. and consequently never endeared itself to me.

My third car I acquired purely as a 'fun machine'. It was a little 1903[2] Humber which I discovered neglected in a chicken run at the back of a pub in Winchcombe. It looked very forlorn for it was covered in chicken droppings, its tyres had perished and there was nothing left of the upholstery except the springs, but investigation showed that mechanically it was quite sound and almost complete. One of my two old school friends, Harry Rose, was at this time working at a garage in Cheltenham and he produced the lorry on which we conveyed the Humber to the shelter of a cart shed at Stanley Pontlarge where I was able to work on it whenever I was at home. I found that the simple little two-seater body was secured to the tubular chassis merely by hook-bolts so that it was an easy matter to remove it, the better to attend to the chassis. My mother helped me to renovate and re-cover the upholstery and, when it had been given a coat of the green paint, which I had adopted as my 'house colour', the little car, with its polished copper radiator, really looked quite smart to my eyes although far below the standard of today's restorations.

The Humber had a single cylinder de Dion type engine of 5¼ h.p. which ran anti-clockwise. A small leather-lined cone clutch of alarming ferocity took the drive to a gear box which gave two forward speeds and reverse, actuated by two levers mounted on the sides of the steering column. A short propeller shaft connected the gearbox to the live rear axle, this last a fairly advanced feature for the period. 'Gas', 'Air' and 'Ignition' were each separately controlled from the column which meant that there were no less than five levers working in quadrants below the single-spoked metal steering wheel. When I found the car, this entire complex steering column assembly was a mass of red rust, but nothing daunted I got to work on it with

[1] This device consists of a spring-loaded ratchet and two pawls, all incorporated in the magneto driving coupling. On starting, the pawls engage with the ratchet, the effect being to impart a vigorous 'flip' to the magneto. When running, centrifugal force held the pawls out of engagement.
[2] I believed it to be 1902 and ran it as such for three years, before it was re-dated 1903 by the Veteran Car Club.

a mixture of metal polish and bath-brick and found, to my surprise and delight, that the original nickel plating underneath was practically perfect. The rust had emerged through a few minute pin-holes in the plating and had spread until it had covered its entire surface.

I was determined to get the car ready in time to enter it in the next (November 1932) Veteran Car Run to Brighton. How I managed to achieve this or precisely how I contrived to get the car to London for the start I cannot now remember. I certainly did not drive it up, for although I had had the engine running, owing to lack of time I had never driven the car more than a few yards. So it was scarcely surprising that I suffered the inevitable fate that awaits those so foolish as to bring an untried car to the starting line.

The start of the Brighton Run in those days was from Moon's Garage in Victoria Street. In my recollection of that November morning, the garage was half-dark and filled with choking exhaust fumes. In this smoke-filled gloom there was feverish activity as heavily muffled figures busied themselves about their strange vehicles which emitted desperate panting, tuffing and wheezing noises. I was glad to be clear of this mêlée and bowling up Victoria Street through an avenue of spectators. Then past the Abbey, past the Houses of Parliament and over Westminster Bridge, the little engine panting away gamely. This was the life, I thought; Brighton, here I come! But elation and hope soon turned to despair. In Brixton the radiator began to boil and overheating brought chronic pre-ignition causing the engine to lose what little power it possessed. Obviously it would be folly—besides being cruel to the car—to attempt to reach Brighton under such circumstances so I rolled ignominiously to the kerb-side, enveloped in a cloud of steam. I must have been the first competitor to fall by the wayside.

I transported my Humber from Brixton back to the Tractor Stores at Hungerford, where I. A. Bennett kindly gave it house-room. There I very soon diagnosed the trouble. One of the few things which were detached from the car when I found it was the gear-type water pump which was bolted to a bracket on the chassis and driven by a chain from the front of the engine. This pump had been dismantled and I had to replace its gears which had worn away. It could be made to revolve in either direction depending on which side of it was made to take the drive. In this my choice had been determined, partly by logic and, decisively as I thought, by the length of the driving chain which I had discovered in the tool-box. I now tried the effect of reversing the rotation of the pump and, hey presto!, all was well. The job was simply and quickly done, but it meant shortening the chain. This remains a mystery to me to this day. The evidence of that chain suggests that the previous owner of the car, Mr Greening, an elderly Winchcombe market-gardener, had run it in its incorrect state. If that was the case I could well believe local stories that it used to take him most of the day to get over Cleeve Hill and into Cheltenham.

In my impecunious state, I had surrendered the licence on the Humber at the end of November, but during the following winter and early spring I was able to drive it on the road thanks to the kindness of I. A. Bennett who lent me his general trade plates. This practice of running on trade plates led to an amusing brush with the law.

For some reason, perhaps because most of my motoring has been done in peculiar motor cars, I have always been harassed by the law and charged with a variety of petty technical offences by men whose time would have been better employed in catching criminals. They have buzzed around me like so many pestilential blow-flies so I am emphatically not one of those who subscribe to the view that our policemen are wonderful. My first brush with them was at Dursley where I was charged and fined for having an illegible front number plate on my G.N., although it appeared perfectly legible to me.

One fine Sunday morning in March I headed out of Hunger-ford along the quiet Wantage road to try out the effect of some 'tuning' of the Humber's engine. Beside me in the passenger seat was a beauteous young Hungerford maiden. I was not particularly susceptible to her charms, but she had badgered me so persistently to give her a ride in 'that funny old car' that I had finally given way to her. Now you hardly expect to find a plain-clothes policeman on the Wantage road on a Sunday morning, so I did not suspect that the man in a cloth cap and a raincoat who was cycling towards us was a wolf in sheep's clothing until he jumped off his machine, signalled us peremptorily to stop and produced his police card. 'Having a nice little joy-ride, eh?' he asked with a mirthless smile and a significant glance towards my passenger. Very fortunately, I realised as soon as he said this that one of the absurd anomalies of our road traffic regulations was that one was allowed to carry passengers on general trade plates on weekdays but not on a Sunday. The

situation was the more unfortunate because it would implicate
the owner of the plates—my employer—rather than myself.
The only thing to be done was to attempt to blind the law
with science. So the following dialogue took place:

SELF: No, this isn't a joy-ride; I'm testing the car.
POLICEMAN: You don't need a passenger for that do you?
SELF: Oh yes I do; I need her to prevent the car from
running backwards if it fails on a hill.
POLICEMAN: Aah! So your brakes are defective.
SELF (Indignantly): Indeed they are not; they are the
external contracting band type which are designed to
work effectively only in a forward direction. To prevent
the car running backwards it is fitted with a sprag.
POLICEMAN (suspecting his leg is being pulled): And might
I ask what that is?
SELF (pointing it out): There it is. You see it can be let
down on to the road.
POLICEMAN (triumphantly): Then why don't you use it?
SELF: Because the sprag was designed for rough roads.
On smooth tarmac like this it doesn't work.
POLICEMAN: All right, get along then.

Whereupon, baffled and furious at being cheated of his prey,
this unpleasant customer remounted his bicycle and pedalled
rapidly away. He had not been quite clever enough, for he
had omitted to ask if the Humber had two independent working
brakes as required by law. If he had, I should have lost the
battle of wits, for the car had a second brake on the transmission.

When I moved from Hungerford to the Foundry at Aldbourne the Humber went with me and, as I had now got it
running extremely well, I licensed it for the month of June. So
on these long, fine summer evenings I made a number of trips to
Hungerford and back to visit friends and in recollection these
were the most pleasant journeys I have ever made with a
veteran car. There were not the crowds or the traffic such
as inevitably accompany an organised veteran car run and make
it a self-conscious exhibition. On the contrary, I was using
the car as it was meant to be used on a delightful country
road which, though it had a smoother surface, can have changed
very little since the car was made and, in those days, carried
very little traffic. Chugging along at a steady 25 m.p.h. through

the warm, richly scented air of those still summer evenings was a rare delight which no modern motorist can experience but which the pioneers must have known. Indeed, in one respect I was more fortunate than the pioneers for their one enemy—dust—was lacking. I was reminded of childhood journeys by horsedrawn vehicle, for one sits *on* rather than *in* a veteran car and has a view over hedgerows into fields or cottage gardens.

The quadrant of the lever controlling the Humber's two forward speeds was rightly labelled 'fast' and 'slow' for the gap between the ratios was enormous, speed in low gear being no quicker than a walking pace. The golden rule was never to attempt to change down until the engine was on the point of stalling. Conversely, once in 'slow' speed, it was useless to attempt to change up until the car was on the level or there was a strong following wind. Otherwise, by the time the engine revs had dropped sufficiently to enable 'fast' speed to be engaged, the car had rolled to a stop. Engine speed was controlled by advancing or retarding the spark, for once you had got its mixture right by carefully adjusting the 'gas' and 'air' levers, you left the primitive Longemaire carburettor severely alone. Fortunately, the eight miles of road between Aldbourne and Hungerford run mainly in the valley of the Kennet and include no hill which the Humber could not surmount in 'fast' gear so that I was able to bowl along happily without any tedious crawls.

I was returning to Aldbourne one evening at dusk after one of these visits to Hungerford, when I had a second encounter with the police, this time in the person of the local sergeant from Ramsbury. A stout, red-faced individual, I met him pedalling slowly and majestically towards me on his bicycle. He evidently decided that so curious a vehicle must be illegal, for as soon as he saw me he dismounted and signalled me to stop. I sat patiently at the wheel while he paced slowly round and round the car examining it minutely. At last, surveying the Humber from the front, the light of triumph brightened his eye and, whipping out a folding foot rule, he stooped and measured the figures of the front registration number, FH 12, which was painted on the bottom tank of the radiator. They were three-eighths of an inch too short, he solemnly informed me. A heinous offence had been committed! Out came the notebook from the breast pocket, the pencil was licked and full particulars taken. I remarked that the figures

had very probably been there since 1903 when car registration
was first introduced and that no one had remarked the crime
before. He accepted this with dignity as a compliment to his
vigilance. I was not prosecuted, but on two subsequent occasions
this zealous man pedalled over to Aldbourne from Ramsbury,
first to see for himself that I had enlarged the figures and a
second time to administer an official caution.

I left the Humber in store at a garage in Hungerford when
my job at Aldbourne died on me in August 1933 and I returned
home. I could not afford to perambulate the country looking
for work, so I must have spent six weeks or more hopefully
writing round to likely firms and receiving monotonously
discouraging replies until, in October, one of these letters bore
fruit and I was offered a job at the Sentinel Waggon Works at
Shrewsbury. With hope renewed, I headed the G.N. for Shrewsbury and found lodgings for myself in a pub at Battlebridge, not
far from the works.

The firm was at that time making the latest and last of
its famous steam waggons which was known as the S Type.
This had the same basic layout as its predecessors with vertical
Sentinel boiler in front and engine slung beneath the chassis
amidships, but it was very much more refined. The engine was
single-acting, a flat four-cylinder with poppet valves, which
drove the rear wheels via a propeller shaft and live axle instead
of by roller chain as on all the earlier models. The S Type was a
fast waggon in its day being capable of maintaining a speed of
50 m.p.h. or more (illegally, of course) on the level.

I went to work in the Boiler Shop, fitting up the boilers
for these S Type waggons and it was interesting to me to see
the changes that had been made in the design of the Sentinel
boiler since those days, that now seemed so long ago, when I
had driven the first Sentinel ploughing engine at Pitchill. Most
notably, internal baffles were now fitted in an attempt to cure
its chronic water-lifting or 'priming' trouble. There was also
a new and enlarged superheater element which raised the steam
to a temperature that was then unusually high, so much so that
a special lubricating oil had to be developed for the engine.
My job was to assemble the boiler, lowering the outer casing
over the firebox, and then to mount all the boiler fittings. When
the job was completed I then had to test the boiler under
steam at full working pressure. This was done in a testing bay
at the end of the shop which was equipped with a Laidlaw-Drew
oil burner.

The Sentinel Waggon Works was an exciting place at this time for a steam enthusiast like myself, for I would sometimes see with awed veneration the tall, white-haired figure of the American Abner Doble, striding across the yard or driving out of the works gate in one of his steam cars. Doble was then regarded as the ultimate champion of steam power against the all-conquering might of the internal combustion engine. He had come over to Shrewsbury, bringing two of his flash-steam cars with him, with the object of developing a similar flash-steam commercial vehicle. Of his two cars, one resembled in appearance a conventional large American saloon of the period, while the other was a very handsome coach-built two-seater coupé. I remember peering round the doorway of the works garage and watching the big coupé, moving to and fro with uncanny silence as it was manœuvred into its parking bay. How I itched to have a run in such a car! But I was merely a humble fitter and knew I had no hope.

I also used to see the one Sentinel/Doble flash-steam waggon that had then been built. This outwardly resembled a conventional petrol or diesel lorry with semi-forward control except that its radiator—which was in fact the condenser—was abnormally large. The full roller-bearing two-cylinder compound engine was mounted in unit with the rear axle and was supplied with steam from the flash boiler at 1500 lbs per square inch and 500° C. superheat. This vehicle was employed on works transport at the time. I used to watch it entering or leaving the works and once, when it was standing in the yard, engaged its driver in conversation. He boasted to me of the number of summonses he had received for speeding. This I could well believe, for the Sentinel/Doble once made the 540-mile run from Shrewsbury to Glasgow and back with a full load in less than 24 hours, no mean performance in the days before motorways.

But as things turned out, this was the last brave gesture in a lost cause. Abner Doble, unfortunately, was one of those inventive geniuses who, unless they can be firmly controlled, will ruin any engineering firm. A perfectionist, he could never be persuaded to finalise any design. Despite its promise, his first waggon had certain serious defects which would have to be eliminated before it became a commercial proposition. Instead of trying to iron out these snags, Doble seemed to lose interest in the vehicle, devoting his whole attention and a great deal of the firm's money to the development of a new triple-expansion engine with inter-stage superheating. The final upshot was that the firm went into liquidation, the company being re-formed under a different title, while Abner Doble returned to America. As for the more conventional S Type Sentinel, it was driven off the English road by a new form of taxation which discriminated against the steam vehicle, although a number continued to be made for export for some years. A slackening in the demand for the S Type waggon found me out of a job again at the end of December after a mere two months at Shrewsbury. It has always seemed to me crazy that the only type of heavy road vehicle using home-produced fuel should have been driven off the road by taxation.

Back at home, a second spate of letter writing eventually landed me yet another job, this time with Thornycrofts at Basingstoke. This was unmemorable and proved equally brief with the result that by April 1934 I had returned home once more. Yet but for this brief sojourn in Basingstoke I should never have become part-owner of a garage only eight miles out of the town. But that was still in the future. For the rest of the year I lived, or rather was based, at home with my parents. It was the longest continuous spell I had spent at Stanley Pontlarge since my school holidays and I kept myself occupied by working on my G.N. and Belsize.

My Humber was still stabled in Hungerford, but I was determined to enter it again for the London to Brighton Run and this was the most memorable experience of these idle months. A friend of mine from Cheltenham, an enthusiastic Austin Seven owner named Mark Newth, very bravely offered to tow the Humber from Hungerford to London behind his early Austin Seven 'chummy'. With some difficulty (for the Austin had no chassis at the rear) we devised a suitable towbar and attachments and headed south to retrieve my car and set off for London. From my high perch on the Humber I could look down on the hood of the Austin Seven and as we drove through London the curious spectacle we presented attracted much ribaldry from taxi drivers. They found us the more mirth-provoking because, whenever traffic brought us to a halt, I would have to leap out and push in order to get us rolling again. For though it performed its onerous task gallantly, the one thing the Austin could not do was to start its tow from rest. Instead it suffered such violent clutch judder that it jumped up and down on its springs without any forward motion.

This gallant effort was not in vain, for this time the Humber ran like a watch and it was with immense satisfaction that I drove on to the Madeira Drive at Brighton well within the time limit. The Brighton road, though it seemed congested enough, was much clearer than it is today and I remember gazing enviously after Blake's racing Napier as it came hurtling past at what seemed an incredible velocity.

One of the two friends I had made at school was by this time working at a garage in Maidstone, and offered to stable the Humber there so, on the morning after the run, we set off in bright sunshine to tow the car to Maidstone. It was a hilly road over the downs from Brighton, but the little Austin struggled along bravely and so we eventually left the old car to slumber for another year with no clear idea as to how I should retrieve it.

The only employment I had during these idle months was totally unremunerative and consisted in endeavouring to sell on commission a patent tractor winch manufactured by the firm of Kennedy and Kempe Ltd to timber merchants in the Forest of Dean. Despite the fact that I staged quite an impressive demonstration of this winch in Priors Mesne Wood in the Forest, I never succeeded in selling a single one and decided ruefully that salemanship was not my strong suit.

I had been introduced to Kennedy and Kempe by Leslie Bomford whose farm was nearby. Colonel Kennedy and I. T. Kempe had been managing director and works manager respectively of the old firm of Taskers at Andover before setting up a business of their own in a disused war-time explosives factory at Longparish in Hampshire. They were both charming men and enterprising and inventive engineers, always keen on developing new ideas, so that I felt mortified by my failure to sell their patent winch. I disappointed them in another way also.

As a result of my experience with the KS lorry I had been cudgelling my brains about possible ways of reducing the amount of black smoke which the diesel engine emitted on heavy load. It seemed to me that if the amount of air drawn in to the cylinders could be varied in direct proportion to the amount of fuel injected, not only would the exhaust become clean but the engine would be more efficient. I had made a section drawing of a cylinder head incorporating a device to achieve this which I showed to Colonel Kennedy. He was keenly interested, advised me to take out a provisional patent and offered to send my drawing and a draft specification to his patent agents in

17. The Kerr Stuart diesel lorry: the prototype at the Mainwaring Arms, Whitmore

THE STROUD BREWERY Cº Lᵀᴰ

18. The Kerr Stuart diesel lorry: a production model standing beside the locomotive erecting shop

19. *Cressy* under way, 1930

20. The engine room of
*Cressy*

21. New toy: on my 1903 Humber at Aldbourne, 1933

22. The G.N. and my Belsize at Stanley Pontlarge, 1933

23. Touring in the West Country in the G.N., 1934

24. The G.N. as a single-seater at Bramshill, 1936

25. My father in his Alvis on the Brecon Beacons, 1926

26. My own £10-worth of Alvis

27. The 'Scuderia Carsoni' at the Phoenix, 1934. Left to right: John Passini, Tim Carson and self

28. 'The Home of the 30/98 Vauxhall': the Phoenix, 1935

29. Filling up the Itala at Gretton Garage just before a Prescott meeting, 1938

30. The Phoenix Special rounds the semi-circle at Prescott, 1938

31. Design for Living: an interior view of *Cressy*

London for a report. Alas for my fond hopes! I still have a copy of that report. In it the agents wrote:

'Specification 334018 (Daimler-Benz, Stuttgart) describes the linking up of the throttle control with auxiliary pistons for varying the clearance whereby any desired variation can be obtained, this being practically the same idea as Mr Rolt's.'

The dream of 'Rolt the Great Inventor' was thus rudely shattered. The fact that I had been forestalled by a name so august as Daimler-Benz was small consolation, particularly when I obtained a copy of their patent specification and found it to be a master patent of principle with no indication of the mechanical means whereby it could be applied. So ended my only venture into the complex world of patents.

During these roving, rootless and largely fruitless years my mind was by no means solely occupied with engineering matters. During my apprenticeship I had been content to absorb experiences and in the previous chapters I have tried to describe as faithfully as possible their impact upon me although I could not have described them at the time. Now, however, my frequent, and sometimes prolonged, visits to my home in between one job and the next gave me an opportunity mentally to digest and ponder over my past with the effect that my brain began to buzz with new and disturbing thoughts and ideas.

Of all my varied experiences, that of my years at Stoke-on-Trent had by far the most lasting effect upon me. It had provided me with my first and most intimate insight into the kind of England that the Industrial Revolution had created. I had been fascinated by the vitality of this world of blackened streets, of spinning wheels, of smoke and steam and furnace flame; so much so that the memory of it did not fade but became more vivid with the passage of time. But because I could recall its every sight and sound so clearly, the contrast between it and the green England that I had known as a child became for me the more significant. The prospect that one day this new black world might grow until it had altogether overwhelmed the green world where I had found such sweet solace seemed to me too terrible to contemplate. And yet, as an engineer, was I not dedicated to such a course of destruction? I realised that this conflict between the black and the green was an internal as well as an external one and that philosophical problems were involved which were far beyond my limited intellectual range. The first thing to do, it seemed to me, was to acquire some knowledge as to how the Industrial Revolution had come about in the first place. Of this I was completely ignorant, for the history I had been taught at school was all to do with kings and politicians, with wars and with revolutions of a bloodier but much less significant kind. In this sort of history the Industrial Revolution appeared to be merely an incidental happening, although it now seemed to me the most important event in human history and one filled with potential menace. My thirst for knowledge was first quenched when I came upon an original three-volume edition of Samuel Smiles' *Lives of the Engineers* in a second-hand bookshop. I read it with avid interest. And so, for the princely sum of 7s. 6d., my self-education began. It was to become a lifelong study.

At the same time, the side of my nature that loved and remembered the world of my childhood found secret refreshment in poetry. Being made to learn dull passages of prose and poetry by rote at school by men who appeared to have no natural feeling for words had very effectively destroyed my appetite for literature. But at some time during these years, precisely how or when I cannot now remember, I discovered the poems of W. B. Yeats and the music and majesty of their language went straight to my heart. This experience encouraged me to read many other poets, ancient and modern, but while I drew much satisfaction from them, Yeats always seemed to me supreme among the moderns and I habitually kept a copy of his poems at my bedside. Later, I read his *Reveries over Childhood and Youth* and *The Trembling of the Veil*; also that strange book *A Vision*.

At this time, too, I felt a strong compulsion to express my thoughts and feelings in writing. Where this literary urge came from is as much a mystery to me as the source of my earlier determination to become an engineer, for there was no literary tradition in my family. Although in her later life my mother became a great reader, my parents read little during my childhood and there were few books in the house at Hay. So, lacking an example, I had read hardly at all, drawing imaginative sustenance from direct experience. I can recall only one book that I read with intense pleasure as a child and that was *The Secret Garden* by Frances Hodgson Burnett. My knowledge of the formal rules of grammar was almost nil, but my immediate liking for the poems of Yeats disclosed that

I had a feeling for the music of words. So I made a first and unsatisfactory attempt to express myself. This was in the form of a novel which I called *Strange Vista*. The title came from a poem called 'The Wheel'; rather a second-rate piece I now realise, but it chimed with my thought at the time.

*Strange Vista* was really very strange indeed and fell far short of its creator's hopes even when it had been completely re-written. The trouble was that the whole idea was hopelessly over-ambitious. It was intended to be a great saga in three parts, past, present and future, with representatives of the same two families playing the leading roles in each. The first part was set in the rural England of the mid-eighteenth century; the setting of the second was the large industrial town which had grown up on the same location. The town was modelled on Stoke-on-Trent and this part was autobiographical as most first novels tend to be. Finally, the last part portrayed the same town in the future. To read it now is a curious experience, for in many ways this town of the future with its tall buildings, its express lifts, its pedestrian subways and shopping 'precincts' has become strangely familiar. So have the manners and morals of its restless, unhappy, neurotic and sex-obsessed citizens. There is one scene where a troupe of girls dance almost naked in a night-club while two characters argue the pros and cons of a 'permissive' society. 'The rules of right and wrong are pretty elastic, they change with the years', says the apologist, to which the other replies: 'You can't go on changing your rules to suit your inclinations.' But I had over-estimated the pace of change. For reasons to do with the ages of my chief characters, I set this future scene in 1954, a date which, in 1932, seemed to a young man half a world away. Even so, in one respect this world of the future remains a Wellsian dream, for in it men had discovered a way of 'broad-casting' electric power. All forms of transport used electric propulsion, private cars being fitted with shilling-in-the-slot meters.

In my book, this hectic urban civilization ended not with a big bang, as now seems probable, but with a whimper. Its neurotic citizens all began to succumb to a sudden, acute and invariably fatal brain disease. The power stations stopped and everything ground to a halt. My hero and heroine, of course, were amongst the few survivors. They sought refuge on the Welsh Border where they proceeded to lead a life of Arcadian simplicity of the kind William Morris used to dream about, resolved to found a new civilization that would be better adapted to man's natural environment and his instinctive needs.

Naïve though it is, *Strange Vista*, painstakingly written in two large lined notebooks, does provide an accurate record of my state of mind at this time. It thus enables me to avoid the danger of attributing to my youthful persona thoughts and ideas which, in fact, he never held at the time. Such a back-projection of ideas is a falsification to which autobiographers are peculiarly subject, often quite unconsciously. During these difficult years of the great depression it did indeed seem to me that the industrial world was changing and might be sowing the seeds of its own dissolution. The writing and rewriting of *Strange Vista* in my spare time throughout this unsettled period of my life was the equivalent of keeping a secret and highly personal journal.

# Chapter 11

# The Phoenix

THE sporting character of my father's 12/50 Alvis was such that no sooner had he acquired it in 1925 than he became an enthusiastic follower of motor racing. From 1926 onward he regularly visited the speed hill climbs at Shelsley Walsh in Worcestershire and, as I accompanied him whenever I was free to do so, I soon became as keen as he was. Naturally, after I had acquired my first G.N. I became a devoted fan of B. H. Davenport who frequently made the fastest time of the day at Shelsley in his single-seater G.N. 'Spider'. On occasion, too, my father and I went to Brooklands in the Alvis. We saw the Grand Prix of the R.A.C. there in 1926, the first formula Grand Prix to be run on English soil.

My interest in motor racing had thus begun at the age of sixteen so I was pleased to find, when I went to Basingstoke eight years later, someone who fully shared it. We also shared the same lodgings in Worting Road. He was an apprentice at Thornycrofts named John Passini and, as motor racing was by no means our only common interest, we soon became firm friends. We both admired what we considered to be the right kind of car and consequently deplored the effect of the great depression on the British motor industry. Many firms had gone out of business, while of the survivors the majority had lost their separate identities by seeking refuge in amalgamations. These new combines sought salvation by adopting, not very successfully, American methods of mass-production. In America, the closed car had become the rule rather than the exception, a trend which had been vastly accelerated by the introduction of the pressed steel body which was cheaper, lighter and stronger than the older wooden-framed coach-built body which it replaced.

The introduction of these American methods to England from

1930 onwards brought about a rapid revolution on the English roads. Hitherto, Englishmen had taken for granted that a closed car was something expensive and heavy to be used as a 'town carriage' and that for long-distance motoring in the country one used an open touring car. My father and mother, for example, thought nothing of setting out to drive from Gloucestershire to Chester in mid-winter in the open Belsize or the Alvis and it would never occur to them to erect the hood unless it was actually snowing or raining. There is an interesting parallel to this in the early cab-less locomotives on our railways. But when the first small 'tin saloons' (as John and I used rudely to call them) came on to the market they proved so popular that within the space of a very few years the open touring car had become a rarity. Because our climate is bad and the average mortal is slothful and comfort-loving, this speedy change was understandable although, along with the hardship, a great deal of the pleasure went out of motoring in the process. It was one significant step in that process by which man has used his technology to cut himself off from his natural environment.

By 1934 it had already become clear that the previous decade was the golden age of motoring in England. Though main roads had become dustless they were then still traffic free. The term 'the joy of the open road' was still literally true and carried no cynical overtones. Compared with their pre-war predecessors, the better cars of the 'twenties had an immeasurably superior performance and reliability so that one could embark on the longest journey without the haunting fear of breakdowns. Because they were designed by engineers to be built by engineers rather than by machines, using methods which would now be considered impossibly expensive in labour and materials, such cars were valued by their owners, not as mere status symbols, but as objects of fine craftsmanship; for the way they handled and for the sensitivity of their response to driving skill. My father valued his Alvis in the same way as he valued his Holland & Holland guns. The experience of driving such a car on the roads of the past has been so evocatively described by Sir Osbert Sitwell in the third volume of his great autobiography *Left Hand, Right Hand!* that any further attempt to do so would be superfluous.

'They would sit together, the two of them,' he writes, 'the man at the wheel, the girl beside him, their hair blown back from their temples, their features sculptured by the wind, their bodies and limbs shaped and carved by it continually under their clothes, so that they enjoyed a new physical sensation, comparable to swimming; except that here the element was speed, not water. The winds—and their bodies—were warm that summer. During these drives, they acquired a whole range of physical conscious-ness, the knowledge of scents, passing one into another with an undreamt-of rapidity, the fragrance of the countless flowers on the lime trees, hung like bells of pagodas for the breeze to shake, changing into that of sweetbriar, the scent of early mornings, and of their darkness, of hills and valleys, outlined and tinged by memory; there was the awareness of speed itself, and the rapid thinking that must accompany it, a new alertness, and the typical effects, the sense, it might be, of the racing of every machine as dusk approaches, or the sudden access on a hot evening of cool waves of air under the tall trees;—all these physical impressions, so small in themselves, went to form a sum of feeling new in its kind and never before experienced. Even the wind of the winter, at this pace snatching tears from their eyes, and piercing through layers of clothes, was something their fathers had not known. The open car belonged to that day. No other generation had been able to speed into the sunset.'[1]

This passage stirs many a nostalgic memory for me, but already, by 1934, it had become clear that the open car belonged uniquely to the past. The new mass-produced saloon cars were appearing on the road in ever increasing numbers. That so far as weight distribution, road-holding and steering were concerned these first British attempts at mass production were some of the worst cars ever made is now a commonly accepted fact. The contrast with what had gone before could not have been more striking. I remember driving one early example which, with two heavy passengers in the back seats, became almost uncontrollable because the front wheels were practically off the road, a defect cured on later models by the crude expedient of shifting the engine forward over the axle.

It must have been one Sunday evening in March 1934 that I returned to Basingstoke in the Belsize after a visit home

[1] *Great Morning*, pp. 234-5.

to find John full of a marvellous pub he had discovered at Hartley Wintney, eight miles out of Basingstoke on the road to London. He had been introduced to it by a curious character named 'Soapy' Monkton, a car salesman from the Sarum Hill Garage just down the road. This pub was called 'The Phoenix' and it was kept by a tall Irishman named Tim Carson. This character had, John informed me excitedly, broken records at Brooklands driving a three-litre T.T. Vauxhall and now possessed a special racing 30/98 Vauxhall which he had built himself. As John portrayed it, the whole ambience of 'The Phoenix' sounded so congenial and inviting that I could scarcely wait to visit it so, on the very next evening, we drove out to Hartley Wintney together. That visit was the first of many during the next nine months, for it marked the beginning of an enduring and fruitful friendship between John Passini, Tim Carson and myself. Because, in Grand Prix racing, the Italian star was then in the ascendant, we styled ourselves jokingly the 'Scuderia Carsoni'.

Although John favoured the Lancia Lambda and I, naturally, the G.N. and the 12/50 Alvis, our taste in cars was very similar and we both enthusiastically shared with Tim his admiration for the 30/98 Vauxhall. The work of the Scuderia Carsoni was done in a humble wooden hut, known as 'the racing shed', at the back of the Phoenix and, so far as I can recall, its first public appearance was at Lewes Speed Trials in August where the stable's No 1 driver ran his 30/98 Special with the enthusiastic help of his two devoted assistants. The next outing that I remember was the September meeting at Shelsley Walsh. The team made the 'Falcon' at Bromyard their headquarters. Our tender car was a standard 30/98 'Velox' tourer in which I had an exhilarating drive up from Hampshire, the back loaded with large Rudge wheels of assorted sizes, feeling that now I really was playing a part in the racing game.

John and I soon discovered that our No. 1 driver displayed a remarkable optimism in matters mechanical. On my very first visit to the Phoenix, Tim had casually offered to give me a run in his Special, an offer I accepted with alacrity, thrilled at the thought of a trip in a fast car driven by a man who had actually taken records at Brooklands. We swept out of the inn yard and turned left on to the straight road to Odiham. Here one fine burst of acceleration was succeeded by dead silence. We rolled to a standstill and opened the bonnet when the cause of this abrupt quietus was immediately disclosed—the magneto had become disengaged from its drive. It was a new one which Tim had just fitted. Finding it too low for its holding down strap by an inch or more, there was a need for a distance piece and the first object that came to hand, namely a roll of insulation tape, had been pressed into service.

Sometimes the consequences of this trait could be much more alarming. On the morning of practice day, Tim roared off from Bromyard to Shelsley, leaving John and me to follow in his wake in the tender car. We were startled to see a large Rudge 'knock-off' hub nut lying in the road, and, on stopping to retrieve it, were even more alarmed to see that it undoubtedly belonged to the Carson Special. We pressed on madly, expecting to see disaster round every turn. Miraculously, however, we found Tim in the paddock, blissfully ignorant of the fact that one rear wheel lacked any means of retention. It then transpired that, unknown to us, Tim had decided to try the effect of smaller rear wheels and as these were suitable for short hubs whereas the hubs of his car were long, he had fitted an improvised packing piece between wheel and hub, thus defeating the whole principle of the Rudge detachable wheel.

On one side of the Phoenix yard, a petrol filling station stood beside the road. This consisted of an ugly corrugated iron building with four manual petrol pumps on its forecourt. It was run in a somewhat desultory fashion by a man named Baldwin, an ex-county cricketer and MCC umpire. At what precise moment during this summer of 1934 John and I determined to go into partnership and acquire this garage I cannot now recall, but it was this decision that accounted for my frequent visits to the Phoenix. We put up the capital in equal shares, this being the last substantial call I would make upon my parents' slender resources. Besides the garage, our purchase covered a range of buildings on the opposite side of the yard which had once been an old coachbuilding business. These included a large building with red-tiled roof, which had originally been a barn, a small office and a paint shop. Behind these was a cottage and a modern brick building standing in an open yard, this last being leased by a firm of car breakers named James and Salmon. Although we acquired all this property for what now seems a ridiculously small sum, its purchase left us with all too little working capital, a fact which was to handicap us seriously in the years ahead. We planned to start business in January 1935 in a far more energetic manner than our predecessor.

Meanwhile, at the beginning of October, a letter had appeared in the motoring press over the names of Colin Nicholson and Ned Lewis suggesting the formation of a 'Veteran Sports Car Club' for the owners of sports cars built before 1931. This idea naturally appealed strongly to the members of the Scuderia Carsoni and we immediately wrote to Messrs Nicholson and Lewis, inviting them to come down to the Phoenix and discuss the project. We were a little disappointed to discover that Nicholson owned an Austin Seven and Lewis a 1930 Morris Minor, which were not exactly the sort of cars we had in mind. I suspect they were equally taken aback by the array of somewhat less conventional motor cars owned by the Scuderia Carsoni. However, we thought their idea was a good one and promised our whole-hearted support. Because the Veteran Car Club somewhat naturally objected to the use of the word 'veteran' in the title of the new club it was changed to 'vintage'—at whose suggestion I do not know—and so the Vintage Sports Car Club was born. The Phoenix became the unofficial headquarters and rallying point of the V.S.C.C. until the outbreak of war in 1939. Each weekend would see a desirable collection of motor cars parked in the yard, and, because closing time always seemed to be pretty elastic in those days, convivial, and frequently hilarious parties in the bar used to continue until a late hour.

Although I have since been concerned in the birth of other clubs or societies formed for one object or another, in no organisation other than the V.S.C.C. have I found such good company or made so many lifelong friends. I have often wondered why this should be. It seems that the vintage car attracts a type of mind that is peculiarly congenial to me. It is not by any means a one-track mind, but one with an exacting appreciation for fine craftsmanship that is by no means confined to motor cars. But there is nothing solemn or portentous about this appreciation for it is combined with a keenly ironic sense of humour that is quite free from malice and is capable of laughing at itself. It is due to this detachment and light-hearted tolerance that the V.S.C.C. can organise its affairs and its events with a degree of efficiency combined with a complete absence of friction, empire-building or officiousness which, in my experience, is quite unique among voluntary associations, whatsoever their object. Despite the fact that its membership has grown eight-fold in recent years the Club still retains the character impressed upon it by that handful of people who used to foregather at the Phoenix thirty-five years ago. Of these people, two exercised an outstanding influence. One was Tim Carson, who has now been Secretary for over twenty-five years, and the other was Sam Clutton. Sam is as much of an authority on the organ, early keyboard instruments and horology as he is on the motor car. Driving down from London in the Frazer Nash he then owned, he was a frequent visitor to the Phoenix in these early days and has been my friend from that day to this. As the first Press Secretary and Editor of the Club's *Bulletin*, Sam drove his pen as forcefully as his motor cars so that it is difficult to say which activity was the greater formative influence.

In January 1935 the Phoenix Green Garage, as we called it, opened its doors for the first time under our joint ownership. John's sister had designed for us the emblem of a phoenix on a nest of flame which our successor uses to this day. Unlike our predecessor, we had resolved to go into the repair business and decided we ought to have a breakdown vehicle. I therefore purchased in Cheltenham for the princely sum of £10 a 1911 Silver Ghost Rolls Royce with a vast landaulette body and, having paid over the purchase money, drove it straight down to Hartley Wintney. I had never driven a Rolls Royce before and delighted in the meticulous precision with which all the controls operated and in the silence of the big engine under the long aluminium bonnet that extended before me to that well-known figure of the winged goddess that topped the brass radiator. This silence was the more remarkable because, when we came to overhaul the engine we found it had been sadly neglected. The sump was full of black sludge of the consistency of butter and when we removed the connecting rods, what was left of the white metal in the big-end brasses fell out in small pieces. Apparently the Silver Ghost engine was too well-mannered to complain even under maltreatment. We cut off the rear portion of the landaulette and substituted a truck body in which we mounted a breakdown crane. The front seats were retained, but for the landaulette roof we substituted a folding hood with roll-up rear portion for better visibility when towing. The result was a very handsome and impressive breakdown vehicle, though such a conversion would be thought barbarous nowadays.

One wet and windy winter night soon after we had opened for business, John and I were working late in the garage overhauling the Rolls Royce when we heard a car coming from the direction of London making the most appalling clatter. 'A job!' we cried, and rushed out into the rain. The car, an old Citroen, had drawn up opposite the petrol pumps, its engine still running and 'Two gallons, please' the driver shouted above the mechanical uproar. 'Hadn't we better see what's wrong?' we asked diffidently when we had pumped the petrol into the tank. 'You can do,' replied the driver casually, getting out of the car and looking over our shoulders as we lifted the bonnet. Through a large hole in the side of the crankcase the bright, jagged end of a broken connecting rod could be seen flailing round. 'O ho!' said the driver, 'I'd better take it a bit steady now.' Whereupon he shut the bonnet and drove off rapidly in the direction of Basingstoke, leaving us standing speechless in the road, watching the rear-light of 'the job' disappear into the darkness. This was only the first of our many odd experiences as garage proprietors.

The biggest job our old Rolls Royce ever had to tackle was to rescue a fallen comrade. This was a Silver Ghost hearse of much later date belonging to a firm of London undertakers. It was travelling to Southampton to collect a customer when, between Hartley Wintney and Hook, a front stub axle broke and it had finished up in the ditch. As originally built, this chassis, like ours, had had rear wheel brakes only, but it had subsequently been fitted with a front wheel brake conversion of a singularly crude kind. It was the ineptitude of this conversion which had undoubtedly caused the failure of the stub axle. However, we decided that this was the owners' headache so we duly wrote off to Rolls Royce for a new stub axle and the other spares which were needed. We had reckoned without Rolls Royce. We received in reply a letter to this effect:

'On referring to our records we find that this chassis has been fitted with brakes of alien manufacture. We regret, therefore, that we cannot supply any spares for this chassis until we receive a document, signed by you and by the owners, to the effect that these alien brakes have been removed.'

This imperious missive filled us with admiration, not only for the exacting standards of Rolls Royce but for the completeness and accuracy of their records. The owners could not do other than comply with this edict and we cheerfully threw the 'alien brakes' on to the scrap heap. This disabled hearse was so large that we parked it in the yard near the Phoenix, seizing the opportunity to play on Tim's superstitious fears by pretending that its empty coffin was occupied. When taking our morning drink in the bar, we would sniff ostentatiously and remark that we hoped the spares would arrive soon.

In our old range of buildings we discovered a number of relics of the coachbuilding business which had once been carried on there. In a bin in the old paint shop, for example, we found a large stock of long, cloth-covered springs which at first suggested that someone had once intended to mass-produce jack-in-the-boxes. In fact, they were carriage lamp springs, their function being to push up the candle as it burned and so keep its flame in the focus of the mirror. Another find was a pattern book of the crests and coats of arms of local families, all beautifully hand-painted, which had once been faithfully reproduced on carriage doors by craftsman coachpainters long since turned to dust. Yet a vestige of the old business still lived on in the person of Joe Attewell, a delightful, elderly rural character who still built farm trailers and repaired an occasional farm cart in the big barn. He was to prove a valuable tenant when there was any woodwork to be done and he built us a very useful car-transporting trailer complete with loading winch.

John was marrying Tim Carson's sister-in-law in the spring when the three of us planned to move into the cottage which was part of our property. For the first three months, while the cottage was being redecorated, John and I shared lodgings near Winchfield Station a little over a mile from the garage. I was driving back to the garage from Winchfield after lunch one day when my faithful G.N. met its Waterloo. Rounding a blind bend I suddenly saw directly in front of me a Jowett car heading my way at a fair speed, obviously making for the old road to Odiham that joined the main road at an oblique angle on my left. There was no time to take avoiding action and we met in violent head-on collision. Because it was a light and flimsy machine, the G.N. literally disintegrated around me and it is remarkable that I was able to step out of the ruins completely unhurt. As I did so I observed with a certain malicious satisfaction that the Jowett, which was a nearly new car, had been savaged pretty severely. Its owner lodged a very substantial claim for damages against me, but this was unsuccessful as it was clearly his liability.

This left me with the Belsize as my only means of transport and, as I considered it was hardly a suitable mount for a founder member of the V.S.C.C., I began to look around for another car. With Tim's help I succeeded in finding a 1924 12/50 Alvis two-seater sports model of the genus known as the 'duck's back' from the rude shape of its pointed tail. Although it was then only ten years old, it looked a sorry sight for it was lying in the open and had been sadly neglected, its polished aluminium body panels white with corrosion. I paid the owner ten pounds for it and we towed it back to the garage to receive proper care and treatment. I certainly got value for my money for, apart from an interval during the war years when it was laid up, I have been driving this car from that day to this and the pleasure and satisfaction it gives me has never palled. It has never been elaborately restored to better-than-new condition as is the modern fashion but is still a workaday motor-car. When I first drove this car on the road it was regarded with awe as a 'racer' by the youthful section of the public. Then for many years my appearance was greeted with shouts and whistles of derision, but now this has changed to admiration again, although not of so healthy a kind. By young and old alike the Alvis has come to be regarded as a sort of flashy status symbol. That I do not drive the car in order to make myself conspicuous or to gratify my ego but simply because I enjoy it seems to be beyond the comprehension of the modern mind.

The earliest motoring events organised by the V.S.C.C. were reliability trials. I have never been able to summon much enthusiasm for this type of event although I did accompany Tim Carson as navigator on the Club's first Chiltern Trial in January 1935. Our car was an E type 30/98 Vauxhall with an unusual wide two-seater body which John and I had recently acquired, the first of a number of similar cars to pass through our hands. With it Tim won a second-class award. In view of the prices that these wonderful cars now command, it is interesting that we subsequently advertised this car ('award winner') for £25 and, as there were no takers after some months, subsequently dropped the price to £20.

What attracted me far more were speed events and I decided to reincarnate my shattered G.N. as a single-seater sprint car. I fitted the engine with two magnetos and two carburettors. The latter dripped petrol over the hot cylinders, producing a haze of petrol vapour which caused Sam Clutton to observe

in the Club *Bulletin* that it evidently assisted in carrying off
heat and would probably carry off me as well. However, strange
to relate, it never caught fire. Unlike the racing G.N.s which
were so successful in the years between the wars with their
potent 'Akela' or 'Vitesse' engines, my car still had the ordinary
touring engine beneath this proliferation of magnetos and
carburettors. Consequently it was never seriously competitive
in the racing class in which, being a single-seater, it had to be
entered. Nevertheless, it was a nice looking little car and gave
me a great deal of fun. I first entered my G.N. for the second
V.S.C.C. sprint meeting at Aston Clinton in Buckinghamshire
in May 1936. The course here was a length of private drive,
appallingly rough and pitted with potholes so that the chief
skill consisted in preventing one's car from leaping off the
road.

This meeting was most memorable for the first appearance,
after many years' hibernation in East Anglia, of the 12-litre 1908
60 h.p. Grand Prix Itala which won the class for Edwardian
cars in the hands of its discoverer, J. C. Pole. Sam Clutton
immediately fell for this great car hook, line and sinker, as
well he might, and agreed there and then to purchase it from
John Pole. Sam has been driving it ever since with such
characteristic and tireless verve that it has become the most
famous car in the Club. No Vintage meeting is complete without
Sam and his Itala. We used to maintain the Itala at the Phoenix
Green Garage; it suffered certain derangements in its gearbox,
I remember, due to a somewhat crude and elementary form
of reverse gear, and we had to have some new pinions made
for it. Driving the Itala on test was a motoring thrill such
as I had never experienced before. Although the big engine,
which entirely filled the bonnet, made a considerable mechanical
commotion, once, with tensed calf muscles, you had gingerly
engaged the heavy clutch and felt the engine take hold, you
were rewarded with a sensation of effortless power such as no
modern car, however potent, can possibly convey. As has been
so truly said, in this respect 'there is no substitute for litres'.
In 1968 I was privileged to drive the Itala round the full
Silverstone circuit on the occasion of its 60th birthday celebra-
tions and, after an interval of more than thirty years, experienced
the same thrill.

My first memorable experience with the Itala was when Sam
entered it for the Shelsley Walsh hill climb and I accompanied
him thither as mechanic. It was the first occasion when a

special class for Edwardian cars had been run at Shelsley and the first time Sam had driven there. We drove up in the car from the Phoenix to Shelsley, stopping the night at Worcester to inspect a small chamber organ in the cathedral. On practice day a mysterious air leak developed in the top of the rear petrol tank and, since fuel supply depended on air pressure, this was most unfortunate. However, such an emergency had evidently been anticipated by the provision in the cockpit of a connector to which a hand tyre pump could be attached. So we borrowed a pump and I accompanied Sam on both his runs, pumping madly.

That heroic figure the riding mechanic has long been extinct in motor racing. He was heroic because, while a racing driver holds his life in his own hands and is far too pre-occupied to feel any sense of fear, his helpless riding mechanic has little to do but watch what, if he has any imagination, seems a series of imminent accidents. No such passive heroism was called for on this occasion, however. As we thundered up to the esses, I was far too busily occupied with that tyre pump to worry whether we should get round or not. In fact, as I discovered then, although the Itala stands so high that its passengers get the impression that it must roll over when entering a corner at what seems an impossible speed, it is perfectly stable and corners impeccably. The car had—as it still has—an archaic low-tension ignition system. There are no sparking plugs as we know them, the spark being produced by the opening of contact points within the cylinder. These points are opened by a cam and closed by a spring. On this occasion our progress up the hill was punctuated by a series of deafening reports whenever engine revolutions approached their peak. I diagnosed that this could only be due to the return springs being too weak, thus causing the ignition points to flutter. So when we returned to the paddock and were asked by admiring spectators to explain these alarming explosions, we answered tersely: 'plug bounce',[1] a reply that sent the inquirers away completely baffled and unsure whether we were mad or whether their legs were being pulled.

Sam's father at this time owned and drove a 1910 Fafnir and it was this driver/car combination which is said to have started

[1] For the benefit of the layman, it is the valves of an engine that normally flutter at high speed if their return springs are too weak, a malady commonly referred to as valve bounce.

the Edwardian[1] car movement in the Vintage Club. This
may have been so, but it is equally true that Sam and his
Itala popularised a movement that his father began and in a very
short time the Club could field an impressive array of Edwardian
cars. There was Anthony Heal in the big Fiat, the Itala's
closest rival, Dick Nash's 15½-litre Lorraine-Dietrich *Vieux
Charles Trois* and Eric Giles's famous 1913 5-litre Bugatti
*Black Bess*.

In some of these additions, John Passini and I were directly
concerned. Just where we managed to acquire a 1907 Renault
'forty-five' racing car I cannot now remember, but we sold
it to one Anthony Mills of Offchurch, near Leamington,
agreeing to take his two cylinder 1905 Renault in part exchange.
Anthony drove down to the Phoenix one Saturday in the little
Renault and, on the following day, departed for Leamington in
the 'forty-five', obviously well satisfied with what was surely
one of the more remarkable part-exchange deals. The big
Renault subsequently appeared in a number of early Vintage
events.

One of our customers, an R.A.F. Squadron Leader whose
name I have forgotten, owned two desirable motor cars, a DISS
Delage with boat-decked body and a very unusual 3-litre
Belgian S.A.V.A. of 1914. We were instrumental in selling the
latter car to an early Club member named Aubrey Birks.
Aubrey became a particular friend of mine who, alas, failed
to survive the war. In 1939 he joined the mercantile marine
and became a member of the crew of a petrol tanker which, as a
result of enemy action, was subsequently lost with all hands.

One day we discovered that our car-breaking tenants Messrs
James and Salmon had acquired for breaking up a 1914 Alfonso
Hispano-Suiza. Nowadays it seems inconceivable that, even in
the mid 1930s, such a car should come to such an end, but it
would undoubtedly have perished had we not purchased it for a
song. Having restored it, we sold this car for £35 to the
late Forrest Lycett, famous for his exploits in his equally
famous 8-litre Bentley,[2] painting the car in his special livery

[1] The term 'Edwardian' is not used literally by the Club but is
used to define cars built prior to 1918. And since few cars were
built in England after 1914, it commonly applies to cars of the
pre-first war era.
[2] In 1959, Forrest, at the age of 74, achieved a speed of over 140
m.p.h. for the flying kilometre, driving his 8-litre Bentley on a
road near Antwerp.

of black with cerise mudguards. Forrest won the Edwardian class in the first Club event in which he entered the Hispano, although both the driver and ourselves were somewhat dismayed when a wheel flew off the car just as it crossed the finishing line. The hubs all had right-hand threads and the security of the wheels depended on a ratchet locking device in the hub nuts; since this proved to be unreliable, it was subsequently modified.

John and I soon found that, where modern motor cars were concerned, the repair business was dreary and unrewarding work. It was also uneconomic. All routine overhauls of such cars were the subject of standard charges based on the use of special tools and equipment as issued to specialist agents and repairers for the particular make concerned. This meant that no small business, relying on skilled hand fitting with the minimum of special equipment, could hope to compete with the specialised service depot. This state of affairs is now commonplace, but it was then a new and novel situation brought about by American methods of mass-production. It meant that, with the exception of a few modern cars belonging to regular local customers, our work became increasingly concentrated on veteran and vintage cars, or on those few high quality equivalents which continued in limited production throughout the 1930s. In the latter respect we benefited from the proximity of the new R.A.F. station at Odiham, with many of its flying officers, owning such cars as Frazer Nash or Aston Martin, becoming our customers.

In addition to the Itala, we had many interesting early cars to work on and in this connection I remember particularly the 1908 single-cylinder Sizaire Naudin and the 1904 Darracq 'flying fifteen', both then owned by Kent Karslake, which were stabled with us for some time. The former was the most wilfully eccentric motor car I have ever driven. It boasted independent front suspension, but in every other respect it was archaic, even by the standards of 1908. It had a design of differential-cum-gearbox on the back-axle of so tortuous a complexity that I will not attempt to describe it. Suffice it to say that, because it always seemed to work while we had the car, we wisely let well alone. It had a quadrant gear change which meant that, assuming the lever was in the top gear position, it was necessary to go through the intermediate gears in order to get back to bottom. Engine speed was controlled by a throttle lever on the steering column which, to the confusion of the driver, constantly changed its position as he turned the steering wheel. Finally, its designers had asserted their lofty independence from the trammels of current convention by placing the clutch pedal on the right and the brake pedal on the left. So instinctive has the orthodox become, that we found that the only safe way to drive the car was with crossed legs; otherwise the wrong pedal was invariably depressed in an emergency. To invite some experienced but unsuspecting driver to try out the Sizaire Naudin provided us with an unfailing source of amusement.

By contrast with the Sizaire, the Darracq was a most advanced car for its date, indeed I regard it as quite the best medium-powered veteran I have ever driven. With a four-cylinder T head engine in a fairly light chassis, by the standards of 1904 it really was a flyer. When we received the Darracq from Kent it had been converted to magneto ignition and the original battery ignition system was out of action. We restored the latter and found that with both systems working together (there was a choice of three sparking plug positions per cylinder) the improvement in performance was quite remarkable.

There was at this time a desperate shortage of suitable— or even unsuitable—courses on which to run speed events. The course at Aston Clinton had been so appallingly rough that it was resolved to find an alternative for the next meeting in July. The country was scoured and finally we succeeded in finding a course right on our doorstep. Sir Denzil and Lady Cope, the then owners of Bramshill House, near Hartley Wintney, agreed to allow us the use of one of their drives. Because this event was held so close to home, the Scuderia Carsoni turned out in force. Tim ran his Special and I my G.N., while John entered our Rolls Royce breakdown truck in the Edwardian class. I also drove the Flying Fifteen Darracq with Aubrey Birks as passenger and the Sizaire was likewise entered.

As may be imagined, there was a record late night session at the Phoenix on the evening following this event. With the Phoenix ablaze with light at midnight and cars being tried out down the road to Odiham, often in a highly illegal condition, it may be wondered what the local police were doing. The answer is that the local constable was not a very zealous policeman in the eyes of his superiors because he made common-sense the yardstick of his conduct rather than the petty, and often absurd, letter of the law. Consequently, evil-doers were his concern, but the sharp eye he kept cocked for the malefactor would become afflicted with blindness when confronted by the technical offender. He was the only policeman I have ever liked and admired; if there were more of his like, England would be more law-abiding than it is today and the police would enjoy better co-operation from the public in their efforts to keep the peace. We kept the garage open late, particularly at week-ends, and often when he was on night duty he would stand airing his bottom before the welcome warmth of our coke stove, gossiping or taking an intelligent interest in the unusual cars that stood around while, clearly observable through the windows, the Phoenix presented an animated scene although it was long after closing time.

In the early autumn of 1935, we retrieved my Humber from its resting place at Maidstone and I entered it in the London to Brighton Run in this and in the three succeeding years. Three times the car made a trouble free run, once with Sam Clutton as my passenger, while John Passini drove Kent Karslake's Darracq. On the fourth occasion, when I was accompanied by Aubrey Birks, we had a bitter struggle against difficulties in pouring rain. One of the rear wheel hubs split, allowing the drive shaft to rotate within it, thus causing a complete cessation of forward motion. By pushing and coasting we got the car to a garage where the hub was temporarily repaired by welding. But alas, this effort was vain for near Bolney crossroads, only twelve miles from Brighton, we came to a standstill once more, this time with ominous sounds of tortured metal coming from the back-axle. When we finally got the car home and dismantled the axle, I found that the differential had disintegrated and had to have a new set of star wheels and spindles made for it. I had never had occasion to dismantle this part of the car before and was amazed by its diminutive size and fragility, the gears resembling clockwork. In theory, one was supposed to maintain the car in precisely original condition, but I made one or two common-sense modifications such as replacing the frail bicycle type ball bearings in the front wheels by plain phosphor-bronze bushes on the model of those used on my G.N.

One morning I was surprised to receive a telephone call from Dursley. It was from the brother-in-law of a girl friend of mine there and I had known him only very slightly. 'Would you like my Vauxhall?' he asked brusquely. Taken aback, I was

a little hesitant, whereupon the distant voice said testily: 'I'm
not trying to *sell* it to you, it's yours to take away if you want it.'
So I set off for Dursley and drove my gift back to Hartley
Wintney. It was a rare model known as the 25/70 having a six-
cylinder engine with Burt and McCullum single sleeve valves
as later fitted to some Bristol aero engines. It represented an
unsuccessful attempt on the part of the English Vauxhall
company to rival the smaller Rolls Royce in the medium-
powered luxury car market. It was, in fact, the company's last
expensive fling before it was taken over by General Motors
of America. The car was fitted with a beautifully built enclosed
landaulette body by Windover and was in perfect condition
having had very little use. The reason its owner had decided
to give it away was that, after many fruitless attempts to get
the brakes to work, he had finally lost patience with it—he was
an impulsive man. The car had the same type of hydraulic
brakes as were fitted to the later 30/98 Vauxhalls. These
brakes looked most impressive and were beautifully engineered,
but when they could be made to work they did so extremely
erratically, causing the car to swerve on braking, now to one
side, now to the other, in a manner that was unpredictable and
therefore decidedly unnerving for the driver. Although in our
advertisements we boasted that the Phoenix was 'the home
of the 30/98 Vauxhall', we were completely defeated by these
brakes. When we overhauled a 30/98 of this type, we used to
consign the entire front axle assembly to the scrap heap and
fit in its stead a Delage front axle with mechanical brakes
actuated by a vacuum servo motor. It has now been found
that when fitted with modern synthetic seals the original
brakes work perfectly. In other words the trouble was entirely
due to the porosity of the leather seals which were the only
type available before the war.

Unlike the 30/98s which passed through our hands, the
25/70 retained its original front axle and we relied mainly
on the handbrake which actuated the shoes on the rear wheels
only. We made the car a garage hack, fitting it with a drawbar to suit a towbar or our car-carrying trailer. This may
sound an unkind fate, but in extenuation it must be said that
the car, though a rarity, was also something of a white elephant.
Although capable of a fair turn of speed, it behaved in a
ponderous fashion, its unusual engine emitting a subdued but
curious sound like the whirr of a sewing machine. My most
memorable experience with the 25/70 Vauxhall began with a

telephone call one dark December evening. It was from one of my Vintage Club friends named John Morley. He explained that his 12/60 Alvis had broken down as he was coming down the Great North Road and he had parked it in a wayside garage. Would I drive over to his home near Welwyn, stay the night, and help him tow the Alvis home next day? It was not until I set out to drive to Welwyn in the 25/70, equipped with a tow bar, that I realised that John had not told me, and I had omitted to ask, the precise whereabouts of the car we were to rescue on the morrow. When I learned on arrival that it was at Scotch Corner, I was somewhat disconcerted, as this meant a round trip of something like 300 miles, and I was even more daunted by the prospect when we awoke next morning to find that snow had fallen, snow that became progressively deeper as we proceeded northwards. There were no prompt remedial measures such as gritting or salting in those days, so that the going was decidedly tricky, particularly in a heavy car with effective braking on the rear wheels only. But at least there was very little traffic on the move, such cars or lorries as there were seemed either to have skidded into ditches or to be stationary beside the road. However, the old 25/70 whirred along steadily and we eventually reached Scotch Corner, hitched the Alvis on the towbar, and started the long trek southwards. Approaching Stamford after darkness had fallen it started to snow again heavily. But at least I was in a closed car whereas John was steering an open sports car with no hood and without even the benefit of engine heat. I began to wonder uneasily whether the Alvis would suddenly veer off the road as a sign that its occupant had gone to sleep as people are said to do who fall into snow drifts as a preliminary to freezing to death. But every time I stopped to clear my windscreen of snow I was relieved to see him grinning broadly, looking exactly like an animated snowman. How John managed to survive that long ordeal I do not know. Incidentally he, like me, still owns the same Alvis to this day.

Another memorable experience of these years was the affair of the Captain, the beautiful damsel and the Rolls Royce. The Captain was a car dealer, but no ordinary one. Only thirty-seven miles from London and on a trunk road, we were within the orbit of London car dealers looking for country suckers. Seedy and furtive in appearance, they were so transparently dishonest that we found them rather pathetic. We used to call them the Mews Rats. The only thing the Captain shared with this fraternity was dishonesty, though his was by no means transparent. He dealt only in Rolls Royces and radiated well-bred affluence and bonhomous charm. He was a very plausible character indeed. He was greatly helped by the fact that he had cut quite a figure at Brooklands for many years and in this way had become acquainted with Tim Carson. He disdained what he regarded as the lesser breeds of motor car and whenever he was forced to accept one in part exchange for a Rolls Royce, Tim allowed him to park it in a field behind our garage. The Captain's taste in women was as extravagant and exclusive as his taste in cars. Moreover, he demanded quantity and variety as well as quality. Most week-ends would find him at stud at his cottage near Camberley. When planning one of these illicit week-ends he would run his eye down the trade advertisements for second-hand Rolls Royces in the motoring papers, pick out the most desirable car, ring up the dealer concerned, and arrange to take it away for the week-end 'for demonstration to a client'. His winning ways were such that he invariably got away with this.

One Monday at noon the Captain swept on to our garage forecourt driving a magnificent Phantom II Rolls Royce with a young woman whose beauty and elegance matched the car. 'Dear old boy,' said he in his fruitiest voice, 'I wonder if you would do me a tremendous favour by driving this car back to London for me. I have another urgent appointment.' The opportunity to drive such an opulent carriage was irresistible, so I agreed and hopped into the back seat without more ado. I found myself reclining in the comfort of the finest Bedford cord and surrounded by fittings and what-nots of ivory and silver. The car, I was given to understand, had been specially built to the order of some eastern potentate who had never taken delivery. Perhaps he had been deposed or assassinated. We drove to the Captain's cottage. 'Go and get your things, my dear', said he, whereupon he flung himself on his back in the cockpit with his head beneath the dashboard and I realised that he was reconnecting the speedometer drive cable. Thus the car would not divulge the true mileage it had covered in his hands. When he had completed this task and emerged looking more red in the face than usual, his companion came tripping down the path from the cottage carrying a small week-end case. It was at this moment that I realised that I was not only to return the car but the lady as well. He gave me the address of a large and well-known firm of Rolls Royce agents in west

London to whom I was to deliver the car. 'But what about your friend?' I inquired. 'Oh, don't you worry about her', he replied, 'I'll fix all that.' So, somewhat mystified, I headed the Phantom II towards London.

I enjoyed that drive. John and I each drew a salary of only £3 a week from the business, so I also enjoyed the experience of masquerading for a brief hour as a rich and fortunate tycoon. I exchanged few words with my passenger beyond asking if I could drive her to her home. 'Oh no, thank you,' was her response, 'the garage will do', a reply which I found slightly disquieting. As we rolled silently to a standstill at traffic lights on the Great West Road I found myself gazing down with an air of remote disdain at the little cars drawn up beside me, receiving in return envious glances that appraised the car and the beautiful woman beside me. It was obvious that, to a world that worshipped material things, we represented the ultimate status symbol; the pipe-dream of every suburban male. Yet if these lesser mortals had only known it I was becoming increasingly apprehensive the nearer we approached our destination. If only I had been told to drop the girl off somewhere before returning the car I should not have been so worried. What would my reception be if I arrived at the agents with her sitting beside me? Surely they would realise that the Captain's 'demonstration' was completely phoney? I began to suspect that I had been had for a mug, that the 'urgent appointment' was a pure fiction and that, by using the bait of a drive on this magnificent vehicle, the Captain had lured me into facing the music instead of himself.

When we eventually drove majestically into the agent's large covered garage I thought for a moment that my worst fears were to be realised. For, on seeing our approach, a man who was standing in the garage turned about and made a hurried bee-line for the office. He is certainly going to phone for the police, I thought, but no; the same individual presently emerged bearing an enormous bouquet of flowers wrapped in cellophane. Opening the car door, he presented these to the lady with a slight bow and a beaming smile. 'With the Captain's compliments', he said. He then ushered her into a waiting taxi, summoned, of course, on instructions from the Captain, in which, with a charming smile and a wave, my fair companion instantly departed. As for me, I might not have existed. No questions were asked and I was left to make my way by public transport to Waterloo. The moral of this story was plain to me.

It was that provided you have sufficient effrontery and *savoir faire* you can get away with murder.

Shortly after this episode, the Captain suddenly disappeared to some unknown destination abroad. No sooner had he performed this vanishing trick than a gloomy business man from Birmingham arrived at the Phoenix and became even gloomier as he surveyed the tired collection of second-hand cars which represented all that the Captain had left behind him. This individual had, it transpired, been induced to invest £5,000 in the Captain's Rolls Royce business of which these cars were now the only remaining asset. He instructed Tim to sell them for what they would fetch, which was not much, and departed a sadder but wiser man.

An altogether more reputable friend of Tim's to whom I took a great liking was Clive Windsor-Richards. Clive was a great 30/98 Vauxhall exponent who owned two of these cars, a special two-seater which he frequently raced at Brooklands— I accompanied him to the Track as mechanic on one occasion— and a rare saloon model which he used regularly on the road. On several occasions Tim, Clive and I attended B.R.D.C. dinners and film shows in London, driving up in the 30/98 saloon. Clive was a fast, fearless and supremely competent driver and these expeditions used to be a little frightening at times, particularly on the Great West Road which then had no central reservation. We used to meet the rush-hour traffic pouring out of London sometimes four or five abreast. On sighting such an approaching phalanx, Clive used to curse under his breath, switch on his big headlamps and drive straight at them. I would shut my eyes at this point, but it was surprising how quickly those cars contrived to scuttle back to their own side of the central white line.

It was with Clive at the wheel that I first experienced a speed of a 100 m.p.h. on the road. This was in a special short chassis 38/250 Mercedes with what was termed the 'elephant' blower on occasion when we were lucky to get a clear road over Hartford Bridge Flats. What with the bellow of the exhaust, the scream of the supercharger and the roar of the wind over the open cock-pit, it was a stirring display of brute force, though by no means so impressive as the sensation of effortless power which one got from a big Edwardian such as the Itala. With this Mercedes, on the contrary, the sense of effort was positively demonic. Nevertheless, this was a memorable experience for although such speeds are now within the capability of quite ordinary saloon cars, in the 1930s, 100 m.p.h. was still a magical figure so far as road cars were concerned.

After one of his trips abroad, we were presented by the racing driver Charles Brackenbury with an unusual firework. Instead of the usual blue touch paper, two thin copper wires emerged from the top of it. We were instructed to position this firework under the bonnet of a car, attach one wire to a plug terminal and the other to earth, and then stand back and watch the effect. We treasured this device for some time before we decided upon a suitable candidate for the experiment. He was the proud owner of a very beautiful 4½-litre Bentley. It was painted British racing green and had little Union Jack emblems on its sides. He used to drive this car down from London at a very sedate speed wearing whiter-than-white racing overalls and white helmet with a similarly attired girl friend seated beside him. Arrived at the Phoenix, he would park the car as conspicuously as possible in front of the door, stroll into the bar and behave in what we thought an insufferably superior fashion. Such conduct, we decided, was not in the true spirit of the V.S.C.C. so, on one occasion when this individual was holding forth in the bar, John and I duly fixed our infernal device beneath the bonnet of the Bentley. We then joined the admiring throng inside who had been informed privily that some mischief was afoot. When he announced his departure, our friend was obviously flattered by the fact that everyone trooped out to see him off. He and his girl friend clambered into the cockpit. He adjusted his helmet with care, drew on his string-backed racing gloves and pressed the starter button. Immediately there was a tremendous report followed by a strange whistling sound, while thick black smoke seeped out through the bonnet louvres. This whistling noise continued for some time while the occupants of the car sat wide-eyed and petrified. Then there was a second loud bang and silence. It was some time before the owner could be persuaded to open the bonnet, such was his fear of the ruin that would be revealed. This despite the fact that no internal combustion engine could ever produce a succession of noises so farcical that it was extremely difficult to maintain an expression of suitable gravity. Our victim took the point; he abandoned his ostentatious ways and afterwards became a valued member of the club.

In 1935, accompanied by Tim Carson, I paid my first visit

to France to see the Circuit de Dieppe. The last motor race to be run on that circuit, Alfa Romeos of the Scuderia Ferrari filled the first two places in the hands of Chiron and Dreyfus. Tim and I also went to see the 1937 Donnington Grand Prix in which the German Mercedes and Auto Union racing cars competed. All who were fortunate enough to see this race agree that it was the most spectacular and thrilling motoring event ever to be organised in this country. Certainly it was an experience which I shall never forget. It was chiefly made memorable for me by the inspired driving of the winner, that legendary figure Tazio Nuvolari driving an Auto Union, a car that was comparatively strange to him and was obviously a handful. To see the Donnington course today and compare it with the racing circuits currently in use is to marvel that such powerful cars, developing over 600 h.p., could ever have raced each other on such a narrow and twisting road so beset with hazards. Modern racing cars may be faster, largely due to incomparably better handling and road holding, but the sheer power of these German monsters and the skill required to control them made a spectacle which can never be surpassed.

At this time the lack of suitable courses on which to stage speed events continued to exercise the minds of the members of the V.S.C.C. Bramshill was a 'once only' event and the next meetings were held on a flat stretch of new 'unadopted' concrete road which had been constructed to serve a new housing estate at Littlestone-on-Sea. All the courses we had so far used had been more or less flat and therefore rather dull. What the new club really needed was a speed hill climb course like Shelsley Walsh. But we could not use Shelsley because it was the exclusive preserve of the Midlands Automobile Club. In this dilemma I bethought me of the drive up to Prescott House, only a mile away from my home. Some years before, this house had been owned by an elderly couple named Royds who were friends of my parents and I had welcomed any excuse to visit them in my G.N. because motoring up their drive was such an exciting exercise. The house stood high on a hillside above the public road and its approach drive wound this way and that in order to ease the gradient for the horse carriages for which it had been designed. It included one hairpin bend so acute that it could not be negotiated on one lock and I used to get my G.N. round by sliding the tail, a process made much easier by the absence of a differential combined with a loose and dusty surface. In view of the fact

that this and other corners were made completely blind by
dense shrubberies, it was perhaps fortunate that the Royds
owned no car and that, in this part of Gloucestershire, trades-
men's delivery vans were extremely rare. Otherwise these
sporting ascents might have been marred by some disconcerting
confrontations.

Early in 1937 I learnt that Prescott House was empty and
that the estate had been bought as a speculation by the Gloucestershire Dairy Company of Cheltenham. This seemed to bring the
prospect of acquiring Prescott for a speed hill-climb within the
bounds of possibility, so one fine Sunday morning after the
May Shelsley meeting I led a small party thither which included
Forrest Lycett, Sam Clutton and Tim Carson. After they had
driven up the hill in their several cars, they pronounced it
distinctly promising provided it could be widened and re-
surfaced.

While Sam Clutton and Kent Karslake investigated the
possibility of floating a company to acquire the property on
behalf of the Club, I obtained an estimate for the necessary
work on the road from a Mr Stokes of the Beaufort Quarries in
Dean Forest with whom I had been put in touch by my friend
Mark Newth. Mr Stokes was enthusiastic about the project
and his estimate was extremely reasonable. So far, so good,
but it was reluctantly though wisely decided that the scheme
was too ambitious for a small and youthful club to undertake.
It was Sam Clutton who saved the day. He knew that the
wealthier and more established Bugatti Owners Club were as
dissatisfied as we were with Aston Clinton and were looking for
some other course to take its place. He proposed that he should
divulge our Prescott scheme to Eric Giles of the B.O.C. on
condition that, if his Club brought it to fruition, the V.S.C.C.
would be permitted to hold one meeting a year on the new
hill. This was agreed by the committee of the V.S.C.C., which
used to meet in Forrest Lycett's house in London and of which
I was then a member. Things now began to move fast. In
August I received a letter from Eric Giles and put him in touch
with Holborow of the Gloucestershire Dairy Company and with
Stokes of the Beaufort Quarries. Eric Giles and his brother
bought the estate on behalf of the B.O.C. and the Beaufort
Quarry Company set to work on the hill to such purpose that
by the following spring it was ready for racing. A small
informal party was held to celebrate the opening of Prescott
at which those present were each allowed to make a timed ascent

of the hill. Many of the drivers and cars who took part in this celebration are now no more, but it is interesting that three drivers are still driving the same cars today that they drove then. They are Sam Clutton, Itala; Ronnie Symondson, Bugatti and myself in my 12/50 Alvis.

Meanwhile, John and I decided to build a special sprint car more worthy of the Phoenix Green Garage than my old G.N. Like all good 'special' builders at this time, we made no working drawings, though I did go so far as to produce a general outline of the proposed car on a drawing board, re-shaping it by eye until I judged that it 'looked right'. This 'Phoenix Special' consisted of the rear half of my G.N. married to the front half of a Bugatti. It was fitted with a 1½-litre Brescia Bugatti engine supercharged at 20 lbs p.s.i. by a large Roots blower and running on dope fuel. We took crude but effective precautions to prevent the cylinder block from being blown off the crankcase as a result of the excessive pressure generated within. We designed and built the car entirely ourselves, the only exception being the single-seater bodywork. We made the light metal framework for this but prevailed upon two professional panel beaters from Windovers to come and fill in the spaces with light aluminium sheeting. The way those craftsmen shaped the curving panels of the tail was a joy to watch. The finished article was no string-and-sealing-wax special but, for the period, a very business-like looking racing car. It was painted black and it bore on its front cowling our badge of the phoenix rising from the flames. Unfortunately, however, it did not fulfil the promise of its looks although it might have done so had not the war supervened. As it was, its racing career was extremely brief. Our garage was commandeered during the war and not surprisingly, by the time it was over, the Phoenix Special, which had been stored in the paint shop under lock and key, had disappeared without trace.

To have run such a car on the road at Hartley Wintney would have been too much even for the accommodating local constable, so it was completely untried when it made its début at Prescott. On my first practice run, I left the starting line in an exhilarating burst of acceleration and torrent of sound. But gratification soon turned to despair when, after covering a mere fifty yards, the engine suddenly cut out completely and there was a humiliating silence. The car was coasting to a standstill when my head was jerked back as the engine suddenly burst into full song once more. Then it fell silent again and so I proceeded up the hill in a series of fits and starts. The explanation was simple. Running on dope fuel, the car needed an excessively large main jet in the carburettor. This jet was actually larger than the aperture of the needle valve which admitted fuel to the carburettor float chamber. Consequently, the engine took one large gulp of fuel and then waited for the float chamber to fill up again, just as one waits impatiently for some tardy lavatory cistern to refill after it has been flushed. Testing the engine on the bench under a light throttle, this elementary fault had never manifested itself.

This defect was easily cured, but there were other troubles of a much more fundamental kind. The rear half of my old G.N. strongly resented the unprecedented amount of power it was asked by the front half to transmit. The back axle whipped alarmingly, particularly when getting away from the starting line, and this caused the driving chains to ride up on the sprockets with a most disquieting ticking sound. We fitted heavier and stronger chains, but in vain. What was really needed was a central bearing on the axle. Although we subsequently ran the car at Prescott as well as at Lewes and Poole, I don't think I ever crossed a finishing line without disgorging a broken chain somewhere on the course, thus depriving me of one or other vital gear ratio. Moreover, that ominous sound of protesting chains from the rear made me instinctively ease my foot from the throttle. Thus, from memory, the best time the car ever made at Prescott was in the region of 54 seconds, whereas the record for the hill was already well down into the forties. Nevertheless, despite this serious fault, which we could have overcome had time allowed, the Phoenix Special was immensely satisfying to drive. It was the first really potent car I had driven, it handled beautifully and, because we had designed and built it ourselves, it was the source of more satisfaction to me than any 'off the peg' racing car, however fierce, could ever have been. Nowadays, when Prescott Hill climb is as renowned as Shelsley Walsh and earnest young men in full racing fig drive up the hill at dizzy velocity with immense expertise, I look back with a certain nostalgia to those happy-go-lucky, regulation-free days before the war when one jumped into a car and drove up the hill without even bothering to put on a pair of goggles, let alone a crash helmet.

This account of life at the Phoenix Green Garage must

suggest that it was all play and very little work. This was very far from the case. The garage was open long hours for seven days of the week and at one time we tried the experiment of remaining open day and night. As we only employed one mechanic for most of the time, John and I could never leave the garage together but took it in turns to attend Vintage events and other spare-time activities. Though we did much work that was interesting, there was a lot of pretty dull routine work to be got through as well. For example, I took it upon myself to keep the books and send out the monthly accounts, a task I found most uncongenial and one calling for great self-discipline, particularly when there were interesting things going on in the yard outside the little office.

We learned a great deal about the seamier side of garage life. Very soon after we set up in business, a chauffeur-driven car belonging to an elderly local lady drew up at our petrol pumps. The chauffeur asked for four gallons, saying in a lordly fashion that he always got his petrol here and that when he asked for four gallons we should book six to his mistress and split the ill-gotten gain with him. When told in no uncertain terms that he had come to the wrong shop, he strode away in high dudgeon, vowing he would take his business elsewhere. Fortunately for us, however, he got the sack shortly afterwards and the business returned to us, though whether his employer had found him out we never knew for certain.

Getting in the accounts was another constant worry. The local farmers, I am sorry to say, were the worst payers. One of these offenders, when at last he did pay up, used to delight in knocking off the odd shillings and pence from the account. I must confess that if this customer's account amounted to—say—£12 18s. 6d. I would contrive to increase it by one pound. Thus he was given the pleasure of knocking off 18s. 6d, little knowing that he was making a payment that was slightly over the odds. Nevertheless, despite gruelling work and long hours, despite the fact that we failed to make money, our accountant warning us each year that we were under capitalised and were what he termed 'over trading', on the whole these were happy and memorable years. Best of all, they brought me many friendships which I have valued ever since.

# Chapter 12

# Anna

THE previous chapter may have given the impression that from the moment I first visited the Phoenix in the early spring of 1934 my mind became totally absorbed by motor cars. Although the Phoenix Green Garage and the V.S.C.C. activities that were closely associated with it certainly claimed the lion's share of my time, this was not so. Throughout my life I have admired people of catholic taste and liberal intellect and have felt a strange antipathy towards any specialist, even though he might be capable of doing some one thing superlatively well. Only the discovery that a specialist was what I may term a bridge-builder, that he took an intelligent interest in subjects or skills that appeared to be divorced from, or only remotely connected with, his specialism, could induce me wholeheartedly to admire his particular expertise. Such discoveries of unexpected diversity, either in people themselves or in their writings, have always been a particular source of delight to me. In short, I have always abhorred the one-track mind and have therefore instinctively resisted any tendency to become one-track minded myself. One of the few remembered books from my childhood, Robert Louis Stevenson's *A Child's Garden of Verses*, contains the little jingle:

> 'The world is so full of a number of things
> I'm sure we should all be as happy as kings'.

It has always stayed in my mind. I think these simple lines contain a truth which, later in my life, I was to find much more profoundly and eloquently expressed by Thomas Traherne in the *Centuries*. Traherne resolved to spend his life in search of happiness, but the modern world has changed the meaning of that word. What Stevenson and Traherne meant was a purposeful quest for felicity and not an aimless, hedonistic and, in the last analysis, fruitless pursuit of pleasure. The world is so filled with riches and life is so brief that to spend it locked away in one small compartment has always seemed to me criminal folly.

In a world of professionalism, a world that venerates specialists who know more and more about less and less, this is an unfashionable view. Consequently I am often regarded as a Jack-of-all-trades with the inevitable uncomplimentary corollary. Also, because I tend to veer away from any interest once I feel there is a risk of its becoming obsessive, or so demanding as to threaten the overthrow of my mental balance, I am sometimes thought a mere dilettante lacking purpose and tenacity. This has never worried me very much. For I believe that no worldly interest should gain such power over a man that he has not the strength of mind to break free from it. Such an inability is often egotistical. An undertaking begun out of a genuinely disinterested concern can all too easily become, by insensible degrees, a little dunghill on which we delight to crow and flap our wings. The individual identifies himself with the project and his unwillingness to step down in favour of others becomes no longer a matter of selfless concern, but is due to a reluctance to forgo the petty sense of power and authority which he feels he has acquired. Too often in this imperfect world, human organisations founded with the worthiest aims become little empires for frustrated egos.

Happily, as I stressed in the last chapter, the Vintage Sports Car Club has never taken this sorry course, perhaps because of the breadth of mind of its members. Nevertheless, most of those members did not live with motor cars to the extent that I did, so that I felt an urgent need for diversity to restore the balance.

In another way the impression created by the last chapter may be misleading. For, if the truth be told, I found the ambience of the Phoenix in some ways strangely disturbing. So close to London and bordering the great trunk road to the west of England, the immediate district was to my mind, neither true town nor true country but a mixture of both that I found wholly uncongenial. From the scrub oaks on the common land not a hundred yards from our garage, on still nights in early summer there would come the sound of a chorus of nightingales. Yet their voices had to compete against the fretful roar of cars and lorries. For already the A30 was carrying a volume of traffic that far exceeded its capacity,

particularly at holiday times. At summer week-ends streams
of cars would pour out of London nose to tail like so many
lemmings racing for the sea. And because the road was too
narrow and most of the cars were small modern saloons with
chronic unroadworthiness built into them, there were all too
many horrible accidents. Our old Rolls Royce would have to
pull the ghastly wrecks apart, looking like crumpled and
bloody sardine cans. And meanwhile there would be a hubbub
of activity in the brightly lit bars of the Phoenix; a blue haze
of cigarette smoke, laughter and the clink of glasses; the
mingled voices of men and girls competing with the sound of
the radiogram playing Louis Armstrong or Duke Ellington or
the latest jazz hit, 'These Foolish Things' or 'Night and Day'.
Then, through the open door would come the throaty exhaust
note of some car engine starting up and the sickly-sweet smell
of Castrol 'R' would come seeping in to mingle with the
scarcely less cloying perfume of the women.

All this added up to something feverish and fretful, it had an
ominous quality which used to fill me with foreboding. Such a
hectic party must surely be followed by some dreadful morning
after. For this was the period of the rise of the great dictators
and although I never had the time or the inclination to read
the newspapers, like everyone else, I could not fail to be
conscious of the ominous thunder clouds that were gathering
over Europe however much we tried to reassure ourselves that
such a storm would never break. A verse of *1919*, one of my
favourite poems by Yeats, used often to be running in my mind
at this time:

> 'Now days are dragon-ridden, the nightmare
> Rides upon sleep: a drunken soldiery
> Can leave the mother, murdered at her door,
> To crawl in her own blood, and go scot-free;
> The night can sweat with terror as before
> We pieced our thoughts into philosophy,
> And planned to bring the world under a rule,
> Who are but weasels fighting in a hole.'

But it was not only in Europe that signs of coming storm
were appearing. In reaction against a Conservative 'establishment' most of the intellectual young men of my generation held
decidedly left-wing views. Several whom I knew went to
Spain to join the International Brigade in its fight against

Franco and one of them never returned. On the other hand, the second mechanic whom we engaged latterly, a pleasant, open-faced farmer's son from Dorset, was a member of the British Union of Fascists. He had been lured by the B.U.F.'s specious agricultural policy, a hook baited to catch such honest but simple men as he, and he proudly wore his Union badge of an encircled lightning flash. In the lunch hour, we would find him sitting on the bench reading *Action* and occasionally, when he went off to London of an evening to police some B.U.F. meeting, we used to tease him unmercifully. 'Got your rubber truncheon?', we would ask and, as he drove off, we would shout 'Heil!', click our heels and give him the Fascist salute. His response to this light-hearted badinage was frightening. His normally placid and kindly face would harden and his eyes blaze with anger. It was indeed no laughing matter.

For my part, I had no time for politics, extreme or moderate, left or right. It was not that I was indifferent but rather that, to my way of thinking, the policies of both left and right appeared equally inadequate and misguided. For a brief period at Stoke-on-Trent I had held Socialist views, but experience had soon disabused my mind on that score. Now, whenever politicians spoke of 'the workers' or 'the working class' I would remember the fate of those men who had worked beside me at Kerr Stuarts. With the alarmingly rapid growth of big business—the motor industry was only one example—the increasingly impersonal and powerful commercial world of the 'right' was robbing such men of their only real asset and source of true satisfaction—their skill—by substituting machines for men in the interests of mass production. This, and many other changes which I deplored, the waste, the ugliness, the deterioration of standards, was coming about because the whole industrial system was increasingly dominated, not by people who understood the men who made its wheels go round, but by economists and accountants. Blinded by figures, they were unable to see that their financial logic made brutal nonsense in human and natural terms when translated into action.

So much for my view of the 'right'. For the apostles of the 'left' I had even less time. For they appeared to think that they had only to take over the commercial machine of the 'right' and operate it in the sacred name of the State and hey presto! all the ills of modern industrial society would disappear. This so-called solution appeared to me to be ridiculously naïve and simplistic and at the same time highly dangerous. I had learned to hate commercial power, but at least, so long as it was divorced from Government, there existed two opposing forces and in that balance of power there seemed to lie what little was left of individual freedom and hope. But let the two amalgamate and the result would be an all powerful State, a monster beyond any individual power to control, a prospect which I dreaded. For it seemed to me that such a State would possess, in a vastly magnified form, all the faults of the huge commercial empire and none of its few remaining virtues. The economist would not be de-throned and the working man would be worse off than before under such a State system. So when Socialists held forth to me about 'the workers', I was not impressed. Some were Oxbridge intellectuals whose heads were filled with abstract political theory and dogma yet were completely ignorant of the class they claimed to champion, having never dirtied their hands or eaten fish and chips out of a newspaper in their lives. Those who had a working class background seemed of that jumped-up sort such as my mates at Kerr Stuarts had despised. Claiming to be plain men speaking for their fellows, they were in fact insufferably arrogant in their dress of brief authority and greedy for power. My arch enemy was that 'funding system' which William Cobbett hated and my views at this time were a mixture of old-fashioned radicalism, distributism and social-credit.

I managed to do quite a lot of reading although the demands of the garage were such that most of it had to be done in bed at night. Among the books that impressed and influenced me were H. J. Massingham's *Shepherd's Country*, which my mother had given me, and Aldous Huxley's *Brave New World*. Massingham's book is an elegy on the traditional rural culture of the Cotswold country, then perishing under the brutal impact of an urban and industrial society and now quite dead. It so impressed me that I read all his subsequent books. Massingham, who was later to become my friend, was fair game for those who believed in a technological utopia because he was inclined to overstate his case. Yet he continued to make that case to the end of his life with passionate eloquence and conviction and, had he lived, he would have found that the present confirmed his gloomiest predictions. At least Massingham was in a class apart from those authors of cosy country books who wrote as though there had never been an Industrial Revolution and the English countryside was the same as it had always been. For this 'There'll always be an England' school I felt nothing but contempt. As for *Brave New World*, I thought it quite brilliant. It seemed to me to portray the kind of future to which I felt that industrial man was heading. Of all the prose writers of the period, it was Huxley who most appealed to me. He revealed in his writing precisely the type of wide-ranging liberal intellect that I most admired and which I felt that an over-specialised age so sorely needed. When his *Ends and Means* was published in 1938 I at once procured a copy and found it equally stimulating and thought-provoking. Unlike other artists and intellectuals, Huxley did not subscribe to any facile political dogma, nor did he run away from the crucial problems posed by the march of science and technology by pursuing art for art's sake. I was later to admire the work of Arthur Koestler for the same reason. The Severn novels of Francis Brett Young were the only works of fiction which I remember reading with great pleasure, partly because they were set in country that I knew well and emphasised the contrast between the Black Country and the familiar landscape of the Welsh Border. They were weak in characterisation, but I thought, and still think, that his descriptions of landscape, of weather and season are masterly evocations. Brett Young obviously had a deep love and understanding for the country he described, otherwise he could never have distilled its essential quality and beauty so faithfully. Because technology has now alienated us from a natural world whose beauty and diversity it is rapidly obliterating, regional writing of this order no longer exists because it is no longer possible. They cannot write about Eden who have never experienced it.

One of my ex-school friends, visiting the ballet for the first time and asked what he thought about it, replied: 'Oh it was just a lot of bloody pansy boys with gold tits prancing about.' I, too, was not untouched by this characteristically Philistine attitude to the arts which a public school education had engendered. All artistic activities were considered 'cissy' and to indulge in them was something almost as shameful as masturbation. Thus my own attitude to the arts at the time I went to the garage was a curious love-hate relationship, ambivalent and even hypocritical. I still delighted in poetry, but I read it secretly in my room at night and divulged this activity to no one. My partner John Passini was of mixed English and Austrian parentage and had spent his youth in Vienna. With this background, he had no such inhibitions and was a frank devotee of classical music, opera and ballet. He used to play classical records on the radiogram in our cottage of an evening. He particularly admired the music of Stravinsky and now that I fully share that admiration it seems extraordinary that his record of the *Firebird* should have seemed to me then no more than a discordant and incomprehensible noise. I suppose this was because I subconsciously resisted any attempt to understand or appreciate it. John often went to the opera at Covent Garden and when Colonel de Basil brought the Russian Ballet company to London it drew him as surely as a magnet and I was left in charge of the garage night after night. I did not resent this; let him indulge his odd whim, I thought, though now I bitterly regret a lost opportunity. But this inhibited resistance to the arts was soon to be broken down with far-reaching results. The agent of this change was a woman whom I will call Anna with whom I had an affair at this time.

Although my association with Anna was of comparatively brief duration, when I look back on the first thirty years of my life I can think of no single person other than Kyrle Willans who had a greater influence upon its course than she did. In many ways she was a most remarkable woman, unforgettable both in appearance and personality. Although she was small and slight she had that mysteriously magnetic quality which, for want of a better word, we call presence. She was not in any way ostentatious and yet one sensed the moment she entered some crowded room that everyone present, women as well as men, had become instantly aware of her. This quality was the more remarkable because, although she carried her head proudly, almost arrogantly, and all her movements were naturally graceful, she was not beautiful in any conventional sense. She had high and prominent cheekbones, her dark hair was Eton-cropped, which lent her a boyish appearance, and although she had fine eyes, dark and expressive, her mouth and chin were ugly. Yet somehow these defective features, by eliminating any suggestion of mere prettiness, added great character to her face. She possessed the most beautiful hands. Small and long-fingered but capable, they were more like miniature man's hands in the way they revealed their bone structure and their veining. Of this last attribute she was not unaware, for she never made the mistake of gilding the lily by loading her fingers or wrists with elaborate jewellery. There was no need for such artifice.

Anna was ten years older than I was and far more sophisticated and worldly-wise. It would be more truthful to say that it was she who had an affair with me rather than I with her, though precisely why she should have picked on me of all people is something that will always remain a mystery to me. I can say this without false modesty for at this time, to anyone of the opposite sex, I must have seemed a very uncouth, gauche, untidy and unattractive young man. By a kind of inverted snobbery with which I was then afflicted it had become almost a point of honour with me not to appear 'smart'; not to betray any sort of pride in my personal appearance. My finger-nails were in perpetual mourning and my hands in-grained as a result of delving in the innards of elderly motor cars. My grease-spotted flannel trousers hung perpetually at half-mast. Like many of the Vintage fraternity in those early days, my pride was reserved for my cars. Had I spared for myself a fraction of the care and attention I lavished on them, my appearance might have been more prepossessing. Moreover, although I had some sexual experience by this time, I was still very much a man's man who found the exclusive company of the opposite sex an almost totally inhibiting embarrassment. Women seemed to me to inhabit a different world in which I could find no area of common interest, and since I have never been capable of carrying on a polite conversation about triviali-ties, in their company I would soon lapse into morose silence. For this, as for my attitude towards the arts, I believe the ethics instilled into me at my public school were responsible.

No closed communities of monks and nuns could have been more strictly segregated than were the boys of Cheltenham College and the girls of the neighbouring ladies college in my day. In the 'pie-jaw' that all boys customarily received from their housemasters on the eve of their confirmation, we were led to believe that sex was something shameful, a purely male indulgence which no 'nice' girl could conceivably enjoy. We were told always to respect and honour such nice girls, remembering the pain and suffering which our own mothers had endured in bringing us into the world. The result was that I left school with the fixed idea that any girl of my own class with whom I might have formed a normal relationship based on common interest and friendship was strictly taboo and un-touchable. Consequently, I sought the company of working-class girls with whom, unlike their menfolk who were my workmates, I could find nothing whatever in common. In these circumstances, physical intimacy seemed just as self-indulgent and shameful as I had been led to suppose it would be and as, indeed, it was. Such encounters used to leave me riddled with guilt.

In my attitude to the arts and to sex, therefore, my school days had tied some pretty complicated and firm knots in my psyche and I am eternally grateful to Anna for the fact that she unravelled them with such complete success. She was bi-sexual and was thus equally attractive to members of either sex. She had a masculine cast of mind which was capable of regarding the foibles and flirtations of her own sex with amused and ironic objectivity. This was the reason, I now believe, why I, who had never felt truly at ease when alone with a woman before, now found her friendship so enriching and enjoyable. I never felt constrained by the so-called 'sex war' but was always perfectly contented and at ease. I was never in love with her nor she with me; it was the absence of this frequently agonising emotional tension that made our friendship so intimate and so free from constraint. Nor was there anything cold-hearted about our physical relationship. In this, apart from a completely uninhibited enjoyment, she was wholly feminine. That a friendship so close should express itself in such a passionate way seemed entirely natural and logical. Anna showed me that, when two people are completely *en rapport* as we were, there can never be any feeling that one partner is using the other merely to gratify an appetite. In this way any sense of shame or guilt I might have felt was effectually exorcised. She also taught me that, given infinite finesse and consideration on both sides, physical love can become itself a form of art and a most subtle means of self-expression and communication. I count myself extremely fortunate to have been taught such lessons by so able a mistress, for the tragedy is that they can so seldom be learnt without causing misery or heartache to others, often inflicting permanent psychological damage in the process.

What was more important in the light of my future, Anna very soon drew the psychological cork which had hitherto bottled up my artistic inclinations. She regarded with amused tolerance the peculiar motoring activities at the Phoenix, particularly the women who were to be found in the bar at week-ends. They had driven down from London with their men-folk in a manner less romantic than that portrayed by Sir Osbert Sitwell, suffering agonies of discomfort from a combination of hard suspension, buffeting wind, exhaust fumes and tearing noise, only to find themselves huddled in a corner of the Phoenix while the men clustered round the bar talking unintelligibly about blowers and compression ratios or laughing uproariously at some strange joke. Anna had little time for all this, though she did come away with me in the Alvis for a brief but memorable holiday one fine September. We stayed at Chipping Campden, motoring to and from Stratford-on-Avon to visit the Memorial Theatre.

School had not only implanted in me the notion that a liking for art was cissy, but had done its best to put me off Shakespeare for good and all. It did this not only by forcing me to learn long passages by heart before I was of an age to appreciate or even understand them but, like the rest of the school, by making me attend compulsory special matinees of Shakespeare at the Cheltenham Opera House. These performances were decidedly second-rate. On one occasion in *King Richard II*, owing to a sudden structural failure backstage during Act III, Scene iii, the unfortunate King, accompanied by the Bishop of Carlisle, abruptly vanished from view behind the plywood walls of Flint Castle with a resounding thud to the evident dismay of Bolingbroke and his retinue. On another, a performance of the *Dream,* the curtain rose to disclose a wood near Athens in which two elderly scene-shifters in shirtsleeves and braces were in the act of setting down, with great deliberation, a rustic bench. Not until the house became convulsed with laughter did they realise that they were discovered. Their reaction was then even more diverting. Such incidents might appeal to a schoolboy's sense of the ridiculous, but they were hardly calculated to encourage an appreciation of Shakespeare.

But now, on this pilgrimage to Stratford with Anna, it was quite otherwise. Apart from the handicap of education, where appreciation for the arts was concerned I was obviously a slow developer and must have reached just the right mental age to be swept away on the tide of the plays' magnificent language. From a pose of affected contempt, I swung to the opposite pole of uncritical admiration and in this euphoric state I was fortunate in my companion. For Anna's interests were centred in literature and the arts and of this world, which was only just opening to me, her knowledge and experience was considerable. This had given her a highly developed critical sense which supplied a wholesome corrective. For a lately converted philistine at large in a new-found world there could have been no more discerning guide. Her taste, reflected in her possessions, was impeccable and she could unerringly detect the second-rate, the meretricious, the sentimental or the banal and demolish all such 'kitsch' with forthright and devastating effect. The ironic mockery with which she punctured the merely pompous or bogus reminded me of Kyrle Willans.

I discovered that in art and literature, Anna always tended to prefer the small and exquisite to the mighty masterpiece; the private to the public voice; the miniature rather than the broad canvas. In literature it was the prose of Sir Thomas Overbury, in music the last quartets of Beethoven. Until I met her I had never heard the last quartets, while all that my school had told me about Sir Thomas was that he had the misfortune to be slowly poisoned in the Tower on the orders of Lady Essex. With such a taste it is not surprising that, much as she loved the plays, Anna should have considered the Sonnets Shakespeare's finest work. They were her favourite reading. She thought that the sonnet, though so seemingly simple, was the most difficult of all poetic forms and Shakespeare the one absolute master of it. Reading the Sonnets in the privacy of my room at Hartley Wintney at night was a revelation; I could understand the reason for Anna's preference. I had never read them before. At school we had only 'done' the history plays and had certainly never heard of the Sonnets—maybe the school authorities considered them improper. The theme that love, like all created things, is born to perish echoed and re-echoed through the poems. This made them seem infinitely poignant to me. What made them great was that Shakespeare never allowed himself to be defeated by such a tragic awareness of the human condition but pitted his art against it with superb, at times almost arrogant, assurance:

'And all in war with time for love of you,
As he takes from you, I engraft you new.'

This seemed to me like a brave man who, before some last desperate and fore-doomed encounter, bids all the trumpets sound.

Another part of my education was to be given the freedom of Anna's small but fine library. Browsing here it was interesting to me (as it always is in other people's libraries) to discover which writers she admitted to her shelves. She collected first editions and I was intrigued to see uncut volumes with reading copies of the same titles arranged on the shelf beside them. No bibliophile myself, and thinking that the whole purpose of a book was to be read, this mystified me. One thing we could share from the very start of our relationship was our admiration for the poetry of W. B. Yeats—Anna herself was Irish born. The poems of his 'Celtic Twilight' period which I had so much admired now seemed too cloying for my taste, too preoccupied with the music of words rather than with their meaning. But as my taste matured, so Yeats' style developed and tautened until it attained a superb, muscular eloquence, a style from which the last ounce of superfluous verbal flesh had with the highest artistry been pared away till every word that remained supported a tremendous weight of meaning. I have on my library shelves the slim first editions of *A Full Moon in March* and *The Herne's Egg* which Anna gave to me at this time. They recall the excitement we both felt as the later poems and plays began to appear.

One reason why I found the company of Anna so intensely stimulating was that her keen sense of humour was combined with an astonishing gift of rapid repartee such as I have never heard equalled. My conversational gifts have always been limited. It is only when I recall a conversation that I think ruefully of some brilliant thing I *might* have said at the time. It is such slow-wittedness that makes us doubt the spontaneity of many of the sayings attributed to such renowned conversationalists as Oscar Wilde. One feels they must have thought them up beforehand and then waited for—or created—an opportunity to lob them into the table talk with suitably devastating effect. But having listened to Anna when she found some opponent worthy of her art, I doubt this. It was the verbal equivalent of watching a first class tennis match.

We used to frequent a certain variety theatre where it was our custom to join the artistes in the theatre bar after the performance. On one of these occasions the star performer was a famous comedian noted for his 'blue' jokes. By the standards of the 1930s, his act was certainly near the bone, but we both thought it both humourless and vulgar. When Anna crossed swords with him in the bar afterwards he was soon reduced to sulky speechlessness, proving that he had no natural wit but merely the ability to put over the lines fed to him. But when, shortly after this, Nervo and Knox visited the same theatre it was quite the reverse. Not only was their act so funny (it included an unforgettable parody of *Spectre de la Rose*) that it reduced us to helpless tears of laughter, but their cross-talk with Anna in the bar afterwards was a brilliant verbal firework display as witty as their act.

Although John and I frequently complained of the amount of traffic on the A30, outside rush-hour periods it was then still possible to cover the 37 miles to the West End in the hour, so Anna and I used to meet in London fairly frequently. She introduced me to an urban society that was then completely foreign to me. Being country-bred and having an ineradicable dislike of crowds, I had never enjoyed London. I felt oppressed by the vast size of it. To me it seemed a great desert, cutting me off from the natural world, and I could understand only too well why Falstaff had babbled of green fields as he lay dying at the Boar's Head in Eastcheap. But although I have never been able to accept Dr Johnson's famous saying that a man who is tired of London is tired of life, at least Anna made me understand what he meant by it.

One of these nights that I spent with Anna in London stands out in memory because that evening King Edward VIII announced his abdication. For those who did not experience it, it is difficult to convey the extraordinary effect which this news had upon the people of London. It made me realise that the monarchy, though shorn of its power, was nevertheless still a most potent force. No news of the unexpected fall of a government could have caused so universal a sense of bewilderment and loss. All London seemed conscious of the fact that the throne was empty and everyone seemed to be discussing the situation. Since we had arranged it beforehand, it was a strangely apposite coincidence that Anna and I should have gone that evening to the play *Charles the King* which dealt with the trial of Charles I. There was an extraordinary moment when the curtain came down. The audience rose to its feet expecting the National Anthem, standing in silence while an embarrassed, whispered colloquy took place between the conductor and the leader of the orchestra. Then the members of the orchestra began to pack up their instruments and the audience, realising that at that moment there was no King for God to save, filed silently out of the theatre.

Sympathy for the King seemed to be almost universal and feeling was running high. We took a taxi from the theatre to the Café Royal where the most extraordinary talk was circulating among the tables. Maybe it was because my head was still full of the play, but it seemed to me to be a Cavalier and Roundhead situation all over again and that it would take only a little more heady drink and even headier talk to set us all marching on Westminster chanting Royalist slogans.

Because Anna could always be sure of finding acquaintances there, we used often to go to the Café Royal. It was then in its original state, an elaborate stage set which had been designed to attract the writers and artists of the English Decadence by reminding them of their beloved Paris of *La Belle Époque*. To the end—and this was so nearly the end—it still retained something of the atmosphere of a raffish and Bohemian club. Although the people occupying the famous red plush seats below the encircling balcony looked very different, one was still reminded of the paintings of Degas, Manet and, above all, Toulouse-Lautrec. There were still one or two striking figures to be seen: Radcliffe Hall in her wide-brimmed Spanish hat; bearded Augustus John looking like a tramp who has been sleeping rough. Nevertheless, with rare exceptions, I realised that these habitués were but pale shadows of those who had frequented the restaurant in former years and I was at once fascinated and repelled by the glitter of this wholly artificial world, a world so foreign to my previous experience. My life at No. 439, London Road, Stoke-on-Trent, or at the Aldbourne foundry might have existed on a different planet; even my present life at the Phoenix seemed completely divorced and remote. I revelled in such diversity. I was not dazzled by this sophisticated London life—far from it—but I relished keenly the piquancy of the contrast it presented.

The companionship of Anna induced in me a sensation of living upon some higher plane of being where all one's faculties become sharpened and so more receptive to the apprehension of the beauty and richness of life. But I remained wary of this sensation as of a too-potent liquor. It was, I believe, such a sensation as Walter Pater had in mind when he wrote that: 'To burn always with this hard, gem-like flame, to maintain this ecstasy, is success in life.' Finding the new industrial society ugly and hostile, the artists of the Decadence, taking their cue from Huysmann, had accepted this delusive philosophy as though it were some sacred canon, seeking refuge, not in the natural world, but in a highly artificial environment where sensation was created to feed imagination. The result had been tragic for, in their vain efforts to keep Pater's 'hard, gem-like flame' alight, they had resorted to drink, to drugs and to sexual debauchery, a desperate course that can lead only to despair. In London in the 'thirties I saw for myself the pitifu end of this road. For most of those who frequented the Café Royal at that time, though highly intelligent, seemed to be either perverts, alcoholics or drug addicts. I used to find this state of affairs infinitely sad and depressing; it seemed such an appalling waste of life and talent. It was also evil.

The one thing that repelled and disturbed me about Anna's milieu was its all-pervading scent of *Fleurs du Mal*. A hint of debauchery may seem wickedly attractive when we encounter it in literature or art. It is present in the writings of Wilde and in the drawings of Beardsley, suggesting that they are old in experience, having tasted forbidden fruit. But debauchery experienced at first-hand is as nauseating as the scent of the Pyrenean lily. For although this flower, when growing en masse, can fill the distant air with sweetness, at close quarters its blossom exhales a sickly stench of rottenness. I used to wonder why Anna failed to notice such a scent until I realised that she could not detect it because she herself was touched by it. Not that she had succumbed to drink or drugs—she had too much natural zest for life for that—but she made no secret of her sexual promiscuity. I was aware that I was regarded with a certain critical interest by her acquaintances as her latest young and bemused capture, nor was I so conceited as to suppose that our relationship was in any way special or different where she was concerned. These things did not seriously trouble me. I was content in the knowledge that, so far as this particular liaison was concerned, I was at the receiving end. For I could give her very little in return for all she gave me in the way of knowledge, experience and, above all, in critical appreciation.

I used to think it sad that Anna did not apply her undoubted talent to some creative purpose. She was certainly working on a biography of Queen Caroline at this time. But 'Poor Queen Caroline is lying about in folders and she'll never get done, poor girl', she wrote, and, so far as I know, she never was. For I think that Anna preferred to expend her gifts, as some spend money, in the encouragement of talent in others and that when this produced results she was as pleased as though they were the product of her own creative effort. She as good as admitted this in a letter to me when she wrote: 'I am incurably experimental, and I like juggling about with other people's brains. Think of the kick I shall get out of it if anything does come of it.' In this case she was referring to my unfinished novel *Strange Vista*.

As though they contained the most outrageous pornography, I had kept the two dog-eared books in which this novel was written most securely hidden from every prying eye. Yet it was not long before Anna had read them. In showing them to her I felt as diffident as I had done when first we had stepped out of our clothes, for the book had not been aimed at the public but had been written under a compulsion to set down on paper my reactions to my experience at Stoke-on-Trent. This analogy between mental and physical intimacy is apt, because I knew my style to be so unpractised and clumsy that, as a means of expressing my feelings, it must surely have seemed to Anna woefully inadequate. In both situations, she must have sensed that the future of our relationship was balanced upon a psychological knife-edge; that I was too conscious of my own shortcomings not to detect the falsity of mere flattery; too serious-minded to accept even the most affectionate ridicule. The merest suspicion of either might have sent me bolting back into my private burrow, never to emerge again so far as she was concerned. So she paid me the sincere compliment of treating me seriously, with an eye to future promise rather than present performance.

Anna read my text thoroughly, making perceptive and constructive critical comments. I realise now that the most conscientious of publisher's readers could not have done the job better. Most of them would never have got beyond the first page. No matter how sharp the criticism may be, nothing can be more encouraging to an aspiring young writer than to find his 'prentice work taken seriously by someone whose opinions he has learned to respect. It must have been at least two years since I had last touched that book, and until now I had never seriously thought of writing for publication. But when, after reading *Strange Vista*, Anna wrote: 'the futility of your doing what you are when you should be writing would be enough to make one weep if one didn't see the necessity behind it', I was made to think again. But aspiring authorship did not mix with running a garage and, despite all Anna's encouragement, *Strange Vista* was eventually relegated to the lumber room. So she never got her kick out of it. But she had implanted in my mind the idea of becoming a writer and so unwittingly plotted my future course for me.

So immersed was I in this new and rewarding relationship that I was content to live from day to day and never paused to think how it would end. Had I been more experienced I would have realised that the end of such an affair is almost invariably anti-climactic and unhappy. Inevitably, friendship cools more rapidly upon one side than upon the other, usually resulting in recriminations so bitter that they can poison the memory of all that has gone before. Anna, older and wiser than I was, did not wait for this melancholy ebb but wrote an abrupt 'finis' to our affair while it was still in full flood. In recollection, it seems as though one day she was there and on the next she had vanished. I would only see her once again, ten years later, and then only very briefly.

I remember that at the time I felt hurt and bewildered that a friendship so intimate could be so summarily broken, but soon I realised how right she was. Shortly before the end, Anna sent me a sequence of four sonnets which she had written about our affair. No one had ever felt inspired to write poetry to me before and I was so absurdly flattered and dazzled by such a compliment that I failed to realise that this was her way of saying thank you and goodbye.

# Chapter 13

# Design for Living

Although my interest in railways and steam locomotives dwindled almost to vanishing point during the years I spent at the Phoenix Green Garage my interest in canals did not. Excepting only my experiences in Stoke-on-Trent, it was the memory of my voyages in *Cressy* that remained most vividly in my mind. On hot summer days when traffic surged endlessly past the garage and the air was full of the stench of petrol fumes and hot tarmac I would think of *Cressy* gliding along some narrow ribbon of still water between green fields as a traveller in the desert dreams of an oasis.

When my uncle sold *Cressy* after the Kerr Stuart débâcle, I optimistically wrote to Fortune, the Leicester reporter who had bought her, asking him to give me the first refusal should he ever decide to part with her. At that time it seemed highly unlikely that I could ever afford to buy her and equally improbable that her new owner would want to sell in the foreseeable future, since I knew he intended to live aboard with his new wife. However, I had not been at the garage more than eighteen months before I received a sad letter from Fortune. His young wife had died tragically and *Cressy* held so many poignant memories for him that the sooner he could get rid of her the better. Situated as I was, there was nothing I could do about this unexpected offer, but I promptly passed on the news to my uncle Kyrle. Since the Willans family were still living in the West Country far from any navigable waterway, I scarcely expected any action to result but, to my pleasure and surprise, my uncle promptly got in touch with Fortune and agreed to buy *Cressy* back from him. At the first opportunity he travelled up to Leicester accompanied by my cousin Bill and together they worked the boat southwards, leaving her in charge of Frank Nurser at Braunston Boatyard near the junction of the Grand Union and Oxford canals.

A reunion cruise was planned for the autumn and accordingly, in October 1936, Aubrey Birks and I motored from Hartley Wintney to Blisworth on the Grand Union Canal where we found *Cressy* moored with Bill in sole charge. His father had helped him work her down from Braunston but had had to leave, though he hoped to rejoin the boat later. This was the first time I had set eyes on *Cressy* since the steam plant had been taken out and I noticed a number of changes. Both her original bow and stern cabins had been removed. The fact that she was now flush-decked at the bow greatly improved visibility from the little well deck for'ard. One could now sit at ease there and enjoy an uninterrupted view of the canal ahead. To sit thus while the boat glided slowly along, swinging now this way, now that, as she followed the windings of the canal and the green, ever-changing landscape flowed slowly past, was one of the most delightful experiences I have ever known. From that graceful, curving bow ripples fanned out over the still water with only the faintest chuckling sound. Aft, the new cabinwork had been extended over what had once been the steam engine-room while the length at the stern once occupied by the old aft cabin had also been flush decked and was surrounded by a railing. In the middle of this new aft deck sat a Model T Ford engine, mounted in part of its original car chassis and driving the propeller shaft by double roller chains and sprockets. This unorthodox arrangement was a typical example of an ingenious Willans improvisation designed to make virtues out of a necessity. The necessity was to avoid altering the line of the propeller shaft and stern tube. This had been determined by the original steam engine and was too near the keelson to accept any petrol engine if it were mounted in the orthodox position. Its virtues were unfailing reliability and—unlike most marine installations—the complete accessibility of the engine both from the sides and from below. In addition it created ample covered storage space below deck. The famous Model T epicyclic gearbox, less its low gear band, formed a ready-made marine reverse unit. The one disadvantage of this new installation compared with the old steam plant—noise—was minimised by a water-cooled exhaust manifold, the circulating water discharging into the canal through the exhaust pipe.

Aubrey, Bill and I soon cast off and during the next few days we cruised south down the Grand Union Canal, turning aside down the Aylesbury Branch to spend a night at Aylesbury on the way. My uncle Kyrle joined us near Berkhamsted and we proceeded as far south as Cassio Bridge Wharf, Watford, then thronged with timber traffic, where we winded the boat and began our return journey. Aubrey and I disembarked at Blisworth, leaving my uncle and cousin to work *Cressy* back to Braunston. An experience so often recalled in memory and so keenly anticipated often proves disappointing when realised, but in this case there was no anti-climax. To me this slow journeying was just as magical as it had been on that first maiden voyage from Ellesmere that now seemed so long ago. We had left Aylesbury early to rejoin the main line and it was our gliding over the glass-smooth surface of the long, deserted level of the canal through the Vale of Aylesbury on a still and misty autumn morning that stands out in my memory. Apart from an occasional Harvey Taylor boat trading to Aylesbury with coal, there was little traffic on the branch and so remote and lonely did its waters seem that it was difficult to believe that we were in the populous home counties.

It was shortly after this voyage that my uncle decided that Banbury and not Braunston should be *Cressy's* base. It was planned to move her thither over a week-end and I received a signal at the garage that my help would be welcome. We must have been late away from Braunston on the Saturday, for dusk soon fell and we worked up through the last three locks of the Napton flight in pitch darkness, mooring at the head of the locks resolved to make an early start next morning. We awoke to find a thick fog, but nevertheless we cast off as soon as it was light. This was my first acquaintance with the Oxford canal and I did not then know how incredibly tortuous were the eleven miles of its lonely summit level from the top of Napton locks to Claydon, where the canal begins its descent into the valley of the Cherwell. Even in clear weather, the voyager is apt to lose his sense of direction, so to navigate this wayward summit level for the first time in thick fog was an eerie experience. I felt as though we had lost ourselves in some watery maze and must surely finish where we began. We sounded our horn repeatedly, expecting on every sharp turn and beneath each narrow bridge to see the bluff bows of an oncoming boat looming out of the fog. But we met no other craft in all those eleven winding miles, a fact that increased our sense of complete isolation. However, we eventually reached Claydon, the fog clearing as we locked down the Claydon flight and, just as darkness was falling, we tied up at Tooley's Boatyard,

Banbury. Although I did not realise it at the time, I was to become very familiar with Tooley's Boatyard.

These two canal voyages added substance to an idea which I had been turning over in my mind for some time until it had become a kind of dream of ideal bliss. This was that I should live aboard a boat like *Cressy* and journey slowly about England at will, taking my home with me like a snail. I got busy with pencil and ruler and came to the conclusion that, although the beam of a narrow boat was indeed very narrow, its length of 70 ft. allowed sufficient room for civilised living. As with all such romantic notions, however, there was one very big snag—money. My supply of this was non-existent. How would I earn my living? It was in answer to this question that the seed that Anna had planted in my mind began to sprout. I would live on my boat and write for my living. I was not so naïve and optimistic as to suppose that this solution was as easy as it sounded. I was never taken in by those specious advertisements for correspondence courses promising that I, too, could earn money with my pen. But at least I should be living cheaply with no rent or rates to pay, while writing seemed to be the only occupation which could be reconciled with such a roving existence. It seemed to me to be worth a trial. I decided, wisely I think, that, despite all the help and encouragement which Anna had given me, my novel *Strange Vista* was far too ambitious a bow to draw at the outset of this venture. Instead, I tried my 'prentice hand by writing three short ghost stories, 'The Mine', 'The Cat Returns' and 'New Corner'. The first was based on recollections of a bygone visit to the Snailbeach lead mining district of Shropshire, the second was purely imaginary while 'New Corner' was a motoring variant on the theme of H. R. Wakefield's golfing ghost story 'The Seventeenth Hole at Duncaster'. It was based on Prescott Hill where, by coincidence, a new corner was actually built many years later as described in the story, though happily not with any such dire results. I sent these three tales to a pulp magazine called *Mystery Stories* whose editor rejected the first but accepted the other two, much to my surprise and pleasure. It was a very small beginning, but it gave me quite a thrill to see myself in print for the first time and it made me feel that my new design for living might not be so fanciful after all.

At this time, if the Vintage Sports Car Club attracted a new member it was not long before he or she made a pilgrimage to the Phoenix. Through the long window above our work-bench in the garage which overlooked the inn yard, John and I would inspect these new arrivals and their cars with critical interest. One morning in the late summer of 1937, we were intrigued to see a white Alfa Romeo sweep into the yard, driven by a young girl with blonde hair wearing a white polo-necked sweater. This was my first glimpse of my future wife, Angela. Such a combination of exotic motor-car and beautiful blonde may sound like something out of a James Bond adventure but, so far as the car was concerned, the truth was quite otherwise. For Angela, it appeared, had lately rescued it from the clutches of a well-known scrap dealer at Dorchester in Oxfordshire. It was in that condition which dealers euphemisti-cally describe as 'a runner', meaning that it was just capable of pulling itself off the premises. Anxious to get her new monster on to the road, Angela had carried out a very hurried and superficial face-lift which had included repainting it with what looked like whitewash. However, although it was a tired specimen of a not particularly good car, it was an authentic vintage sports car of the type known as the RLSS of 22/90 h.p. Behind an imposing Vee radiator with its twin Alfa Romeo badges there lurked a large six-cylinder engine with push-rod operated overhead valves, but behind this was a gearbox which was the Achilles heel of the car. The gear ratios were disastrously ill-chosen and it emitted groaning noises reminiscent of some superannuated tramcar ascending a steep gradient.

Although the attraction was mutual so that we saw a lot of each other from that first meeting onwards, I do not know what became of Angela's Alfa. In recollection, it seems as though, having affected our introduction, it discreetly dis-appeared from the scene. It was no great loss for we soon found a far more entertaining toy lying in a scrap yard at Stratton, near Swindon, which Angela purchased for a song. This was a racing Horstman, alleged to be one of the original four cars of that marque to be entered for the JCC 200-mile race at Brooklands in 1921. However, its specification does not seem to tally with descriptions of these four cars, nor with that of the replicas which were built in limited number for sale in 1922. It had a typical light Brooklands aluminium body of the period with a long, pointed, quickly detachable tail and exiguously narrow staggered seats for driver and mechanic. This was mounted on a chassis having ash side-members strengthened with steel flitch plates, cantilever springs all round, no front wheel brakes and cable-and-bobbin steering which was so direct that the lower half of the steering wheel had been dispensed with to provide the driver with a bit more belly room in the cockpit. Power was provided by a side-valve Anzani engine with alloy head and high-lift camshaft. We put the car on the weighbridge at Winchfield station and found it scaled 10½ cwt. with fuel and oil. Angela entered and drove this car in the 1938 Lewes Speed Trials where its performance was mediocre in the extreme despite its light weight. This was not surprising because the Horstman only had a three-speed gearbox, the ratios of which had obviously been chosen, not for sprints, but for circulating the outer circuit at Brooklands at maximum velocity.

I will not bore the reader with the endless minor troubles we experienced with this car, chiefly due to age and neglect. Suffice it to say that Angela and I, taking it in turns to drive, did manage one long trouble-free and unforgettable drive in the Horstman from the Phoenix to Prescott and back. Although, with such a specification it may sound improbable, that little car was an absolute delight to drive. The steering was light and precise, it held the road perfectly and, on the comparatively empty roads of those days we were able to cruise effortlessly at around 70 m.p.h. That this was well within the capability of the car is shown by the fact that the actual 200-mile race car, with a similar Anzani engine, finished fifth at an average speed 82·37 m.p.h.

Angela shared a mews flat in South Kensington with a girl friend named Margot and my visits there became increasingly frequent. In November she came as my passenger in the Brighton Run. This was the last occasion on which I would drive my Humber to Brighton and it was quite the most enjoyable. For once it was a perfect November day, clear and frosty with bright sunshine, and the old car, fully restored to health after its misbehaviour with Aubrey Birks in the previous year, never missed a beat.

In the following spring I mentioned somewhat diffidently to Angela my idea of living on a canal boat and, somewhat to my surprise, she welcomed it enthusiastically. Nevertheless, I felt that we should have a trial run, so to speak, during the coming summer in order to find out whether she liked the idea in practice as much as she did in theory. So I hired for a week a small two-berth cabin cruiser named *Miranda*—she was a converted ship's lifeboat—from her owner who kept her at a mooring on the Warwickshire Avon at the village of Wyre Piddle. This choice of the Avon may seem strange now, but it must be remembered that there were then practically no suitable small boats available for hire on the canals.

The navigation of the Avon between Tewkesbury and Evesham has now been fully restored by the Lower Avon Navigation Trust, but in 1938 it was still the property of the moribund Lower Avon Navigation Company. During that week we were to learn quite a lot about ancient and semi-derelict river navigations. Heading upstream from Wyre in the direction of Evesham, our first surprise came when we sighted Fladbury Navigation Weir[1] ahead. My experience having hitherto been mainly confined to canals, I had never encountered such a thing before. Nor did I realise that this ancient device for raising the level in a river to enable boats to proceed upstream was already a great rarity. The big timber gate set in the masonry weir stood invitingly open so we forged gaily through the gap only to run suddenly and very firmly aground in the middle of the river some thirty yards or so upstream. In this predicament we were wondering what we should do next when we were hailed from a cottage on the Cropthorne bank of the river. A man appeared, rowed across the river in a small boat, closed the weir gate by winding on an ancient, creaking winch, dropped the paddles in the gate and called to us: 'When she floats off, let her drop back and lay her alongside of the weir.' Sure enough, she soon did float off and I came astern as instructed until *Miranda* lay beside the masonry wall. 'Now,' said the man, pointing, 'just you stay where you are until you see the level come up to that bolt on the gate there. Then you'll know there's enough water to float you up to Fladbury Lock.' And, sure enough, he was quite right. Such was our initiation into the gentle—and very slow—art of working navigation weirs.

We passed through Fladbury Lock beside the beautiful mill but were unable to reach Evesham because there was a 'stoppage' at the last lock at Chadbury. Here men were at work patching up the rickety gates so we came about in the river by the tail of the lock and set off downstream to Tewkesbury. There we entered the broader Severn and headed upstream as

[1] This weir and its fellow at Pershore have now been removed by the Trust and the river bed deepened.

far as Stourport. It was when we were returning *Miranda* to her mooring at Wyre at the end of a most successful week that we had our second mildly comical adventure on the Avon when we were within sight of our destination. Wyre lock has a curiously wide diamond-shaped chamber. The water level must have dropped since we had passed through it a few days before, travelling downstream, for when we ran in between the open lower gates we went hard aground on the mud in the middle of the lock chamber. Try as we would, we could not get her off so, as there was nobody in sight to help us, there was only one thing for it. Angela, who was more aquatically-minded than I was, stripped and swam for the shore, closed the lower gates and lifted the top paddles. By the time we finally stepped ashore from *Miranda*, Angela was as enthusiastic as I was at the idea of living afloat.

In the December following this voyage in *Miranda*, my career as a garage proprietor came to an end as a result of a financial crisis in our business affairs. Throughout we had suffered from a shortage of working capital, but now the need for it had become imperative. So far we had run the business on an equal footing, but now, whereas John's family were prepared to put up the necessary money, I could not and I decided I would have to pull out. So I said goodbye to the Phoenix Green Garage in January 1939 and returned home. Very soon after, Tim Carson left the Phoenix Hotel to take over the Sarum Hill Garage in Basingstoke and those memorable Phoenix years were definitely over. In any case, they could not have lasted much longer for the days of peace were running out on us. Since the Munich crisis we had felt, like so many others, that we were living on borrowed time. In the event, John joined the Royal Naval Supply Services while his garage was commandeered. Tim joined the R.A.F. and his Sarum Hill Garage was closed for the duration. He had very kindly offered to store my Humber and Angela's Horstman at Sarum Hill, but although the Humber survived the war, the Horstman did not. Like the Phoenix Special, our Rolls Royce and the 25/70 Vauxhall, it vanished without trace as did many another interesting car during the war years.

So far as the Vintage Sports Car Club was concerned, my last activity was to set out for Wales with a friend and fellow Club member named John Swainson to determine a route for a proposed Welsh Rally and Trial to be held in the spring of 1939. We travelled in John's 3-litre Bentley and headed for

the Presteigne district of Radnorshire which John knew
intimately. It must have been early in the year, for I remember
we had to dig the Bentley out of snowdrifts in the narrow
Radnorshire lanes. However, we managed to plot a suitable
course for a trial and the event was duly held in the spring. It
was voted such a success that it was resumed after the war
and has since taken place every year.

The Presteigne Rally is now looked upon as something of
an institution, not only by the Club but by the people of that
little Radnorshire town. The first Rally was notable for the
extraordinary feat of John Seth-Smith who, alas, did not
survive the war. He had become the proud owner of Kent
Karslake's Sizaire-Naudin, which I described in a preceding
chapter, and he drove this car single-handed 180 miles from
Chelmsford to Presteigne and back again, coping successfully
with a succession of dire mechanical derangements en route.
Only one who had first-hand experience of this wayward and
peculiar vehicle could fully appreciate what this epic drive
entailed. It made the Brighton Run seem an easy Sunday potter.
After this event I fell completely out of touch with matters
motoring and it was not until the summer of 1949 that I
became actively concerned in the Club once more and began to
renew the friendships I had made in the old Phoenix days which,
as a result of the war, by then seemed a world away.

In February or March 1939 I drove over to the Stroud
valley to visit my uncle Kyrle who was then working for an
engineering firm at Chalford. The purpose of my visit was
a momentous one on which my future plans might depend. I
knew that *Cressy* was still lying at Tooley's Boatyard, Banbury,
and I had come to ask my uncle if he would sell her to me.
After a brief discussion he agreed to part with her for £100.
This seemed a large sum at the time because it was almost all
I possessed, but few young men, contemplating matrimony, can
have set up house on so little money. I could hardly believe
that I was now the captain of the *Cressy* and that my long
cherished plan could be put into execution at last. I drove
home in a state of trance, my head buzzing with my plans for
converting *Cressy* from a holiday boat into a comfortable
permanent home for two people.

In April, I loaded up the boot of the Alvis with such scanty
possessions and tools as I had and headed for Banbury, my
intention being to camp on board while I carried out the
necessary conversion work. Angela and I planned to get

married in the summer so there was no time to be lost. I did all the interior conversion work myself, but relied on the willing co-operation of old George Tooley and his two sons, Herbert and George, for such work as had to be done on the hull. As I have written about my own work, the boatyard and the Tooley family very fully elsewhere,[1] it will suffice briefly to describe *Cressy's* accommodation by the time the job was finished, starting at the bow. First of all, opening on to the little foredeck, there was a small dining saloon which I had designed to be readily convertible into a spare two-berth sleeping cabin. Next came the galley with a sink on one side and a cooker on the other. This gave into a large sitting cabin occupying the whole of the midships portion of the boat; its floor was close carpeted and it was equipped with a coal-burning stove, easy chairs and, against the aft bulkhead, built-in bookshelves and a writing desk, this last a most important adjunct in the light of my future activities. This was followed by a double-berth 'state room' or owner's cabin with bedside table, a dressing table and a hanging cupboard. But it was the bathroom with its gleaming copper pipes which opened out of the state room aft that was my chief pride and joy. The bath was mounted high so that it would drain over the side, so I had boxed it in to provide cupboard space underneath it. A wash basin could be hinged down from the cabin side and then slid under the bath taps when required. Opposite the bath was a small independent heating boiler which could provide enough water for a bath in about an hour from lighting up. This installation was supplied with water from a large flat tank on the roof, so designed that it would clear low bridges. When we were at moorings, I used to fill this tank from the canal with a bucket on a line, but when *Cressy* was on the move this could be done from the main engine. For this purpose I had fitted a stop valve on the cooling water outlet. Whenever *Cressy* was passing through a pound where the water was particularly clear, from my position at the tiller I had only to close the valve to divert the water up into the tank. Finally, right aft there was a chemical closet and a small workshop with bench, vice and tool racks from which steps and a hatchway led on to the aft deck. Emptying the chemical closet was the one unpleasant chore and it sometimes posed awkward problems, but I thought then, and still think now,

[1] *Narrow Boat* (1944).

that to fit a yacht type closet discharging solid effluent into a still canal is a disgusting practice.

Apart from small auxiliary electric lights (supplied by the engine dynamo and battery) and the coal stove, all lighting and heating on the boat was by paraffin lamps and stoves. Paraffin is dirty and apt to smell, but I decided that these disadvantages were outweighed by the danger of using gas in the confined space of a boat cabin. The choice of paraffin was also influenced by the fact that one could then buy it in the most remote places, whereas calor gas was by no means so readily available. Such, then, was my design for living.

In my long-abandoned novel, I had attempted to point the contrast between the new urban and industrialised England and that older England whose beauty meant so much to me. It had expressed the conflict between the two sides of my own nature. At the time I wrote the book and for some years thereafter there still existed substantial pockets of rural England where beauty survived substantially unsullied and unpolluted by urban man and where the way of life that had contributed to its beauty, though visibly failing, still possessed sufficient tenacity and strength to give an eloquent meaning to the landscape. In other words, man was still playing his true creative role in the ecology that had produced the beauty. Such a landscape, undefiled by industry, had not yet become either a dormitory for tired city commuters, a pleasure park preserved in the rigor of death, or a wilderness. But what I had wrongly assumed at the time I wrote was that these two worlds, the new and the old, would continue to co-exist. Thus, when the new world came to that apocalyptic end which I had envisaged in my book, my hero and heroine were able to seek refuge in a Welsh Border country very like that with which I was familiar. By the late 1930s, however, such a view had already come to seem almost incredibly short-sighted. For it had become apparent that what I had taken for permanent peaceful co-existence was in fact only a temporary truce enforced by the great trade depression. Now that trade had revived and England was arming herself for war, a war of a less bloody but equally ruthless kind had been resumed against the landscape and the life of rural England.

When I looked back over the first twenty-nine years of my life I realised that the one thing that had solaced and sustained me through every difficulty and disappointment, every black night of the soul, was the loveliness of the English landscape, whether seen in actuality or recalled to the mind's eye. It would remind me of those intimations of beauty and order which had come to me as a child in the Black Mountains.

'Truly there are two worlds. One was made by God, the other by men. That made by God was great and beautiful. Before the Fall it was Adam's joy and the Temple of his Glory. That made by men is a Babel of Confusions: invented riches, pomps and vanities brought in by sin. . . . Leave the one that you may enjoy the other.'

At this time I had not read these words of Thomas Traherne or even heard his name; nor did I believe in God. None the less, I had resolved almost intuitively to obey Traherne's final injunction by enjoying as much of that other world as was left in England before it was finally sullied and destroyed. How to achieve this? My experiences on *Cressy* had seemed to me to supply the perfect answer. Roads could be ruled out at once. The craftsman-built cars in which I had delighted had spawned an ugly crop of mass-produced successors which had become one of the chief agents of destruction. Nor could my other love, the steam locomotive, supply a solution. Even if I would, I could hardly buy myself a steam locomotive and a saloon carriage and trundle round the railway byways of England, stopping where I would. But on the canals and rivers of England we could do just this. They seemed to me then so many secret ways leading into the heart of England, peopled by men who were themselves a part of the English tradition. And at the end of the day there would be no anti-climax, no closing of doors and waiting for the next day, for even in the night time the silence and the solitude would still be with us and we would feel ourselves a part of it. More importantly, perhaps, the canals resolved in an unique way the contradiction in my own nature which worried me increasingly. For they seemed to me the one work of engineering which, so far from con-flicting in any way with the beauties of the natural world, positively enhanced them. This was the thinking that inspired me to work on *Cressy* with almost demonic energy. Like the canals she would journey on, I wanted to make her a thing of beauty inside and out and not a mere aquatic caravan. When she was at last completed and painted I felt well satisfied for, like Cleopatra's barge, she seemed to burn upon the water. But time was running out, though just how fast I could not then know.

'Man proposes, God disposes.' To conceive what one thinks will prove a perfect design for living and to translate such a long dreamed-of conception into reality is itself a form of pride. On this account it is a perilous proceeding. It is tempting providence too far. I still believe in man's free will, but then I held this belief too arrogantly and passionately. One cannot order all things to one's mind. Life is not like that. Even while *Cressy* was building troubles were coming to cloud what I had fondly hoped would be—and might have been—the most idyllic period of my life.

First and foremost there was the growing threat of war. We both hoped against all hope that it would never come, yet knew in our secret hearts that it would. It threw a great question mark, like some dark shadow, over the whole future of our enterprise. The other trouble was the implacable hostility of Angela's father towards our marriage. Looking back on this sorry business, it seems incredible that such a thing could have happened at the end of the fourth decade of the twentieth century. Almost from the outset I had made my parents aware of my attachment to Angela, whereas she continued to keep our association a secret so far as her family were concerned. She loved her mother, but obviously went in terror of her father. I thought such fears exaggerated and was frankly incredulous, but I was soon to learn otherwise.

By 1939, when we had determined to marry during the coming summer, it had become no longer possible to withhold her 'guilty' secret from her parents so, taking her courage in both hands, she told them. The reaction was immediate. I was peremptorily summoned to London to attend a family conference which had been arranged for twelve noon in a private upstairs room at the International Sportsmen's Club. The memory of that dreadful interview remains vividly in my mind. I ascended those stairs with a certain trepidation as may be imagined, but I had too much faith in the goodness of my fellow men to anticipate exactly what lay in store. Angela had driven her mother round from her flat and I arrived to find them already waiting. Angela introduced me and I felt momentarily re-assured for on this, the first and only occasion on which I met her mother, she impressed me as both beautiful and charming. But where was the Great Man? The appointed hour struck and still he did not come. Our desultory conversation faltered and died. In the silence of tense expectancy that followed I noticed that Angela's mother seemed as nervous as we were, her hands restlessly fiddling with her gloves. After waiting in this state of apprehension for about a quarter of an hour (a delay deliberately calculated, I suspect) there was a sound of heavy footsteps approaching rapidly down the corridor, the door was flung open unceremoniously and there in the doorway stood himself, as the Irish would say, regarding the three of us with such a baleful stare that we might have been plotting some assassination or the overthrow of the British Empire. Without addressing a word to us, he turned his head and bawled down the corridor 'Waiter! A double brandy and soda—and quickly!' It is perhaps significant that while I can recall Angela's mother with clarity after all these years, of her father I can remember nothing. Despite his dramatic and unmannerly entry he has become a faceless man in my mind.

When an obsequious waiter had hurried in with his drink and had been dismissed with a curt wave of the hand, the gallant Major (for such he was) seated himself comfortably in a chair, took a deep swig of his brandy and soda and proceeded to berate Angela and myself impartially. What did she think she was doing, a daughter of his, to begin such a shameful liaison with a dirty garage mechanic? As for me, had I the infernal impudence to suppose that he would ever permit someone like myself to marry his daughter? And so on. I am ashamed to say that I came off second-best in this encounter for I was left speechless with amazement—not that speech would have been of any avail. But I reflected ruefully that it was just this sort of ill-mannered arrogance, which is commonly, but wrongly in my experience, attributed to members of the upper classes, that makes people Socialists. In fact, as was true in this case, it is far more commonly a trait of the wealthier middle classes. Angela's mother was far better born than her father. She was an aristocrat, but what she must have thought of such a display, which was as discourteous to her as it was to us, we never knew for she never divulged her true feelings. Like any Victorian wife, she subordinated herself utterly to the will of her husband as head of the household. Later, she paid secret visits to Angela in London and helped her to choose curtain materials for *Cressy*. Such a revelation of sympathy was at once pathetic and heartening, but that was as far as it went. Never, so far as I could discover, did she betray the loyalty she felt she owed to her husband by a single incautious word.

When my parents heard about this frightful interview my

father was furious, not so much on my account as because he felt that the Rolt family honour had been impugned. 'Never heard of the damn feller,' he said testily, 'who the hell does he think he is?' Had our two fathers ever met it would have been a case of Greek meeting Greek, but such a battle royal never took place. My father was over seventy by this time and practically confined to his chair with crippling arthritis which had developed following a fall in the River Usk while he was trout fishing. So my mother, who had not visited London for thirty years and loathed it, very gallantly set off to beard the dragon. This second interview was no better than the first. I never heard the details, but she returned furious, declaring that the Major was the most insufferable man she had ever met.

It was under this heavy cloud of parental disapproval that we went doggedly ahead with our plans. One night, when I was fast asleep on my temporary bunk after a long day's work on *Cressy*, I was awakened by a frantic hammering on the for'ard cabin doors. I stumbled out of bed, switched on a torch, saw that it was the small hours of the morning and, wondering who on earth it could be at such an hour, opened the doors. Angela almost fell into the boat. She was trembling from head to foot and on the edge of hysteria. Realising that we had not been deterred, her father had staged a monumental family row. He had shouted and sworn at her, calling her a whore and a strumpet and finally told her to get out of his house. It sounded exactly like a scene from some Victorian melodrama, except that in Angela's case there was no shameful bundle. But for us, at that time, it was no laughing matter. When she had been shown the door, Angela had jumped straight into her little Fiat and driven desperately through the night to Banbury. It had seemed the only place to go. I managed to console her somehow and she took off for her London flat next morning in somewhat better heart.

In July, we were married at a London registry office with only two people present to act as witnesses, John Swainson and Margot, the girl who had shared Angela's flat. Afterwards, the four of us lunched at the Berkeley before Angela and I set out to drive to Banbury. Inevitably, it all seemed rather furtive and hole-in-the-corner. Angela was scarcely a radiant bride. Her father had seen to that and throughout the years of our marriage he did not for one moment relax his hostility. There was never any possibility of reconciliation. With the wisdom of hindsight I can now see that the fact that our marriage cut her off from her home in this brutal fashion, meant that it laboured from the start under an intolerable psychological burden which it eventually proved incapable of sustaining.

However, notwithstanding this inauspicious start and the gathering war clouds on the horizon, we cast off our mooring lines from Tooley's yard in early August and *Cressy* glided away into the green and gentle landscape of the Cherwell valley with its stooping willows. Soon Banbury was lost to sight behind the high hedgerow that bordered the towpath. The reeds by the margin of the water bowed gracefully in the gentle wash of our passing and cattle, lowering their heads, stood motionless, watching us with wide, dark eyes. The sun was shining and the graceful arc of the old brick bridge ahead seemed to us to be the gateway to the landscape of all England. It was to be our garden from now on. Down in the sitting cabin, beside the folding desk that I had built, reposed the tool of my new trade, as yet unused—the portable typewriter with which Angela had presented me. What, I wondered, as I leaned on a tiller gaily painted like a barber's pole, did the future hold in store for us? Despite every obstacle, financial and man-made, our grand design for living had, it seemed, been achieved at last.